The Survivor

www.penguin.co.uk

The Survivor

JOSEF LEWKOWICZ

with Michael Calvin

bantam

TRANSWORLD PUBLISHERS
Penguin Random House, One Embassy Gardens,
8 Viaduct Gardens, London SW11 7BW
www.penguin.co.uk

Transworld is part of the Penguin Random House group of companies
whose addresses can be found at global.penguinrandomhouse.com

First published in Great Britain in 2023 by Bantam
an imprint of Transworld Publishers

A CIP catalogue record for this book
is available from the British Library.

ISBNs 9781787636293 (cased)
9781787636309 (tpb)

Typeset in 12/15.5pt Sabon LT Pro by Jouve (UK), Milton Keynes
Printed and bound in Great Britain by Clays Ltd, Elcograf S.p.A.

The authorized representative in the EEA is Penguin Random House Ireland,
Morrison Chambers, 32 Nassau Street, Dublin D02 YH68.

Penguin Random House is committed to a sustainable future
for our business, our readers and our planet. This book is made
from Forest Stewardship Council® certified paper.

This book is dedicated to the blessed memory of Tuvia,
who was so tragically taken from us by an accident.
May it be a merit for him.

Contents

CONTENTS

Foreword

by Rabbi Naftali Schiff with Jonathan Kalmus

A starved, enslaved and beaten teenage boy surviving six major Nazi concentration camps is nearly unheard of. This book is already unique for that alone, and it will keep you asking – How? How an orphan, alone, surviving by stealing potato peels and scraps, humiliated by his captors who've murdered his entire family, resists the precipice of Nazi degradation by maintaining his humanity with a mantra: 'I must not become an animal like *them*.' Could a person do any more? He does. Although emaciated, he protests against cruelty by finding the compassion to risk his life and feed fellow starving prisoners. An entire barracks of them. That he also rebuilds his life after the Second World War, we could be fooled into thinking this story's beautifully powerful messages have a simple arc. How this same boy swaps his striped camp pyjamas for a United States army intelligence uniform to net the most infamous mass murderer of Nazi Germany is the stuff of epics. Meet Josef.

There are rare moments in relatively few people's lives when they discover something that almost no one else in the world knows, but should be brought to the world's attention. When I met Josef Lewkowicz and heard about his mostly unknown story in 2018, I knew it must be told. Josef repeatedly proclaims, 'I am a zero, not a hero.' Yet he brought to justice the most well-known concentration camp commandant, Amon Goeth, made infamous by the film *Schindler's List*. The eminent historian Professor David Crowe describes Goeth as 'one of the true monsters in Nazi Germany's devastating war against the Jews'. But exactly how he was unmasked after the Second World War has hitherto been shrouded in mystery.

Josef has a near flawless memory of his role in this critical history. But he possessed not a single document of evidence to prove it. Only an intriguingly unique photograph of that Nazi mass murderer under arrest, which no museum, archive or anyone else in the world seemed to have. This, along with a portrait of Oskar Schindler, signed by the man himself to 'my dear friend Josef'.

The breakthrough to prove Josef's story should be credited to the work of Jonathan Kalmus. A filmmaker, journalist and colleague, he sifted through 100,000 documents to build the essential evidence base to historically verify Josef's past. Jonathan should also be solely credited for the new history unveiled in this book about the capture, identification and eventual trial of Amon Goeth.

But it was the book's author, Michael Calvin, who has diligently woven this research with artful brilliance into stunning historical storytelling, and greatly expanded it to produce a masterfully compelling and complete autobiography by adding the many other aspects of Josef's thankfully long life. The book is true to Josef's voice and spirit, and it has been an honour to see our idea for this work realized by a bestselling yet genuine and humble master wordsmith, whom I've come to know in Michael.

There is much more to Josef's story than solving an historic mystery. It shows he played a key part in defining our humanity – how civilization responds to evil on a monstrous scale and how, we believe, we can collectively continue to keep millions of us safe from it in the future.

There is a terrifying alternate reality that almost happened after the Second World War but for the moral fortitude and daring shared by Josef and enough other people at the birth of an emerging post-war world order. The historical documents where Josef's story is found also lay bare how perilously close humanity came to never bringing any Nazi murderers to a true and fair trial at Nuremberg. The British favoured summary executions without trial, the Russians argued for show trials with weak evidence and predetermined verdicts. Had the American legal representatives not won the argument, by August 1945 the world would likely have never defined crimes against humanity, the rule of international law, or built the global consensus for the creation of universal human rights – some of the most important human values we take for granted today.

Amon Goeth and countless other mass murderers would likely have walked free without war crimes investigators gathering internationally recognized evidence for the newly created international criminal courts. The extent of the calculated, planned and scientific genocide that became known as the Holocaust would never have become one of history's most documented episodes, and so the Holocaust deniers of then and now would have won. We would have stood much closer to the precipice of other holocausts and much further away from the free, hate-free and equal societies we aspire to. That hope may never have been planted within us.

There is even more that humanity stands to gain beyond pivotal history. The more I have considered such survivors my mentors, the more I realize they are all members of a unique cadre of human beings who have so much to teach us. Not just about death and destruction, but about life. To witness their *joie de vivre*, to cherish life and to fight evil with goodness. To miraculously rebuild lives and families after so much tragedy. When you discover his story, you'll see Josef is unique among a unique group of people, so how much more we stand to gain from absorbing his view of life.

As the founder of JRoots, I have dedicated nearly twenty years to help people learn from the stories of survivors. Tens of thousands of young adults have walked with them the paths of Auschwitz and other places of death, but they have also been inspired by the many more places and personal stories of rich life, heroism and heritage before these were destroyed. I know of no more powerful way to ensure a positive future than bringing the next generation to pause their busy lives and really consider the lessons of both the dark past and positive history. But survivors are getting rarer as they age. It was while capturing on film the stories of over a hundred Holocaust survivors in our hope to save their wisdom for future generations that I discovered Josef. Convincing him to give an interview was not easy. Holocaust survivors, I've learned, don't beat around the bush in speaking their minds, and Josef was not unique in this, to say the least. But I implored him to help future generations share his unique humanity, because his survival is witness to the endurance of the human spirit that should prevail in every one of us.

Josef is as bright and shining a living example of this human spirit as we have ever had the privilege to know. In this book you will touch the wonder of his resilience and tenacity, his desire for revenge manifested as yearning to build a better future or save orphaned children. He reveals piercing moral clarity, a sense of duty, and he ascribes much of his endurance to a belief in helping others. As Josef will often say in Polish, 'Being fine, kind and nice will never make you lose.' It saved his life many times over. These are all values he learned as a child, from his mother, from the prevalent Jewish values upon which countless homes were built in the villages, towns and shtetls of Jewish Europe. They are values not for then, but for all time – that if Josef can forge a path in the face of overwhelming adversity, we can too. If Josef can stand up and be counted in history to uphold the values of justice, peace and universal morals with nothing but rags on his back and sheer determination, then we can and we must. It is our hope that anyone who reads this book will not put it down after the last page, but will carry and live Josef's example for the sake of all of our futures.

I am ninety-six, and ready to meet my God whenever He calls me. I thought I was hardened by everything I had been through. I have seen terrible things: ritual hangings, casual shootings, unspeakable cruelty and the depravity of cannibalism. I endured hunger, beatings and torture in six camps, and managed to prevail, so I could bring a monster, Amon Goeth, the butcher of Plaszow, to justice.

He pursues me in a recurring nightmare, screaming that he will kill me because I stumbled into his room when he was eating. I hide in the shadows under a bridge, or cower under the barracks, to save myself. Sometimes Goeth, mainly remembered these days as the sadistic commandant from the film *Schindler's List*, materializes as one of many distorted Nazi faces, swooping towards me like birds of prey. On other mornings I wake panting and sweating, after grappling with a helmeted SS man in a long overcoat. He is trying to shoot me; I am trying to wrestle the rifle out of his grasp.

I am conditioned to violence, whether real or imaginary. I lived in constant fear, became used to danger and degradation. I am a proud Jew, who helped save Jewish orphans after the war. But I broke down at Belzec when I mentioned the names of those I see in my favourite dream, when I am around the dinner table with my family, talking and singing.

My father Symcha is supervising grandparents, aunts and uncles. I know their names, although I struggle to remember some of their stories. I have been giving my brothers rides on my beloved tricycle. I see our mother approaching with steaming plates of food, chicken soup, stuffed fish and cheese pastries. I fall silent, in anticipation. We are allowed to serve ourselves; it is delicious. I would love more, although I am normally a poor eater, but hold myself back.

When I look around, I realize no one at the table has a face. They are silhouettes, ghosts at the feast.

I consider this a happy dream, but perhaps that is why I was so troubled on the way to their place of execution. I remember my mother's warmth and elegance but, to this day, cannot recall her physical features. Despite going through the records at Yad Vashem, the National Holocaust Memorial and Museum in Jerusalem, I do not know the specifics of how she and my three brothers died.

There are lists of displaced villagers, and liquidated towns, but most documentation was deliberately destroyed. Railway records of the time were notoriously unreliable. Only two prisoners survived Belzec. One, Chaim Hirszman, was assassinated in his apartment in the Polish town of Lublin by anti-communist resistance fighters in March 1946, before he was able to provide first-hand testimony.

The other, Rudolf Reder, was saved because of his knowledge of German. He masqueraded as a mechanic before escaping under cover of darkness at the end of November 1942. He changed his name to Roman Robak before spending three years in Israel from 1950, and died in Toronto in 1977, at the age of ninety-six. He wrote of women and children suffocating, as their cries 'became one long, horrifying scream'.

We know the condemned were herded into cattle trucks. Some cars were said to have had piped music, to deceive deportees into thinking they were being transported to a transit camp. Others were connected to motor engines on arrival, so that victims could be gassed with the minimum of fuss. Historians consider Belzec to be a textbook example of the Final Solution, in action. The camp was run by only twenty-three SS men, supported by vicious Ukrainian guards.

The site measures 270 metres on each side. An overgrown railway siding still leads 500 metres from the main station directly to the camp, which was split into two sections. One zone was used to store victims' clothes, and such valuables as diamonds, US dollars and gold, extracted from the teeth of corpses. The other, hidden by fir fronds woven through barbed wire, held the gas chambers and burial pits.

The two zones were connected by a narrow fenced-off path, *der Schlauch*, the Tube. Victims, taken from batches of twenty freight cars and ordered over a loudspeaker on disembarkation to prepare to undress, were forced to run along the Tube by screaming guards, who prodded them with rifle butts and bayonets. The aim was to give them no time to think, to absorb where they were and what was about to befall them.

They had been told on arrival that they were to be showered as part of the adjustment procedure. They were advised to tie their laces together, so their shoes would not be lost. They were encouraged to arrange their clothes in neat piles, so they could easily be retrieved. It was a grotesque, murderous lie.

The Tube led directly to the gas chambers. Once the doors were sealed, trapping up to 200 people at a time, auxiliary police guards started a large diesel engine, which funnelled carbon monoxide into the brick-built building. All were dead within thirty minutes; from reception to death the process took little more than an hour.

Sonderkommandos, groups of Jewish prisoners selected to remain temporarily alive as forced labourers, removed the bodies and hauled them towards mass graves with leather straps. They were quickly covered with a shallow layer of earth. All the while, music was played by a small orchestra formed by temporarily reprieved prisoners.

Around 80,000 Jews were killed in the first three months of operation. By the time my relatives arrived, in September 1942, six gas chambers, double the original number, were in use. It was a production line of death. Heinrich Himmler, the genocidal mastermind, had declared that all Jews were to be wiped off the face of the Earth.

From October onwards bodies were exhumed, tossed on pyres made from railway sleepers, and doused in petrol. Bones were collected, crushed, and thrown into ditches that once served as tank traps. The slave labourers were periodically murdered; the last 300 were gassed in the Sobibor extermination camp in late June 1943, having been told they were being evacuated to Germany.

No buildings at Belzec remain, but the air of menace is unmistakable. Generations have passed through since the war, but people still struggle to grasp what occurred there. I walked down a symbolic death road, an underground passageway designed to replicate the hopelessness of that final panic-stricken stumble along the Tube. The high, rough walls closed in; I felt as if I was alone in the Valley of Death.

It was powerful, very powerful.

I cannot forget those beautiful people who were once around me. My cousins; there were so many of them. Little Bluma Kroner, the girl with the red hair. I did not know what her father did, but he was rich, the first man in the shtetl to have an open-topped car. When he gave us a ride, I felt like an ancient emperor.

Once the Nazis rounded us up, I never saw them again. If I close my eyes I can still visualize them, but it hurts so much. I don't like to think about loss, but it enters my mind, especially when I am alone. Grief taunts me. I cannot remember my mother's voice, or her particular smell. I only have a vague sense of guilt that I defied her by giving my sandwiches away to poorer pupils at school. We should have run away, but why? We had been there for a thousand years. We were rooted there.

We had a happy life, surrounded by friends, siblings, parents, grandparents and great-grandparents. Everyone would come to our home. Some would bring candy; one aunt, in particular, gave us home-made sauerkraut. What became of them? I had so much to learn from them and I missed it all. They did not live long enough for me to get to know them well.

They did not live long enough for me to know myself.

1

Family

The lady mayor was polite, but firm. There was no Jewish cemetery in Dzialoszyce, my birthplace. She sympathized with my plight in trying to locate the grave of my great-grandfather, but could offer no help. As is so often the case in Poland, where darker secrets are protected by half-truths and mysteries, things were not as they seemed.

I knew my mind was not playing tricks. Children of my age, eight at the time in 1934, were not normally allowed to witness burials. But I was so close to my great-grandfather that I was given special permission to be there when he was laid to rest in late afternoon on the day he died in his sleep, just before *Pesach*, Passover eve. No one was quite sure whether he was 105 or 106.

Dovid Leib – my youngest brother was named after him – was a tall, kind-faced man with a long white beard which entranced me, since it danced in the wind. My great-grandfather wore a long black coat and a Yiddish *hittel*, a hat with a brim. I can still hear him saying: 'Never in my life did even a fingernail hurt me.' He died with a full set of teeth, perfect hearing, and no need for glasses or a walking stick.

He was living history.

He told me stories of the Polish kings, like Boleslaw II,

The Generous, Casimir III, The Great, and Władysław II Jagiełło, who awarded Dzialoszyce a city charter in 1409. Like his father, who also reached a great age, he passed down tales of anti-Semitic pogroms, starting with the 1648 Khmelnytsky Uprising, in which tens of thousands of Jews were slaughtered.

My great-grandfather lived through one such pogrom during the Russian Civil War that resulted in the deaths of at least 35,000 Jews at the hands of warlords, White Russians and Ukrainian nationalists. He personally knew Józef Piłsudski, the statesman regarded as the father of the multi-ethnic Second Polish Republic, which was re-established in 1918, 123 years after Partition. The tensions of those times are still felt today.

He was an old man with the heart of a young boy. We would spend long days on his farm, tending his two horses, checking on his tomatoes, and eating freshly picked beans from the vines. He would send me into the attic to collect warm, newly laid eggs from his chickens, and teach me how to make two holes in them and suck out the egg white, to rub into my eyes. It was probably a *bobbemeise*, an old wives' tale, but he was convinced it would do me good.

There is a Hebrew-based Yiddish word, *yichus*, meaning lineage, or bloodline, which expresses the significance of knowing where we come from, who we are, and what we represent. That is why it was so important to me to pay my respects to him in death. The fact that my parents and siblings had been denied a Jewish funeral gave strength to my search.

When I was born, on 21 July 1926, Jews formed 80 per cent of Dzialoszyce's population. They traded in grain, crops, shoes, furniture, skins and clothes. Three tanneries, two oil wells, a brickyard and several tile kilns provided employment. Fairs, on Tuesdays and Fridays, attracted thousands of people from nearby villages and towns.

When I last returned, in 2019, it felt as if I had fallen into a black hole. The roofless shell of the neo-classical Adas Yisroel Synagogue, erected in 1852 and completed in 1876, still stood, but external plaster had crumbled, exposing scarred brickwork. It was colonized by pigeons, which flew noisily through arches that once housed majestic stained-glass windows.

In its heyday it was a beautiful place, with paintings of gold stars on beams, set against a light blue background. Pictures of the twelve tribes of Israel were painted on metal and garlanded with flowers. Paintings of a deer, a lion, a tiger and an eagle were at the edge of the ceiling on the four corners of the hall. Nothing remains. Immediately after the Second World War, in a casual act of desecration, the synagogue was used to store coal, cement and building materials.

I peered through the latticework of locked iron doors and tried to transport myself back in time, to when I sat on benches, *davening*, praying with my father and his father, Jankel, a deeply religious man who was the third of Dovid's four sons. Jankel's wife Esther, my grandmother, was similarly pious; she studied *Tsena Urena*, the women's Bible, and would make butter and cheese after milking Dovid's cows.

So much had changed. The surrounding scrubland added to the sense of decay and to my disorientation, as an old man seeing things from long ago in a different light. Frightening childhood memories of a large river flowing nearby, with a waterfall, which fed the shtetl's only well, were challenged by the realization that it has subsided into a shallow, slow-running minor river, known as the Sancygniówka.

I was compelled to return to the river, to make a blessing for my life, because I had fallen in as a boy, from two loose boards, which acted as a makeshift bridge. I could not swim, started to struggle, and swallowed a lot of water. There was no one around to help; to this day I do not know how I managed to scramble out.

The area was prone to flooding. Dzialoszyce was cut off for eight days in 1936, when the Sancygniówka and the Jakubówka, another river, burst their banks following a cloudburst. Twenty-eight houses were washed away, 130 more were seriously damaged, and six residents drowned. Our house had been flooded to a depth of two metres several years earlier; my parents placed me on top of a wardrobe for safekeeping. For some reason, I still have an image of a ceiling floating by outside, with the light fitting attached.

The solution to the mystery of my great-grandfather's resting place in the graveyard lay in the obliteration of all aspects of the local Jewish community during, and immediately after, the Holocaust. I discovered, after my initial return in 2011, that the cemetery had been wilfully abandoned by Polish residents, who harboured both guilt and grudges. Gravestones dating back to the early eighteenth century had been destroyed.

It became so overgrown it was inaccessible, which, to be charitable, explained the lady mayor's ignorance. At least, I now learn, some kind soul has managed to penetrate the weeds, and place commemorative plaques on tree trunks. The people they honour may be shrouded by the fog of time past, but they deserve to be remembered. May their memory be a blessing.

My grandparents spoke Yiddish, Polish, Russian and German. They had little, but gave freely. My grandfather, for instance, distributed milk, purchased from the *poretz*, a feudal landowner, to the poor, who could pay him only a fraction of what it was worth. His brother Aaron, an estate manager, was so successful he was able to afford a four-horse carriage, the equivalent of today's Rolls Royce. He would give me chocolate treats, and provided support for the extended family.

For someone known by a number in the camps, I have had many names. My given name is Joseph, or Josef, but I was called Juzek or Josek in Polish and Jossel or Yossaleh in Yiddish. In later life, in South America and Canada, I was known as José, or Joe. It all depended where I was living at the time. The original family surname was Lewkow. The 'icz' came much later, and is associated with 'son of'. 'Lew' means 'heart', but also hints at a link to the Jewish tribe of Levi.

It is strange how things turn out; many years later, on a visit to Israel, I was amazed to run into a stranger who told me he had been at my circumcision ceremony, eight days after my birth. I had apparently been named after a learned Torah scholar, Rabbe Yoskele. I yearned to know more, but when I returned to Israel, two years later, I discovered the man had passed away. His reminiscences had never been recorded. Yet another small but significant piece of our heritage had been lost.

My father, Symcha, was born in 1899. He was the eldest sibling, an only son. Hannah, the youngest of his three sisters (the others were Sheindel and Pearl), died at an early age from tuberculosis. He tried, and failed, to avoid conscription into the Polish army during the latter stages of the First World War by deliberately injuring his leg.

13

Resistance to military service runs in the family. In the 1950s fate delivered me to a great-uncle, Israel, a fun-loving man who had run away nearly forty years earlier. He had built a new life in South America because he did not want to join the Polish army.

My father spoke little about his combat activities, in Russia, Ukraine, Belarus and Germany, but had taken the precaution of becoming engaged to my mother, Sheindel, before going to the front. Her fine features hinted at her French ancestry, but she was born in Dzialoszyce in 1902 and was considered the greatest catch in the community.

I hope you forgive me the indulgence of providing a thumbnail sketch of her qualities. It means a lot to me, as a dutiful son, doing my best to bring her back to life through my words and deeds. In addition to her natural beauty, she made the most of a good education, being an avid reader in Polish and Hebrew. She was able to do rapid mathematical calculations in her head, without the need for a pencil to take notes.

Clothes looked good on her, though she was very particular about little things, like the angle at which she wore her hat. She had a passion for well-made shoes, usually those manufactured by her brothers, Leibish and Yossel, ultra-orthodox Jews who ran a successful export business. I used to play hide and seek with my friends in their factory, which smelled of fresh leather.

She could be very stubborn, both a blessing and a curse that she passed down to me, but was quietly spoken, warm and kind. I continue to try to live up to her instruction: '*Na grzecznosci nikt nie traci.*' 'By being nice to others you will only win.' Her caring side probably came from her mother,

Pearl, who was a prominent *shidduchim*, matchmaker, in the neighbourhood.

I miss my mother every day, and still mourn the misappropriation of her pride and joy, a needlepoint of Adam and Eve in paradise, which was stunning in its detail and creativity. It took her many nights of careful, loving work to complete and it adorned the main wall of our house which, as you will learn later in the book, was stolen from us.

Her father, Yitzhak Isaac, made a good living. He manufactured quilts and pillows from fine goose feathers, collected in large sacks by a network of pluckers in surrounding towns and villages. He also used duck down in a range of other products, finished off at my grandfather's factory. That was the way of things: family came first, especially when it was strengthened by marriage.

My parents went through a formal ceremony at the *shul*, the synagogue. I can't be certain where the wedding feast was held, because the guests were part of our lost generation and the details died with them, but it was either in the local fire station or a grand municipal building. The food would have been simple, but plentiful.

As a child I loved the joy and pageantry of such occasions, where a Chasidic band would play *klezmer* dance music until the early hours, when the men would still be dancing in circles. The wedding procession became a community event: doors would be flung open in appreciation as the caravan of colourful horse-drawn wagons came past, with guests singing Hebrew and Yiddish songs. These are the tunes of the sages, songs for the ages.

I love singing, though friends are probably being too kind when they tell me I have a good voice. I love the stories the songs tell, and the culture they celebrate. I love the memories they stimulate, and the innocent enjoyment they provide. I can still hum, unbidden, the waltzes that used to mesmerize me as a boy.

One of my few family heirlooms is a photograph of around a hundred of my father's forebears, a wedding party assembled in front of a building I do not recognize. Some of the men are smartly suited; others wear more traditional dress. It captures several generations; babies and toddlers are in the same frame as elders like my great-grandfather, who is standing erect and wearing a long tan coat.

They were not to know the terrible fate that awaited them.

I didn't appreciate it at the time, but now I can evaluate how my parents wanted to bring us up in the right way. Just as my *eema*, my mother, preached consideration for others, my *abba*, my father, taught me the values of diligence, frugality and honesty. He lived those values, rising from a humble millworker to a grain trader, and on to owning his own mill, purchased by his savings and a dowry from his in-laws.

He bought his grain from a *poretz*, transporting it in 100-kilogramme sacks using horses and a buggy to his water-powered mill in the neighbouring village of Lysowiec, where it would be ground, and sold as flour to local bakeries and shops. He was not well off, since his customers could not always afford to pay him the full amount due, but he was hugely respected.

Mother helped the family finances by running a provisions store on the main street, selling such things as tea, coffee, jam, condiments, cigarettes, bread, vegetables, fruit, sweets, soap and cleaning supplies. Some items, like salt and sugar, had their prices set by the government. Most were sourced, after careful negotiation, by my father. I tended the shop when she

Rab Koppell sat in front of us with a whip, which he flicked at anyone he saw dozing, or not paying attention. It wasn't as brutal as that sounds: it didn't hurt, and was designed to embarrass. I got it a few times, for talking, interrupting the teacher, and playing with a toy under the table.

We sat at that big wooden table, learning Hebrew and reading from the *siddur*, a book of service, and the *Chumash*, which contains special readings from the five books of Moses. We were taught to treasure our holy books. We were told not to place them on the floor, sit on them, or, shame upon shame, write in them. Rab Koppell was a powerful figure in the community; a steady stream of people, suffering from such problems as *ayin harah*, the evil eye, came to the house.

When I was seven, he chose me to be the class *chazzan*, the cantor who leads the prayers in synagogue. This is a great honour but, with the ignorance and audacity of youth, I told him I didn't want to do it. The sting of his slap across my cheek has stayed with me throughout my life; I still take the responsibility very seriously and have fulfilled the role across the world.

I am what is known as a *ba'al tefilla*, a master of prayer. That is not a reflection on the goodness of my ways, but more of a commentary on what others feel is the pleasing nature of my voice. Unlike a professional chazzan, I have never accepted a penny for my contributions. I am simply a volunteer who primes the prayers of his fellow worshippers.

There were around a dozen boys in class. We became very close, and often went back to my house, where my parents had left us cookies, snacks and treats like home-made blueberry pastries before going out to work. We would review our studies and do a quiz to ensure we knew we would be ready, if the teacher tested us on our lessons the following day.

We made small toys and wagons from scraps of wood decorated with pebbles and shells. We also made a lot of noise, which alerted Zisale, our housekeeper, who took delight in bossing us about. She was an orphan, and became such a part of the family my parents eventually acted as matchmakers, and found her a husband, a local carpenter.

We were happily behind the times. When we saw a motorcar for the first time, we ran after it in wonder. I remember hearing a speech about an aeroplane. An iron bird that flies? How could that be? There was no television and only the extremely wealthy had a telephone, but I never had the sense we were missing out. Our ignorance was bliss.

In the summers we would play outdoors, at a large house owned by my uncle, a coal merchant. We also went to Stawiska, a local sports ground, where we staged running races and catching contests. I was never a great sportsman but have never forgotten the sense of awe when my father took me to my first football match.

I suppose this is typical, but I have no memories of the match itself, other than a boyish sense of wonder that the men could run so fast around a pitch that seemed so large. I was fascinated by the noise and the colour of the crowd, but nothing came close to the magic of the lemonade and ice cream bought for me by my father. That made the day.

Rab Koppell believed in the benefits of exercise, allowing us to run free during a brief break from lessons, which he would frequently interrupt to explain the extracts we were reciting. He was a wonderful storyteller, regaling us with tales from the weekly *parsha*, a passage of Jewish scripture, which I would share with my parents over the evening meal.

In the mornings I would accompany my father on the five-minute walk to the *shul*, which doubled as a community centre. We read from the Torah on Mondays and Thursdays. On Friday afternoons Father would invariably take me to *mikveh*, a ritual bath in which I would be immersed as part of a purification ritual.

It was very hot and steamy, and occasionally involved being massaged with a *besiml*, leaves that had been tied together and dipped in soapy water contained in a *wessle*, a wooden dish. I would then be expected to shine my shoes and prepare my best clothes for *Shabbos*, the Sabbath. As the eldest son, I had the responsibility of taking my brother Meir Wolf, and the family two-handled pot, containing *cholent*, a traditional stew, to the baker's oven.

The stew consisted of meat, potatoes, barley, beans and *kishka*, sausage, but Mother added her special ingredient, *yapstock*, patties formed from ground raw potatoes, with herbs and spices added. It simmered overnight, together with the contents of hundreds of other pots from other households, and was the main Sabbath meal.

Mother had set the tone on Friday evening, handing out specially prepared *bulkelach*, small cinnamon rolls, to the poor on our doorstep. She lit candles and laid the table with our finest dinnerware. My father would say *kiddush*, a Jewish benediction, over a glass of home-made wine, fermented from raisins. Some relatives would bring apple wine.

We blessed the *challos*, braided bread, before tucking into fish, *kugel*, a casserole made from egg noodles, and *tzimmes*, a stew made of sweet root vegetables. The air was thick with the scent of cabbage, either from soup or stuffed rolls. Between courses, and in preparation for the meat, we would have a small shot of vodka. We would then sing *zmiros*, hymns that can date back a thousand years.

On Saturday afternoons, between services at the synagogue, we would visit our grandparents, or I would go for walks in the hills with my friends. We were without a care in the world, and should have paid more heed to the worried tones of our elders, quietly discussing the growing menace of Hitler and a diseased form of German nationalism.

The thought of invasion, death and destruction was beyond our imagination, yet all those friends, boys who laughed at Charlie Chaplin films and had so much to live for, were doomed. None survived. Our community might not have been rich, materially, but it was blessed spiritually. It worked because of a thousand tiny interactions between people, who represented the values which so scared our oppressors.

These were the sort of people the Nazis said were subhuman. I am here as their witness. This is the lifestyle the Nazis tried to incinerate. I am here to share the pain, though I still cannot comprehend how little time we had left. Our world was about to be consumed by unthinkable disaster.

2

End of Innocence

Age brings a degree of serenity. I'm intrigued, rather than offended, that my heritage has become a tourist attraction, centred on the cherished places of my childhood. Kazimierz, the Jewish quarter of Krakow, where I lived between 1934 and 1939, has, like so many areas, found a way to marry the old and the new.

Open-sided trolley buses take visitors around cobbled streets once stained by blood, on a tour that starts in the old town and ends at Oskar Schindler's Enamel Factory. I often wonder what the lonely man who came to me for reassurance, in the chaos that followed liberation, would make of his business being turned into a museum of contemporary art.

We lived at 36 Szeroka Street after I had spent some time with my maternal grandparents, expanding my education in the big city at the Talmud Torah, where I learned arithmetic, Jewish history, and how to read and write in Hebrew and Latin. My father occasionally commuted to his mill, an hour away in Dzialoszyce, after closing mother's store and renting out our house in the shtetl.

Szeroka is more of a square than a street, a medieval marketplace originally established as the centre of a twelfth-century village, Bawół. We lived two doors away from the famous Ramuh Synagogue, built in the 1550s to honour the family of Rabbi Moshe Isserles, a world-renowned scholar who believed 'the aim of man is to search for the cause and the meaning of things'. Until the Second World War, thousands of pilgrims visited his grave in the adjoining cemetery annually to mark the anniversary of his death.

A guidebook from 1938 sums up the spirit of the area, and of the era: 'Kazimierz is at times reminiscent of the cities of the Orient. Its people spend their lives outside their houses, where raucous conversations are filled with rich mimicry and gestures. Towards evening on feast days Kazimierz grows quiet. Jews in long robes and fox fur-trimmed caps walk along the streets, and candles gleam in the windows. The houses of worship fill up with people at prayer.'

People felt like kings. They felt holy, happy, spiritually elevated. The plaza was full and hummed with life. Families mingled, children played, and crowds gathered to hear speakers at the fifteenth-century Old Synagogue and the seventeenth-century Popper Synagogue, where I went with my father. It was a small but richly furnished place of worship, with doors depicting an eagle, a leopard, a lion and a buck deer, which symbolize the traits of a devout man.

It now serves as a bookshop and art gallery. The square is beautifully presented, with vintage clothing stores, touristic shops, restaurants and bars they tell me are 'shabby chic', whatever that means. A hotel features a sixteenth-century *mikveh* (a bath for purification) in its basement. There is, at least, an emphasis on Jewish tradition; we were granted freedom of worship, trade and travel by Boleslaw V, The Chaste, in 1264.

Occasionally, almost out of nowhere, the past finds its voice. In the northern part of the square, beneath a ring of maple trees thought to be a plague burial ground, there is a small monument hewn from a large rock. The inscription marks it as a 'place of meditation upon the martyrdom of 65,000 Polish citizens of Jewish nationality from Cracow'.

Our three-storey house was fronted by my mother's new store, which expanded from household goods into elegant furniture, fixtures and fittings. We rented out space to a brush-maker, and a cousin lived in the basement. We entered our living quarters through the back door, after walking down a side street that bears our name, Lewkowa.

Today, that entrance is a protective grey steel gate at the rear of a police station. The house itself, which my family abandoned during the occupation, taking anything we could carry when the persecution became too much to bear, fell into disrepair and was demolished. In contrast to the impeccably presented square, the high garden walls are cracked and dis-coloured. Scruffy saplings and weeds grow in the crevices.

The police were very welcoming when I took my passport to them on my last visit, and explained the situation. They allowed me to wander around the footprint of the old house. It felt odd, like walking on someone's grave. The gable end of the police station was supported by large struts, buried into the ground.

Like so many things, lost in the anarchy of war and subse-quent political regime changes, original ownership counts for little. Perhaps my grandchildren will one day return, and win their right to reclaim the family property. I will not be around, though my spirit will remain. I pray the youth will continue to be proud of who they are, and where they came from.

I became Hasidic after being captivated by the melodic poems and prayers, sung on the Sabbath by my new school friends. I could hear the happiness in their voices as they spoke of their devotions under Grand Rabbi Ben Zion Halberstam, the second in his dynasty, from a community established in Bobowa, a small town in the southern Polish province of Galicia.

I was determined to share the experience with my friends and neighbours in the Wagner family. Father was opposed to me making the long journey from Krakow to Bobowa, since he wanted to teach me himself, but mother recognized the surge in my faith, and argued that I should go, since the knowledge imparted by such a renowned scholar as the *Rebbe* (a spiritual teacher in the Hasidic movement) would be an ideal preparation for adulthood.

Typically, she baked me a cheesecake and roasted a goose so that I would not go hungry. I was too excited to eat on the three-hour train journey and shared it when I was settled into a rented thirty-bed room. We could not wait to receive the blessing of *Sholem*, peace, from the *Rebbe*. I was in awe of him from the moment he walked into the wooden hall.

I remember it as if it were yesterday. He had a holy face. The crowd pressed forward to meet him. His sharp, all-seeing eyes intimidated me, but drew me in. I crawled through everyone's legs to put myself at the front of the congregation. He noticed me, shook my hand, and asked my name, which he never forgot. To my astonishment, I was asked to join him and his grandchildren.

He handed a piece of challah bread to everyone around the table, and I was in a state of bliss. This was a huge honour, and I didn't know why I had been singled out until later, when I learned the Wagner family had told him I was descended from, and named after, Reb Yoskele. This stimulated my curiosity; I found two pages devoted to him in a history book, *Megillas Yochasin*. His name was Yosef Dovid Friedman and he came from the Cohen clan.

By the time of my second visit to Bobowa, a couple of years later, I was a devout follower, a *chasid*. I wore a silk *bekishe*, a frock coat, with a *gartel*, a prayer belt, and had grown *payos*, my sidelocks. When the *Rebbe* asked what I was studying, and who my rabbis were, I proudly told him about the *shtiebel*, a place of prayer in our street, above a foul-smelling cheese factory.

It was in Bobowa that I formed a lifelong friendship with his son and successor as Grand Rabbi, Shlomo. He was struggling to grow his first beard at the time, but would go on to re-establish the Hasidic dynasty in the United States after the Second World War. We reconnected when he visited me in Buenos Aires, and I would often see him in New York, where he worked out of Borough Park, Brooklyn.

We shared the scars of Holocaust survival. Shlomo used a network of followers to avoid arrest, and was smuggled to safety on forged papers through Hungary. He remarried and had six more children with Frieda Rubin after his first wife Bluma and two of their three children, daughter Hentchi and son Mordecai Dovid, were murdered in Auschwitz.

At the time of his death, aged ninety-two, in the summer of 2000, Shlomo had grown the dynasty so that it had branches in New York, New Jersey, Montreal, Toronto, Antwerp, London and Jerusalem. He was succeeded by his only remaining son from his first marriage, Naftali. He had saved his life by sending him to the Holy Land as a teenager before the war; Naftali died in 2005, aged seventy-four, and was buried beside his father in Floral Park Cemetery, New Jersey.

Like me, Shlomo never got over his father's cruel end. When Lvov, where he went to live under Soviet authority and the apparent protection of the Molotov–Ribbentrop Pact, was invaded by the Nazis on 30 June 1941, he hid in a secret room behind a bookcase for nearly a month, while his followers unsuccessfully attempted to evacuate him to the United States.

He left his refuge only when a friend made the fatal mistake of assuring him that his papers, which marked him as a foreign resident, would guarantee his safety. They reckoned without the viciousness of the pogrom carried out by local peasant farmers and Ukrainian police, under Nazi supervision.

The peasants began to gather early in the morning of 25 July, and set out from police stations, attacking any Jews they encountered with clubs, knives and axes. Some were taken to the Jewish cemetery and murdered. Police, in groups of five, consulted lists of Jewish leaders and intellectuals, and sent looters to break into specific buildings. One of them housed the first-floor apartment in which the *Rebbe* had been encouraged to live, openly.

The *Rebbe*, his son Rabbi Moshe Aaron and other prominent individuals were rounded up that afternoon and forced to march, three abreast, at a fast pace. He walked with a cane, could not keep up, and was whipped as he fell to the back of the column. He collapsed, was beaten around his head and face by rifle butts, and only reached Gestapo headquarters because he was held up by Eliyahu Avigdor, a disciple, and his son Moshe.

The following day three of his sons-in-law, Yecheskel Halberstam, Moshe Stempel and Shlome Rubin, all rabbis, were also captured. All five family members, and Mr Avigdor, were among an estimated 20,000 Jews shot and thrown into mass graves in the Yanover forest on Monday, 28 July, one of many days that should live forever in infamy.

The *Rebbe*'s wisdom involved a terrible prescience. He understood the historic consequences of Germany exiling Polish Jews living in the country in October 1938. I can remember his open letter being read out at the synagogue, asking the community to help the refugees, so-called *Ostjuden*, Jews from the East, who had arrived with nothing.

We took in two displaced families, and spread blankets, coats, sheets and anything else that could be used as bedding across the floors, so they could sleep. We fed them, felt their fear and bewilderment. They were broken people, with nowhere to go, dispossessed and thrown into poverty through no fault of their own. The mood in Krakow was dark and frightening.

Groups of adults gathered in the square, quietly asking an awful question: who would be next? The answers became unavoidable the following month, after Kristallnacht, the night of broken glass on 9 and 10 November, in which nearly 200 synagogues across Germany were destroyed, and 8,000 Jewish businesses were looted. The Nazis began transferring 30,000 Jewish men to forced labour camps.

The Jewish community was ordered to pay a one billion Reichsmark 'atonement tax' and the regime rapidly strengthened or enacted 400 anti-Jewish laws and edicts. Jews were thrown out of work and forbidden to operate as doctors, lawyers or journalists. They were non-citizens, banned from riding on trams and trains, prohibited from owning radios or even a dog.

I was still too young to fully understand what was going on, though I can remember receiving the news of Kristallnacht, and my parents' concern was obvious. We smelled the rat. I heard the name 'Hitler' so many times I shivered when it was mentioned. We realized we were unprotected, because the violence had extended into annexed Austria, and the Sudetenland in Czechoslovakia, which had recently been occupied by German troops. Poland was in the line of fire.

Despite the nervousness, life went on, and adulthood beckoned. I had a low-key *bar mitzvah* when I was thirteen. The community wished me *mazal tof*, after I had recited the blessings on the Torah for the first time. My father shared *lekach*, a honey cake, and a small bottle of vodka. I tried to keep my brothers occupied, singing and playing games, but it was impossible not to be distracted by Polish soldiers suddenly appearing on the street.

On 3 May 1939, Polish Independence Day, we watched the army march past, complete with full military band. There was something particularly empty about the pomp and ceremony. The Polish Citizens Organization was urging people to dig trenches in which to hide, during pitched battles with German soldiers that failed to materialize.

Some of the younger children began to be billeted out to surrounding villages during school holidays in that disastrously interrupted summer. My family decided to stay in Krakow, though some friends reckoned it would be easier to hide in the countryside. We were together as a unit, and drew strength from one another. We hoped for the best and dreaded the worst.

No one expected the Germans to arrive with such speed, and without a shot being fired. I was out digging one of those useless trenches when word came that we had to find shelter. Explosions signalled that bombers were targeting important municipal buildings. We could not contain our curiosity, once the drone of the aircraft became fainter, and sought out the still-smouldering craters.

It seemed so unreal, and yet became a new form of normality. We learned to respond to sirens, and watched the low-flying Luftwaffe planes doing as they pleased. The Germans invaded at dawn on 1 September 1939, and, with Krakow being relatively close to the Austrian border, their troops were in town before Polish soldiers had time to put on their uniforms.

Like all males under the age of fifty, my father had been mobilized. He set off for the recruiting office, only to find the Germans had got there before him. He returned home, while I was playing with two or three friends in a local park. We hid in trees and bushes when we heard the sound of tanks, and peeked out to see them being followed by trucks, motorcycles and armoured cars.

The troops wore body armour and had a variety of guns, impressive to any boy. They marched through the streets singing songs of victory. We were in awe of them, too immature to be afraid when a tank stopped in front of us. A soldier opened the hatch and beckoned us over. Not knowing what to say, I simply said 'Hello' in my best German.

He was brisk and to the point. '*Wo kan ich kaufen Crème Nuvua?*' he asked. He wanted to buy skin cream. When I pointed him in the direction of the apothecary, he smiled, thanked me, and disappeared down the turret. How could these be the monsters we had heard so much about? It didn't take long to find out.

We were immediately forbidden to gather in the streets, or talk in groups. Posters warned of dire punishment for disobedience. Loudspeaker announcements of new restrictions, in German and Polish, were a daily occurrence. I returned to school briefly, but abandoned my studies when the routine was disrupted. Within a month the mood became sinister.

At first the two-man patrols were relatively unthreatening. They ordered us to be quiet, but preferred to observe, rather than provoke or persecute. When circumstances began to change, the visibility of the more Orthodox Jews made them particular targets. The German soldiers made fun of our dress, laughed in our faces, and insulted us with increasing venom.

'*Schmutziege Jude.*' You didn't have to speak German to know you had been called a dirty Jew.

The persecution intensified, and my parents insisted I remove my *payos* for my safety. The Germans continually pushed us off the sidewalks, and randomly hacked with scissors at the beards and sidelocks of believers. I have never forgotten coming across four Nazis burning the beard of an elderly man with a cigarette lighter. They laughed as he screamed in pain and panic, and left him weeping in the gutter.

The persecution became progressively more distressing. Troops began to slash traditional clothing with their bayonets, deliberately drawing blood. I still wore my silk *bekishe* on the Sabbath, but reverted to ordinary clothing during the week, so I did not stand out. From 1 December, we were ordered to wear white armbands, with a blue star of David, to distinguish us as Jews.

Everyday life was relentlessly extinguished. The invaders restricted the number of hours we could be outside, and ordered Jews to clean the streets, where beatings were administered mercilessly, without reason. This was the start of

Zwangsarbeit, forced labour. My father undertook heavy, dirty work, designed to weaken and demoralize.

Our family had stockpiled food before the invasion, but as shortages began to bite and prices began to spiral out of control, often doubling overnight, I stole out to wholesalers and surreptitiously bought whatever was available. In normal times this would have been smart business practice, but in reality any money we made temporarily from selling the surplus was worthless, since it had lost all value.

Every second or third evening, before the 9 p.m. curfew was imposed, I wrapped myself in a blanket and slept as best I could on the pavement outside the bakery. There was no option but to queue overnight since the shop's capacity was reduced to fifty loaves a day. The queue stretched around the block, so hundreds were disappointed; each lucky customer was restricted to one loaf.

Hunger was growing, and we remembered our sacred pledge to generosity, giving pieces of bread or a little soup to beggars who came to our door. Our stomachs are not made of glass, so you cannot see whether they are empty, but the eyes of the famished reveal all. There were days when I wished we were animals. We would have received better treatment.

The Nazis had been quick to establish supposedly neutral trustees, *Treuhaendler*, for the biggest businesses, which invited greed and corruption. Jews were banned from traditional trades, in textiles, cotton or linen goods, leatherwear and shoes. Their bank accounts had been blocked. By the end of 1939 any gold, silver and jewels that could not be hidden had been confiscated.

Many shops closed. Others were looted by Polish residents, who smashed windows and hauled goods out onto the sidewalk, so anyone could take what they wanted. On one occasion, walking near the square, I noticed a commotion around a wooden barrel and, because I was small, I was able to wriggle through the scrum. People were fighting over chocolate, so I did likewise, and grabbed as much as I could.

War was stripping away the pretences of dignity and decency. An ugly strain of anti-Semitism, among those we had previously valued as neighbours, began to manifest itself. Even before the war, when I would see graffiti saying 'Send Jews to Palestine' or 'Jews are Communists', it had barely been beneath the surface.

German soldiers helped themselves from Jewish properties, and some in the community even spoke of German citizens coming across the border to steal. The tales of previously poorly dressed individuals leaving town in smart suits and laden with jewellery and household goods were too common for them to be fantasy.

It is only in later years, sharing my story with researchers at Yad Vashem in Jerusalem, that I truly began to understand the roots of such outrages. On one level, Jews are seen as forever guilty of the crime of killing Jesus Christ for money, thirty shekels of silver. On another, they are loathed because allegedly they want to take over the world.

Many sleeping memories were stirred by the images of suffering and mass murder at the memorial centre in Jerusalem, but one exhibit summed up how basically the poison was applied. The exhibit was a popular German board game from 1936, *Juden Raus*, 'Jews Out'. The aim of the game was to expel these dirty, ugly beings from your country. You win by taking over their stores and stealing all their goods.

Give anyone power, and there is a good chance they will misuse it, even among their own. The Gestapo controlled Jewish affairs through the *Judenrat*, a so-called Jewish council, also known by the Hebrew term *Kahal*. They, in turn, employed a Jewish police force, the *Jüdischer Ordnundienst*, the OD, which executed the orders of the SS.

The police were as bad as the Nazis. They provided them with local knowledge, and seemed to take pleasure in the persecution by leading the round-ups, pulling people from their beds. What began as almost a bureaucratic exercise, in fulfilling work quotas, became a murderous tool of oppression. On one occasion, 300 Jews were taken. We never heard from them again.

One of our neighbours, Moszke, was hated and feared when he became a member of the OD. We knew we needed to stay away from him, because he was openly collaborating. Loyalty to a former friend or neighbour meant nothing to him, because he was eager to serve new masters. He was a former customer in mother's store, but there were no benefits to be had from associating with him.

It was terrifying. No one knew when there would be a knock at the door. Members of the *Judenrat* demanded large bribes. If these so-called 'contributions' were not paid, more people disappeared. The OD helped the Germans, and themselves, during the confiscation of valuables, foreign currency and anything of interest, like a fur coat or radio set.

It all literally came too close to home when my uncle Leibish was arrested and thrown into the notorious Montelupich prison, north of Krakow's old town. He was being beaten up during a search of his house when a young girl, a relative on his mother's side who had been lodging with his family, panicked and told the police where he had hidden some British currency.

Being small, agile, and reckless enough to want to prove myself a man, I was given the job of getting him a note, which contained important information about the attorney defending him. I climbed a wall, pushed a bread-and-butter sandwich through the barred window of his cell, and told him, as loudly as I dared, to look inside.

Miraculously, and no doubt by greasing the appropriate palms, he was eventually released. His hair had grown long and matted. It was infested with lice. Before he was taken to jail, he had been a wise, smart and successful man. Now he was weak, demoralized, broken. It was heartbreaking to see him in such a state.

The Nazi stranglehold grew tighter, and more deadly. Food was running out. Stores were empty. There were no raw materials and farmers had to supply almost all their harvest to the authorities. Residents of surrounding villages did not dare to enter the town, and those who tried to flee the other way were risking their lives.

My parents faced a terrible dilemma. Stay and slowly starve, or flee and put us in danger. Once rumours began to circulate that all Jews were to be herded into a ghetto, there really was no choice but to try and escape to Dzialoszyce. As far as he knew, my father still owned his mill, so he reasoned we would still have a means to eat.

On one dark night, we stole out of our house and headed for a pre-arranged boat on the Vistula River. Never had its folk name, the Mother River, seemed so appropriate. She held us close, and by morning had delivered us to an uncle's house in the village of Nowe Miasto, where we had been told the German presence was not as threatening.

This involved travelling north, instead of west, but it seemed a good staging post. For six weeks or so we kept ourselves to ourselves, and life was tolerable. Father was clean-shaven, and wore a suit rather than traditional dress, but when he was brutally beaten in the marketplace by the SS for no apparent reason, his mind was made up. We were no longer safe. It was time for the family once again to run away, and trust in fate.

3

The Last Goodbye

I was growing up far too quickly, a boy masquerading as a man. Part of this was down to necessity so that, being young and slight, I didn't arouse suspicion, like older, more mature youths. I had always been resourceful and strong-willed, and now, with all life's certainties ended, I made a virtue of the ability to think on my feet.

Our plight was immediately obvious when we arrived in Dzialoszyce. The shtetl was filling up with those who had made similar journeys from nearby towns such as Lodz, Pinczow and Zaglebie. The Nazis were effectively trapping us from the start of 1940, by banning Jews from taking up a new address without express permission.

We had no option to begin with except to lodge with Sheindel Chaba, my father's sister, and her husband Meir. This meant the entire family sharing a small room, while my parents tried desperately to reconnect the shattered strands of our pre-war existence.

It took time, and a considerable amount of horse-trading, to get back into the apartment that Father had rented out when we were in the capital, but it turned out that was the least of his, and our, worries. His mill had been given to a

Polish man, a non-Jew, because, under the rules of occupation, Father was forbidden to own and trade from it.

The Polish usurper quickly went back on his promises to give us a little grain as compensation. He was arrogant and unfeeling. When Father returned to beg him to reconsider, the man reluctantly sold him a small amount of flour at an extortionate price. There was no option for Father but to swallow his pride and accept the deal.

When Mother went to make bread she discovered she had no salt. We looked everywhere, but there was none to be found locally, so she made the best of it. What can I tell you? We were like hungry wolves, but the loaves tasted awful. They were dry and it felt like we were chewing straw. Since our stomachs were empty we ate slices of bread with our eyes closed.

We had to count our blessings, because other refugees were crammed together in unsanitary conditions, often without running water. Around a thousand people were housed in the synagogue and the adjoining *bet midrash*, our study hall, where families slept on shelves, with only thin sheets of linen to protect their privacy. Even without the worries of war, it was a struggle to keep body and soul together.

The Germans had arrived in Dzialoszyce on 8 September, a week after their armoured cruise into Krakow. Their district headquarters were in Miechow, around twenty-five kilometres away, so although the Jewish community had to endure the usual criminal activity by troops, who stole at will, the harassment was a little less intense, initially at least.

There had to be some way to look for food and other goods, even though, from late January, we were forbidden to travel outside the area for any reason whatsoever. I had heard of people disguising themselves as Gentiles, visiting neighbouring towns and villages, buying a range of goods and selling the surpluses back at the shtetl for a very good profit.

This, of course, meant removing the hated armband with the Star of David. It wasn't until recently that I realized the historical burden this represented. I learned, through Yad Vashem, that symbols have been used to target Jews since the Middle Ages; in France, for instance, they were forced to wear a circular yellow patch.

It is a form of violation. Your identity is no longer personal or private, but intended to be a public source of shame. We were being branded like cattle, but defiance was very dangerous. If you were caught without the Star of David you were usually shot, no questions asked. I was naïve and impulsive. I reckoned it was my duty, as the eldest son, to search out food, wherever it could be found.

It began with a search for salt in surrounding villages. People often told me that I didn't look Jewish, so I wore regular clothes, including a beret, and tucked my *tzitzis*, the tassels worn by observant Jews, inside my clothing. This was enough to prevent me from being recognized immediately, so I went around knocking on doors, trusting in God's will.

I was very careful, but very lucky. I felt a surge of pride and relief when I returned safely, with enough salt to ease mother's baking needs. It cost a lot, but money wasn't really an object, because there was so little to spend it on. In order not to pay with my life, I needed better protection.

This came in the form of false papers, provided by my uncle through a salesman called Zadon, who had taken over his shoe factory in Austria at the start of the war. Zadon had been the company's main sales agent in Germany and was trusted by the regime, since he had been a member of the Nazi Party from its earliest days.

He proved the point by showing us his membership card, which had a very low registration number, but promised he would look after us. On the face of it, this was madness, but uncle regarded him almost as a member of his family. Zadon often ate at my uncle's *Shabbos* tables in the apartment in Krakow, and loved to join in the singing of *zmiros*, which celebrated the Creator.

The fake documentation identified me as a Polish worker in Zadon's newly acquired shoe factory, which had a contract to supply leather boots to the German army. It didn't have the damning 'J' on it, to give away my faith. I was still taking huge risks, but this at least persuaded my parents that I was not entirely on a fool's errand. I quickly became an efficient smuggler, and an expert in the black market, a source of flour and yeast.

I bought anything and everything I could. Farmers sold beets, barley, beans, cabbages, cucumbers, carrots, potatoes and onions. The family had first pick; once we stocked up, I sold on the rest for triple the price to fund another round of bargaining and purchasing. Lessons learned in the street outside my mother's old store were being put to good effect.

I wasn't infallible, though. I once bought a large sack of beans from a village just outside Krakow, and congratulated myself for the profit they would inevitably bring. I hired a taxi and hid them in the engine compartment, a huge mistake since when I got the beans home they stank of petrol. We washed them continually before boiling them, but they were inedible. They still tasted like gasoline.

We tried spreading them out on the roof to dry and cleanse

them, but the fresh air, and the spring sunshine, did little good. We eventually gave them away to the desperate or the destitute. I heeded the first lesson of business: never dwell on a setback, however avoidable. Focus on the future, and new opportunities.

Those came when I noticed everyone's shoes were starting to wear out. People complained about holes in their soles, so I used uncle's contacts to source small pieces of leather. This required a cloak-and-dagger visit to Krakow, where I figured that taking a taxi would leave me less exposed to checks by highway patrols. The driver looked the other way as I used the old trick of hiding the supplies under the hood, close to the engine. This time, at least, the goods could not be spoiled.

These small pieces of leather obviously provided only temporary relief, though, so I set out to exploit a gap in the market by getting hold of rubber soles. These were scarce, since they were a fairly new item, so it required a bit of lateral thinking. I heard of a factory selling rubber in long, wide sheets, which I hid by bending them around my waist and stashing them under my coat.

I must have looked a comical sight, small, fat and round, but I went from house to house, selling the rubber by the slice. Once the sheets were cut up into small pieces, people couldn't get enough of them. I then remembered my brief time in school, where I'd learned to sew, and had bought up needles and thread, so clothes could be repaired.

If I travelled on a train, I would hide my bags beneath the bench. Fortunately, the only time I was confronted by the Germans, I was carrying a false suitcase, containing only a few pieces of ragged clothing. That was enough to throw them off the scent. I had spotted an increased level of surveillance at the station and taken the precaution of hiding my illicit goods in other carriages.

I was afraid, but we had to live. I felt guilty that my father had become a victim of the local *Judenrat*, which had set up a special Labour Department. This introduced a supposedly fair rota of all able-bodied males above the age of fourteen to do whatever menial work the Germans demanded. It was meant to exclude the heads of large families, and special social cases.

This was theoretically a good idea that became another excuse for extortion. Wealthier families simply paid bribes or gave poorer folk a daily salary of between five and ten zlotys to act as substitutes for their sons and husbands in the work gangs. To give you an idea of the pittance represented by that payment, the minimum bribe that occupation authorities would accept was 500 zlotys.

The Germans brought in a supervisor named Mucha to clean up the streets. Father collected garbage, dug sewage ditches, cleared snow, and worked in the fields. He was regularly beaten for supposedly not working hard enough, from dawn until sunset. I occasionally went in his place so he could recover, since it was extremely physical, unforgiving work.

We cut grains and harvested potatoes by hand, and were ordered into the forest to cut down trees and chop them up for firewood. Often Jews were snatched off the streets by the Jewish police, the hated OD. They boasted that our bodies were their property. They could do whatever they wished with us. The SS took pleasure in other indignities, such as banning beards. This caused great distress and led to many risking punishment by refusing to shave.

Some of the younger men were taken to labour camps near

Krakow, and ransoms were demanded. Others were made to work for the German firm Richard Strauch, which seemed eager to profit from human misery. Working conditions were terrible; the *Judenrat* at least attempted to organize food parcels and warmer clothing. Once again, if the right palms were greased, sons were reunited with their worried families. Bayerlein, head of the local Gestapo, was the most notorious crook.

Dzialoszyce was groaning beneath the weight of additional refugees. Hundreds of families squatted in public buildings. The synagogue, banned from staging services or Torah study sessions, became a magnet for the displaced. Zionist youth movements went from house to house, collecting clothes, blankets and pieces of furniture, but food was the biggest priority.

A public dining hall was set up in a wing above the *Bet Midrash*, serving hot meals and bread. Most of the volunteers were eventually murdered in Belzec. It is the least I can do to honour them by relaying some of their names, recorded in a resident's journal:

> Salomea Gertler, wife of Shlomo
> Joseph and Solomon Shulimovitch
> Shlomo and Hayyim Kaczka
> Moshe Kamelgarten
> Mottel Rozenek

I weep for them.

By the end of 1940 thousands were taking advantage of their charity, but the lack of sanitation and overcrowding meant there were increasing health problems. Those who lived in the study hall had no toilets, and water had to be brought in from the well. It was a hard winter; fuel was scarce. Still more people poured in, as the Nazis forcibly deported residents from other towns and villages.

It was such a breeding ground for contagious disease that typhoid and typhus epidemics took hold in 1941. There was no hospital, and the lack of public hygiene resulted in an additional outbreak of dysentery. The *hekdesh*, a poorhouse close to the cemetery, was used to isolate the worst cases.

We discovered that heroes are not only found on the battlefield. It is no exaggeration to say the community was saved by a Jewish doctor, Dvora Lazer. She joined Dr Grambovsky, the only other doctor in town, in 1940, but had primary responsibility for overseeing the health of more than 10,000 people. She became a one-woman epidemic controller, forced to cope with constant shortages of medical supplies.

She was faced with a fiendish dilemma, knowing that if the Germans learned of the extent of the outbreak, as they were supposed to under the rules of occupation, their response would doubtless have been murderous. Dr Lazer quietly set up a Sanitary Committee, and established fumigation centres, cleaned daily with sulphur. All refugees and their belongings were disinfected in high-temperature steam rooms. Mercifully, the epidemics eased before the Nazis could appreciate their extent.

I am often asked why I did not run away during my smuggling expeditions – but where would I have gone? Though there were many honourable exceptions of local families who courageously sheltered Jews, at terrible personal cost, the majority of Polish residents actively informed against us, and, as I was to discover, would slam their doors in the faces of anyone who asked for help.

I reached my sixteenth birthday on 21 July 1942. I was now older but not that much taller and barely wiser, even if enforced work made me slightly more muscular. Our limited version of the news, delivered through Yiddish papers and illicit radios, was dominated by tales of German triumphs. Holland and Belgium fell. France succumbed. Hitler was sweeping eastwards. Who would stop these masters of the universe?

About a year earlier, leaders of the Zionist Youth movements, like the Kaczka, Rozenek and Shulemovitch brothers, secretly discussed setting up an underground Resistance movement. There were few organized Polish partisans in the area, so a supply of weapons was an obvious problem, but, as a rash teenager, I was all in favour of such defiance.

The Shulemovitchs were distant cousins. I was especially friendly with them and the Rozeneks, but lost contact later on after occasionally coming across them in one concentration camp or another. It was another local youth, Moniek Sarna, who enticed me into an operation to blow up a bridge near the train station. 'We have to do everything we can to hurt the Germans,' he told me. 'I'm ready, I'm ready,' I exclaimed, oblivious to the risks.

We were still freethinkers and had not been worn down by the yoke of slavery. Another friend, Yosek Tenemal, whom I had met in Yavneh, an Orthodox Jewish youth group, was with us. He survived the war, and I visited him many years later in Toronto, where he called himself Joe Tanenbaum, and was happily married to a successful sculptress.

So it was that we assembled silently late one afternoon. I was told to hold a long fuse wire for some engineers, partisan fighters who welcomed our help. I was a novice and didn't really know what was going on, but my job was to keep the wire tight, so there were no kinks or angles as everything was connected.

Eventually the professionals, who carried the explosives in a backpack, slipped away to finish the job. The next thing I knew the darkening sky was illuminated by the flash from a huge blast. We ran away in all directions, seized by a strange combination of terror and exultation.

The Germans quickly surrounded the area. We heard a lot of shooting and screaming. I figured my best chance was to lie low, hiding in the undergrowth. I chewed long grass, sucking out any moisture I could find, for two days, before gambling that the coast was clear. I wasn't really thinking clearly. Predictably, I was quickly picked up by the Nazis, as I walked along a country road.

I thought on my feet, explaining I had been visiting a family known to my parents, but the Germans were not gentle with me. They handcuffed me and threw me into the notorious Montelupich jail in Krakow. I sat there for more than a week, denying any involvement in sabotage. There was little food, and I was doused with cold water under questioning, so that I shivered uncontrollably.

It was all I could do to resist the thought that this was what happened to people before they vanished, without trace. I was saved by my parents, who were able to get me a lawyer. He had taken the precaution of paying off the family, who contacted the authorities and provided me with an alibi. After ten days or so of worry and discomfort, I was freed.

How could I be so blind to the dangers? As throughout my life, I prayed to God, *HaShem*, and trusted in His heavenly protection. I should, though, have also picked up on the concerns of my elders and betters, who, as time went on, began hearing rumours of entire Jewish communities being expelled, and disappearing to unknown destinations.

Panic was mounting. In late August 1942 the shtetl shuddered at news from Zaglembie, where 12,500 Jews had been sent to a camp at Auschwitz-Birkenau. Rumours of a similar pogrom in another nearby town, Sosnowiec, began to spread. Members of Dzialoszyce's *Judenrat* went daily, with special permission, to the German headquarters in Miechow, but were told nothing.

I was working in a field in the village of Nieskow on 2 September when, at around midday, the *Ordnungsdienst*, the Jewish police, arrived and ordered us to down tools. They announced Dzialoszyce was being made *Judenrein*, Jew-free. I was terrified of that word. It felt like a signal that the end of the world was nigh. We were to return home, under their supervision, and await developments.

My first instinct was to escape. Since there was no roll call, I wasn't missed when I chose my moment, and slipped away into a nearby stable, where I stayed until nightfall. All the old bravado had gone; I felt alone and vulnerable as I glanced out, across dark, empty fields. The only sign of life was a flickering light in what turned out to be the window of a farmhouse.

It wasn't a case of me summoning courage to knock on the door; I was desperate for a drink, and something to eat. Hard eyes looked out from behind the door, which was barely open, and quickly shut in my face. I walked on, into a settlement, and was given the same treatment. Apart from one home, where I was given a small cup of milk, it was clear that Jewish beggars were unwelcome.

Each contact carried the danger of betrayal, discovery and death. There was nothing I could do but retrace my steps to the stable, where I lay among cattle and pigs in straw alive with rats that nipped at my feet. In those endless, sleepless hours before dawn I realized I was beaten. I begged for food soon after dawn, again without success, and had no alternative but to try to make my way back to Dzialoszyce.

It could easily have been the last journey of my life. The shtetl was under siege from the Germans. They surrounded the town and were taking no prisoners. My best chance was the *Koleika*, a small train which usually ferried workers to and from the area. It would slow to a crawl as it negotiated a steep hill, which allowed me to jump on and edge into a gap between two carriages.

I frantically tried to keep my balance as the cars swayed alarmingly and unpredictably, and almost fell under the wheels when the train lurched as it gathered speed. I lost a shoe in the process, but managed to cling on until we reached Dzialoszyce, where I was able to jump down and into the shadows.

There were soldiers all around, so I hid in doorways and pressed against the walls on side streets, trying to make my way to the town centre. I had arrived in Hell. There were bodies strewn across the road; I could see men, women and children clustered in courtyards. I knew my fate if I was spotted, and pressed on, step by haunted step, towards my parents' house.

I never reached it. It meant going through the market square, which was illuminated by harsh floodlights and reflectors. Orders were being screamed out, over loudspeakers. Everyone had to gather there at six o'clock the following morning. Each Jew would be permitted ten kilogrammes of luggage. Anyone found in their homes after that deadline, or anyone who dared peek out from their windows overnight, would be shot on sight.

My salvation came in the form of a house at the edge of the square, which belonged to my mother's cousin, Mordechai Joseph Latash. His family were startled to see me, but offered refuge as they went about their awful chore, of deciding what necessities they would take with them, all too soon after dawn. No one slept; my news helped to see to that.

The square was a pathetic sight at 6 a.m. Men and women, the old and the young, shuffled along, carrying their burdens as best they could. Their faces were pinched with dread. Guard dogs barked and sprang forward. Entire streets joined the throng, as the sun rose higher in the sky and I crawled around on all fours, looking, with increasing fearfulness, for my family.

Someone I recognized as a neighbour gestured towards a group huddled on the floor. I saw my parents and brothers, and lunged towards their embrace, mercifully without attracting the attention of guards who were under orders to shoot anyone who stood up. We did not so much weep, but wail in relief and anguish. What was happening? Where were we going?

Polish residents were banned from the area. They stayed in their homes, behind curtained windows, which featured a Cross to proclaim their difference. They might as well have been vultures, waiting on a wire. Once the despicable deeds of the day were done, they would emerge, to loot and scavenge what was rightfully ours, but forcibly left behind in the evacuation.

Eventually, in mid-afternoon, we were told to get up, form a line, and march to the station. Those who found it hard to walk, the old, the weak and the infirm, were taken out and loaded into horse-drawn carts, driven by Polish peasants under SS supervision. We never saw them again. About an hour later, we heard sustained bursts of machine-gun fire in the distance.

Around 1,200 people, including Itzhak Halevi Staslovsky, a prominent local rabbi, were meeting their end in the cemetery, where they were shot and thrown into three mass graves. The slaughter had started. A fog began to descend on our minds, blotting everything else out but the seeming certainty of death. How had it come to this? Why had we been so cruelly deserted?

Many of us were herded into overcrowded cattle cars. The rest were loaded into open trucks. Our destination was a large open field on the outskirts of Miechow, which, in my confused state, seemed to continue as far as the eye could see. Once there, it was obvious we were not alone. There were hundreds and thousands from other towns like Skalbmierz, Wodzislaw and Wielki, also awaiting their fate.

Members of the *Judenrat* and lackeys of the OD were among us, but now as prisoners. Nazi promises that they would be protected had meant nothing.

We felt numb, physically and mentally, as night fell. The cold crept into our bones. We were terribly thirsty. I cannot remember too many families having the foresight to take food with them, as part of their allowance, because most carried clothes and valuables. That meant most of us suffered from hunger pangs.

My father withdrew into himself. He complained of feeling

weak and sucked on a sugar cube to restore his spirits. The rough ground of the field on which we sat, already damp with the dew, became increasingly wet; when we lay down our hair was quickly soaked. As the grass became increasingly water-logged, my father suddenly stirred, and realized what was wrong.

He knew of a flour mill nearby. This drew water from the river, which was dammed. The Nazis had opened the sluices, so, by the time dawn began to break, everyone was freezing, sitting waist-deep in water, under pain of death not to move. What diseased mind could come up with such a cruel plan? The torture had obviously been worked out well in advance.

The aim was to demoralize us, stun us like animals arriving at the abattoir. In late morning everyone was told to undress to the waist and form twenty lines, which seemed to stretch for-ever. They must have contained around 16,000 people. At the head of each line was an SS officer, flanked on either side by armed guards.

He dispensed life and death wordlessly, with a casual flick of his whip. We approached, arms raised, in batches. My father was sent to the left, my mother to the right. I joined my father, while my brothers, cousins, aunts and uncles were pushed towards my mother. Everything happened so fast; there was no time to say goodbye.

My mind seized up, through shock and grief. Crying was the easiest thing we could do, but we were beyond tears. We were cold, hungry, scared, demoralized. No one should know such a feeling. It was inhuman. There was no farewell, no kiss, no hugs or holding hands.

All my father and I could do was make a fumbling gesture, and give our belongings to my mother and brothers, since father reckoned warm clothing would be more useful for them than us. We did not know it at the time, when we were hustled towards the group of 800 or so unwittingly selected to live, but we had given my mother an unnecessary burden that she carried until her death.

I still, to this day, feel a sense of guilt, almost shame. That is why the faces of my mother and brothers are hidden from me in my dreams. They are living ghosts, who speak silently to us all.

4

Desecration of the Dead

My world was in ruins. I was scared, bewildered, exhausted. I might have thought of myself as a man, but I needed the simple comforts of childhood. My father held me by the hand as we trudged into the unknown, throughout the longest of nights. My stomach ached and my brain was muddled. I walked with my eyes closed and craved sleep.

Whenever I stumbled, I felt my father's body stiffen. He had seen the fate of others who had shown such weakness and fallen to the ground. They were beaten, brutalized by screaming SS guards. If they did not respond, and were unable to resume our forced march, they were dispatched like a dog that had outlived its usefulness.

My senses were scrambled. I tasted freshly disturbed dust at the back of my throat and guessed we were on a path, or a road. At other times, when I probably strayed into a ditch in the darkness, it seemed as if I was wading through long grass, or weeds. As dawn broke, we arrived at a place called Liszki. It was only fifteen kilometres east of Krakow, but it felt like the end of the Earth.

We were herded into an empty building and ordered to lie down on straw. Famished and frightened, we seized on the small mercy of a cup of what our captors called soup.

Compared to the steaming bowls of chicken broth or cabbage soup served by my mother, it was dishwater, but it was all we had.

That was then, this was now. My former life was slipping away.

I had no idea of the agonies my mother, brothers and other relatives were going through during those hours, in the death factory at Belzec, but her memory was still too recent and too painful to bear. For almost the next three years, until liberation and the bitter betrayals of my return to the family home in Poland, I lived closer and closer to the edge of existence.

Later that day, we were marched to nearby fields, which were waterlogged and foul-smelling. They put us to work draining the swamp, digging channels and hauling pipes. Once again, the contract had been given to a German firm, Richard Strauss. Their employees took pleasure in ordering us around and treating us just as badly as the guards did.

I was too young to realize this, but their casual cruelty foretold the torments that were to come. They saw us as being beneath them, and knew they didn't have to care that, in a previous life, we were like them. We, too, had our everyday problems, frustrations and ambitions. They enjoyed the power to punish and humiliate that war had given them.

It doesn't take much for such callousness to eat away at what remains of your conscience, so that killing a fellow human being becomes as thoughtless a process as swatting a fly.

It was back-breaking work. We dug for up to fourteen hours each day, slowly sinking until it was difficult to stand. The mud reached our waist and oozed into our underwear. Bugs and worms crawled across our skin, which grew raw and scabby. I still, to this day, bear the scars of being bitten by insects and tiny irritants. They are very faint, but I still have an urge to scratch them.

Priorities changed, as our plight worsened. There was a growing temptation to succumb to despair, and wallow in what we had lost. Food had never been plentiful during the years of occupation, but our bellies had never been this empty. The obsession of even half-filling our stomachs started to take hold.

We began to measure time by the distance between a hunk of bread, distributed early in the morning, and the dishwater soup, or a warm liquid, weak coffee or chicory, which, together with another piece of bread, passed for an evening meal. Compared to the camps that awaited us, this was a banquet, yet still completely inadequate for our needs. Our bodies were being starved of fuel.

Our group was reinforced continually by survivors from the cull of other local communities. Many traumatized newcomers retreated into themselves, but some were eager to speak, though mostly in murmurs or whispers, when our labours were over, and we were expected to sleep as best we could on the floor. One, who recognized my father, brought truly terrible news.

The uncle who had given us refuge on our return to Dzialoszyce, Meir Yacov Chaba, owned a textile shop, which he handed over to a regular customer, a Polish non-Jewish resident of a nearby village, when he was no longer permitted to trade. This man arrived at our door one evening with a horse and cart, which we filled with rolls of cloth and other personal belongings that my uncle had promised him.

In return, the man vowed to protect my uncle and his

family if the worst happened. When it did, and the *Judenrein* order was issued, my uncle, his wife Sheindel and their children risked everything by stealing away to the man's home, where, as part of the bargain, they were hidden. They were spared deportation, but were not out of danger.

Their unwilling host was frightened of being betrayed by his neighbours, or being discovered by the SS, who were ruthlessly hunting down anyone who attempted to flee. He told my uncle he feared for all their lives, and urged him to ready his family to move to another hiding place. They would need to move under the cover of darkness.

The man promised it would be a temporary arrangement, until things quietened down, but instead he took them into a nearby meadow and murdered them all, before burying them on the spot. It is impossible to keep such a monstrous crime entirely quiet, because he must have needed assistance. Word somehow reached surrounding villages before they, in turn, were stripped of any Jewish influence.

Our companion in the labour gangs explained he felt it was his duty to tell us the truth. I felt sick to my stomach, thinking of my innocent cousins and my dear, kind aunt and uncle being butchered. My father was not a violent man, but he swore vengeance. He knew the murderer and the location of the killings. He never let go of the thought of what he would do to the attacker, and his family, if he survived.

I made the same promise to myself, envisaging setting fire to the man's home while he slept or bringing him to justice so that I could watch him suffer, without realizing the mental toll that captivity would bring. The daily ordeal of staying alive scoured my memory in strange ways. I could recall certain individuals and events with great clarity, but lost dates and details of other incidents as if they never existed.

So, when I returned to the area on my liberation, I found I could no longer remember the murderer's name, or the village in which he lived. No one, and nothing, could trigger my memory. This caused me tremendous pain, because I had failed my family, after being spared to fulfil the duty of at least finding the last resting place of my innocent cousins, aunt and uncle.

When we speak about the Holocaust we refer to millions of victims, but the numbers are almost too big to comprehend. Each of those fatalities had a name, a place and a life, however short and cruelly curtailed. There is no reminder or confirmation of what happened to my aunt, uncle and cousins apart from these words. They were just another family, thrown into an unmarked grave in a desolate field. Another group of victims denied the respect of remembrance.

Death, I learned quickly, offered no protection from the inhumanity of our oppressors, who decided to build an *Arbeitslager*, a slave labour camp, in Plaszow, a southern suburb of Krakow, on the site of two Jewish cemeteries. Jeruzolimska was the oldest, having been established in 1887. The second was barely ten years old, and had a beautiful *Ohel*, a form of tomb built in the Byzantine style.

The Nazis were not content with taunting, and killing, the living. They refused to let the dead rest. Dozens of us were ordered to line up behind huge earth movers, which levelled the headstones and gouged out the graves. It was my job to shovel up remains, bones, skulls, teeth and scraps of humanity, into a wheelbarrow pushed by someone who ran along to my left.

Everything had to be done at speed; we were shouted at, whipped across the back and shoulders, and threatened with being shot if we paused or stopped. The disturbed bodies, or what was left of them, were dumped into a hastily dug hole and covered with earth. The sights and smells of such desecration were revolting, and our ears rang with constant abuse, but we were learning not to think, never to question or register emotion.

If we had done so at the time, we would have realized that even the subsequent use of the headstones was a calculated insult. They were recycled as paving slabs, set in front of administrative offices, and also formed pathways to the homes of SS officers. The camp originally covered twenty-five acres of rocky ground, which was marshy in places. By the time it became a fully fledged concentration camp, in January 1944, it had grown to eight times the size.

Eventually it housed 25,000 prisoners, ten times the number it was initially designed to take. We initially lived in tents on the cemetery grounds, and were joined by gangs of slave labourers, the so-called *Barrackenbau* Jews, who commuted from the Krakow ghetto during the early stages of its liquidation. They told us, in snatched conversations, of persecution and starvation beyond our imaginations.

No one mentioned the obvious, that we were building our own prison. We merely prayed that we would not be killed when we were surplus to requirements. We dug out the sewage system, helped build wooden barracks, and tied barbed wire around nails with our bare hands to form double fencing, which, when the camp was fully extended, measured nearly four kilometres. We cemented wooden poles in at regular intervals; the guards patrolled a five-metre corridor between the wires. Machine guns were installed in watchtowers.

You may be aware of a Hollywood version of the camp, as depicted in the movie *Schindler's List*. This was created in the nearby Liban Quarry, which also served as a labour camp for Poles between 1942 and 1944, where typhus and malaria were rife. The life expectancy of prisoners was measured in weeks.

Steven Spielberg's film set included thirty-four replica barracks and watchtowers, remnants of which can still be seen alongside the genuine artefacts, like an abandoned gunpowder warehouse, rusty machinery, fence posts, and triangles of barbed wire. Graffiti artists have somehow scaled the refinery towers. One scrawled message simply says: 'I care about you.'

The quarry was designated as a protected ecological area in 2022; it is largely overgrown and unstable. Waterfowl nest on hidden ponds, and birds of prey soar above limestone cliffs. It extends to the boundary of the former concentration camp. The movie captured the menace of that place, the sense of emptiness and hopelessness it was designed to generate, and the crimes that were perpetrated within.

Today it is also a nature reserve, with thinly wooded hills and open, scrubby grassland. Only the stone entrance arch remains. I shuddered as I stood beneath it on my recent return, because I felt the force of its secrets. As one of the signs on the perimeter says, 'Please respect the grievous history of this site.'

No one can be entirely certain, since the Nazis, led by *Kommandoführerin* Alice Orlowski, a vicious high-ranking female SS officer, destroyed all records in the face of Russian advances towards the end of the war. But it is estimated that the remains of between 8,000 and 10,000 prisoners, or victims of the Krakow ghetto clearance programme, are still located here.

When I was last there, in May 2018 on a bright day with high clouds and a gentle wind, boys rode their bikes across and around the mounds that mark ten mass graves.

The Memorial of Torn-Out Hearts stands on Plaszow's second mass execution pit. It depicts five figures, representing the dead of five nations, killed there. Their heads are bent under their burden, and the stone block from which they are carved has a horizontal crack, across their chests. This symbolizes lives abruptly ended.

The text on a stone obelisk at its base reads, 'In memory of those murdered, whose final scream of anguish is the silence of this Plaszow graveyard.'

There were no gas chambers or crematoria, so mass murder was carried out by shootings. I know, to my cost, that the elderly and the sick were the first to be sacrificed, because I received confirmation, long after liberation, that my mother's parents, the Lataczs, were among the first groups to be murdered there on 31 October 1942, three days after the ghetto clearance began.

Normally, that sort of information offers closure. Yet I still cannot get a nightmare image out of my head. If I am honest, I sometimes wonder if my mind is playing tricks on me. Yet when I found myself back on an otherwise unremarkable hillside named Hujowa Górka, a former Austrian military rampart from the First World War, it all seemed so real.

A modest wooden cross, with a symbolic crown of barbed wire, stands above what was once a hexagonal pit, five metres deep and fifty metres in circumference. It was here that the condemned arrived, usually in covered lorries. They were told to undress and lie down before being shot in batches, through the back of the head. Their bodies were stacked in layers, alternating head to toe, and covered with lime, sand and soil.

Eventually, when the Krakow ghetto liquidation was at its height, all camp inmates, including children, were forced to watch executions on an almost daily basis. But on this particular day, ordered to assemble there in the early weeks of the fiendish pogrom, no one really knew what to expect. Murderous routines were still being established. We saw bodies, lying in a little valley, and were ordered to undress them.

One group had the job of tearing the clothes apart at the seams, to find any hidden valuables, like gold coins and jewellery. I was among those who had to remove the clothes and place them in a pile. As I did so, I could have sworn I noticed a bloodstained photograph of my family. I couldn't bend down to examine it, or slip it into my pocket, because there were too many SS eyes on us. One rash decision, a hasty reflex action to retrieve it, and I would have joined my grandparents in eternity.

Maybe part of the brain shuts down out of self-preservation in such circumstances. I must have looked for my grandparents, because that would have been a natural reaction, but I have no clear memory of recognizing their corpses. Perhaps that is a blessing. All I know is that when I was by myself that night, after working on autopilot, I shivered.

We had no option but to do so many dirty, terrible jobs. Our actions may be inconceivable in what passes as normality in today's world, but they kept us alive. I didn't pray as regularly, because we didn't have a *siddur*, a Jewish prayer book that contains our liturgy, but I sought strength from my faith in God.

I wanted to celebrate Him when I returned to Plaszow as part of a study visit organized by Rabbi Naftali Schiff, whose JRoots charity had received the donation of a *Sefer Torah*, our Book of the Law, from a family in Manchester. To those of you unversed in Judaism, this is a sacred piece of parchment on which the first five books of the Old Testament are written in Hebrew by a qualified calligrapher.

I had the honour of writing some of the letters, and felt a wave of great joy break over my sadness. Surrounded by 100 young Jewish students, realistically the last generation who will hear our testimony first hand, we danced and sang the old songs. Who knows who heard them, because He does, indeed, work in mysterious ways.

Seventy-five years beforehand, my father and I were among a group of around a hundred prisoners, suddenly sent from Plaszow to the salt mines at Wieliczka, which have been operating since the Middle Ages. It is now a UNESCO World Heritage site, a tourist attraction with an underground lake, a chandeliered place of worship and a spectacular chamber, with carved walls depicting wooden chapels built by early miners.

Back then, it was a labour camp that descended 300 metres. The Nazis had designs on its 2,000 chambers as a potential underground armaments factory. Our job was to use picks to hack away rock salt, which was in varying shades of grey, rather than the white you might expect, and shovel it onto wagons.

Relatively speaking, this was a reprieve, since we were usually guarded only by two SS men. They didn't seem thrilled by their underground posting, but nor did they have to prove themselves to superiors by beating us indiscriminately, so they left us pretty much alone. I didn't tell father, but I resolved to escape if I was given the chance.

The opportunity arrived one day, when I travelled to the surface with a load of salt with the intention of transferring it to a truck. Emerging from the elevator, I realized there were no guards about. Surely this was too good to be true. I scanned the area again and saw a single SS man. He was busy in the corner lying on top of a woman, and looked to have only one thing on his mind.

I thought fast, and ran faster until I reached a nearby cornfield. I hid among the tall stalks until nightfall emphasized my sense of isolation. The other prisoners had returned to barracks, and I faced a familiar dilemma. Temperatures had dropped alarmingly. I was cold, hungry and reliant on the goodwill and generosity of strangers.

I walked for what seemed miles, seeking lights in the darkness. In my naïve fantasy world I would be fed and watered, given fresh clothes and perhaps even a haircut, to rid myself of the shaved stripe down the middle of my head, which gave away my status. In the real world, full of pain and paranoia, I again had doors slammed in my face. Some pitiless souls did not even bother to respond to my urgent knocks.

There was nowhere to go. Other escapees were more fortunate. They found allies, and a series of refuges. They were given bread, and something to ease their thirst, by good people. I, on the other hand, was friendless. Defiance seemed pointless and was certainly dangerous. I knew I *had* to retrace my steps, pray that I hadn't been missed, and try to re*join* my gang.

I spent the night fretting in a pigsty, chewing on potato peelings left for the animals. Hiding underneath a truck the following morning, I spotted the work party marching from the camp, back to the mine. I waited for the SS guard to go to the far side of the line, so that I was out of his field of vision, and gambled with my life that he would not see me sprint towards his prisoners.

They knew what was going on, but no one said a word as I tried to look inconspicuous, in the middle of the group. My companions plodded on, without making a peep. My father noticed my return, but remained silent until we were safely underground in the salt mines. He warned me about taking unnecessary risks, and made me promise never to make a run for it again.

The opportunity never arose, because a couple of weeks later we were sent back to Plaszow, without suspecting the terror that was about to overtake us. It began almost immediately, in February 1943, when the camp commandant *Oberscharführer* Franz Müller was replaced by Amon Goeth, an Austrian sadist who had risen quickly through the ranks of the SS because of his ability to round up, and exterminate, Jews. He had played a key role in establishing such death camps as Treblinka.

He was six foot four inches tall, with a hard face, a gravelly voice, and a twisted vanity. He was the embodiment of evil, the personification of fear and death. His terrifying reputation was established on his first day in charge, when he ordered us to assemble on the Appellplatz, where we held roll call.

He stood on a box, barking, boasting and lecturing, giving a tremendous speech – in his own mind. I barely registered his words, because they were garbage. I suppose he could have

The Germans needed the iron gates and metal fencing for the war effort. My job was to demolish the square pillars, brick by brick. Since I was small and agile, I was hoisted to the top, where I would use a pick to remove the bricks, without damaging them, before tossing them down to a companion to stack.

Goeth, who had quotas to fulfil, passed by with Wilek Chilowicz, the commandant of the OD, the Jewish police, who acted as his right-hand man. He stopped and stared as I prised out a brick and threw it gently down to my workmate. Forgive me, I cannot remember his name. By that stage a name was nothing. Men came and went, lived and died. They were there today, gone tomorrow.

It was a simple process, repeated countless times during a fourteen-hour working day, but, petrified by the monster's presence, my companion made the fatal mistake of dropping the brick. Goeth shot him in the head without a word or a flicker of emotion, and then looked upwards. He ordered me to throw him a brick, promised to catch it, but deliberately let it fall to the ground.

'*Komm runter!*' ('Come on down!') He was suddenly screaming, acting crazy. At such a moment it is impossible to react normally, to be in control of your faculties. The pillars were about fifteen feet in height, but in a panic I slid down the sides, opening cuts on my arms and legs.

I quietly recited *Shema Yisroel*, the first prayer that parents teach their children to say before they go to sleep at night. It is the most important part of the prayer service in Judaism, the ultimate declaration of faith. It is a *mitzvah*, a religious commandment, that we must recite twice a day. If a person is able, it should be said in the moments before the soul leaves the body:

Hear O Israel, the Lord is our God, the Lord is One.

Blessed is the name of His Glorious Majesty forever and ever.

Goeth raised his revolver until it was about two inches from my face, and pointed it between my eyes.

So this was how I was going to die.

5

Prisoners of Fate

My prayer was answered. I woke up in the camp hospital a couple of days later, with no recollection of what had happened. The pain was as intense as my puzzlement and relief. My body was broken, swathed in bandages which soon became bloodstained. My face was swollen, my torso badly bruised, and my skin was raw. I was extremely hungry but knew better than to linger in my bed.

The *Lagerarzt,* SS doctors, were known to administer lethal injections to patients. One, Max Blancke, was particularly notorious. He had worked in Dachau and Buchenwald and was responsible for the killing of disabled, sick and elderly prisoners in Plaszow. He committed suicide with his wife on 27 April 1945, just before the end of the war, after ordering the death of 360 inmates of the Kaufering sub-camp. Many were burned alive.

I preferred to take my chances in our barracks, a wooden hut into which hundreds of inmates had been stuffed. I rested as best I could on the third of four levels of cots, on what looked more like a rickety, open-sided chest of drawers than a place in which to sleep. The trade-off, that I had to return to work details when I was far from fit, was better than the risk of remaining in the sick bay.

The mystery of my miraculous survival was solved by chance, when I came across Wilek Chilowicz for a second time. He was known as a *Lagerälteste*, a senior prisoner, but he wielded enormous power as commander of the OD, the so-called 'Jewish brigade'. 'Ah!' he said in mock surprise. 'You're alive. Do you know what happened to you?'

My ignorance, and perhaps the chance to show off to those around him, pleased him no end. 'Goeth was about to kill you, so I started beating you up. You fell unconscious, so I told him to save his bullet because you were already dead. I saved your life.'

Each person tries to survive in his or her own way.

I owed my life to a rush of blood, and shameless flattery. For most of the time I was just trying to exist, to hide, to focus on nothing more than my next slither of bread. It was safer not to be exposed to anything. Drawing attention to yourself was dangerous and occasionally fatal. But bear in mind I was still only sixteen, in many ways a silly little boy.

My impudence got the better of me one fateful day, when I approached Chilowicz. 'You know, for such an important man your boots are very dirty,' I told him. 'Let me polish them for you and I will make them shine like the sun.' That could have been a fatal mistake, but mercifully a slow smile passed across his face. 'Make sure you do then,' he said.

I would go to him twice a week and scrubbed those boots so hard I imagined I could see my face in them. Every time I did so, he gave me something, a chicken bone or a piece of bread. Sometimes he even put a little soup, the good stuff from the bottom of the pan, into my *menashka*, the bowl I kept on my belt. He was a cruel and vicious man, but for some reason I benefited from a hint of humanity.

Some do bad things to remain alive. By collaborating with a butcher like Amon Goeth, always being at his right hand, and killing on his whim, Chilowicz betrayed the Jewish people. He went against his own, ignored accepted morals and ethics. However tempting it is to do that, when it is kill or be killed, can it ever be forgiven?

I repeat a fundamental article of faith: only God decides life and death. Chilowicz had no idea of the fate which awaited him: it had a telling twist. He was just an exaggerated version of the murderous Jewish policemen who took his orders during the Krakow ghetto clearance, or the Kapos, mainly former criminals who wore a green triangle to mark their status and were desperate to find favour in the eyes of the SS.

Why did they do it? Some of them were simply prepared to do anything to get an extra piece of bread or another ladle of soup. Indirectly they became inhuman, and as we saw on Goeth's murderous first day, expendable. Despite the indignities and the cruelties, they were unable to survive. No one mourned their loss.

The worst guards were Ukrainian members of the SS. Most came from *Schutzmannschafts-Bataillon* 206. They were involved in atrocities in the early years of occupation and came to Plaszow from various extermination camps. Though brutal in carrying out their principal task, preventing escapes, they were never wholly trusted by German officers, who regarded them as second-class citizens.

Goeth would kick them, beat them, scream at them, but didn't kill them while he needed them. He was a danger to everyone around him, because nothing was beyond him. That led to a strange, continually tense situation, since even those who killed for him knew their debasement offered no protection. They were as afraid of his random rages as we were.

By contrast, the relationship between Polish and Jewish prisoners was very good. The *Jüdische Unterstützungsstelle*, a support group tolerated by the Germans in the days when Plaszow was a slave labour camp, offered medical assistance that we willingly shared. In return, food sent by the Polish Welfare Organization was divided with the Jewish inmates.

In some ways, though, we would have been better off had Plaszow been officially regarded as a concentration camp. These operated on the principle that only Hitler had the ultimate power over life and death. Camp commandants had to send telegrams to Berlin, requesting permission to conduct executions, and providing personal details of the intended victims.

Plaszow was a lawless place. A death was simply noted with the word '*Abgang*' ('departure'). No clarification was provided, since it was invariably murderous. Goeth's driver, a Ukrainian Kapo named Simleiner, known to us all as Ivan, killed on command.

My father took an insane risk by keeping a couple of gold coins in the lining of his original clothes, which he kept on arrival, after having had a 'J' painted on them as a distinguishing mark. He used the coins to bribe guards to give us a job in the boiler room, shovelling coal into the hot-water furnace. This task was highly sought after, since it was inside, had a measure of independence, and meant we had limited contact with the SS.

Goeth stole meat, flour and bread intended for the prisoners, and sold it, or exchanged it for luxury goods, on the black market. Our rations consisted of one-sixteenth of a loaf, morning and night. We were given two spoonfuls of jam a week. This consisted of rotting fruit and decaying beetroot, marked 'Nur für Häftlinge' ('only for prisoners').

It was no surprise that people took desperate measures, despite the dangers. Food became a deadly weapon to be used against us. When bread was found in a clerk's drawer, Goeth had him and the four other workers in the administration office sent to the shooting range at Hujowa Gorka and killed. Another work party, found with food on their return, were savagely beaten. Two died when their skulls were smashed with half-bricks and rocks.

Poor Mr Kanner – may I be forgiven, since I have forgotten his first name – was found with a piece of chicken on him. As usual, hundreds of us were summoned to the Appellplatz and whipped by the SS, who ordered us to watch his execution. Goeth gave another unhinged speech, screaming that we would all be hanged if we ignored his orders.

The rope around Mr Kanner's neck broke as he dangled from the gallows, and he fell to the ground, unconscious but apparently still breathing. I thought this meant he would be spared under international law, but Goeth stood over him and shot him in the head several times. Something similar happened to a man who came back with a loaf of bread from a work party on the local railway; he begged for mercy when the rope snapped, but the hanging was repeated.

It was meant to scare and demoralize us, but I'm almost ashamed to admit that the more crazy, spontaneous acts of cruelty – such as Goeth making a boy with diarrhoea eat his own excrement before shooting him – had greater impact. We did not necessarily need to see such things; we quickly heard about them.

I don't know if I became conditioned to the horror, but it was relentless. The rope snapped on another occasion when a boy of my age, Haubenstock, was being hanged for singing a Russian song. He again pleaded for his life, in vain. While he was being bundled back up to the gallows, an engineer named Krautwirth, condemned for speaking back to his guards, slit his wrists with a razor blade.

Krautwirth was unconscious through loss of blood, but Goeth made a great show of ordering that he should still be strung up. On the same day a Kapo, Beim, was also executed, for accepting bribes.

I wanted to forget about such things for so long after the war. The memories pursued me, and I wanted to ease the pain. I worried that normal people would not believe me and question the evidence of my own eyes and ears. Sometimes I even hoped I was mistaken and that my imagination had got the better of me.

But I was there. It did happen. I have material from the war crimes trials as proof. You cannot shut my mouth. You cannot silence me. I will talk to those willing to listen, even though the stories are too horrible to contemplate. Even after nearly eighty years I still bear the scars from Goeth's two dogs, Rolf and Ralf, which he had trained to attack prisoners on command.

The physical scars have faded, over time, so they are now a thin white line. When the dogs, a Great Dane and a German Shepherd crossbreed that never went anywhere without their master, jumped on me, I covered my face with my left hand because I was scared they would take my eyes out. They bit deep, to the bone, but I was fortunate to survive.

During interrogations Goeth would set these Hounds from

Hell on defenceless prisoners, strung up by their legs from a specially placed hook in the ceiling. We heard their screams across the camp as they were torn limb from limb. Even those looking after the dogs were not safe; when Goeth's paranoia became so bad he suspected the animals preferred a particular handler, he had the man brought before him and shot.

The greatest agony was endured by a man called Olmer, a Jew from Miechow, accused of obtaining Peruvian nationalization documents that existed only in the commandant's warped imagination. He was completely innocent yet was beaten badly as part of a group of seventy suspects, including men, women and children. He alone was left outside when the rest of the prisoners were returned to their cells.

'Run,' Goeth ordered. As Mr Olmer did so, the commandant ordered the dogs to attack. One leaped on his back and began to tear at him, ripping his flesh. He staggered on for a few more strides, screaming with pain as the second dog grabbed him, before he collapsed. As he was being savaged, Goeth walked slowly towards him and pumped several bullets into him.

I did not witness this, but I know it to be true.

The mass shootings of prisoners became even more nightmarish. Victims, ordered to jump from the edge of the ditch that was to serve as their mass grave, were shot by the Ukrainian SS guards as they did so. Those who hesitated were knocked into it with rifle butts, and then fired upon. Many were only wounded; their bodies writhed as they went through their death throes.

Our clothes were bloodstained. Our ill-fitting wooden shoes had holes in them and quickly caused terrible sores on perpetually wet feet, yet we cradled the shoes as we tried to sleep because they were often stolen by those desperate to find relief. Everywhere stank of decay. Many became ill and died. Even the more robust prisoners were in obvious physical decline. Toothache was common; we would pull teeth out ourselves.

As you might have guessed, it did not take long for the guards to sell our places in the boiler room to someone else. They knew we wouldn't complain, because that would have been suicidal. Any hint of a problem and they would have killed us, to cover their tracks. The fate of Beim told them of the consequences of discovery.

We were not allowed to gather in groups but exchanged furtive words with our neighbours in the work gangs. New-comers carried rumours of the state of the war, especially the Eastern Front, but we were contained in our misery and isolated from the outside world. Our brains were dulled. Everyone had a different interpretation of such unreliable news, but few of us had much hope that mass extermination could be avoided.

There were so many ways to die that we were enslaved by the task of surviving. We were terribly tired but couldn't sleep because the lice were burrowing under our skin and eating us alive. You can scratch them, without catching them, and you long for the respite of the morning roll call. Just as we prayed at night for it to be the day, during the day we prayed for the release of nightfall.

Can you imagine such a life? No day, no night, no food, no hope, no respite. A piece of bread is your redemption. You are frightened every waking minute that something could happen, a random shooting or a vicious, unprovoked attack. Imagine living for years like this, day after day. How can I fully explain what that does to you? How can I expect you to fathom the depths of our degradation?

It seems pointless to strike up a conversation, even in the relative safety of the barracks, because all that does is remind you how hungry and downtrodden you are. Try as you might to keep your brain active by discussing politics or religion, there is simply not much else that seems worth talking about. Surviving each hour is a challenge when you cannot control what is happening to you and those around you.

I did what I was told and followed orders, knowing that if I resisted, I would be wiped out.

Obedience didn't guarantee security, so when I was pulled out of the line by a Kapo, on one morning roll call, I feared the worst. Our selection, of around a hundred prisoners, was sent to the camp on the outskirts of the city of Mielec, which provided slave labour for a factory that produced German bombers and the He-297 fighter plane.

Between 1,500 and 2,000 inmates were woken at 5 a.m. and worked under the authority of the Factory Protection Police, supervised by the SS. Some operated the production line for aircraft parts. Others were used as cleaners, or for loading and unloading cargo. Since daily rations, seven ounces of bread, a black coffee for breakfast and cabbage leaf soup for lunch and dinner, were so meagre, many collapsed through malnutrition.

We were not tattooed in Plaszow, because Goeth's superiors in Berlin had rejected his request to brand us, despite his argument that he wanted to make the identification of escapees easier. Things were different when we reported to Mielec and were hustled into a line in front of a visibly bored and increasingly irritated SS officer, who sat with a typewriter to take our details.

'*Name und Geburtsdatum.*'

Name and date of birth. Simple you might think, but I didn't know the secular date on which I was born, only the year, so I made it up on the spot and chose 15 March 1926. That white lie was a matter of record for years – I didn't discover the correct date, 21 July 1926, until I retrieved my birth certificate from the Polish government in 1967, when I was living in Canada – but it saved me from guards who whipped us around the head to speed up the process.

That was the less stressful part of registration. We were pushed towards another table, where another SS officer ordered us to roll up our sleeves. He carelessly tattooed 'KL', short for *Konzentracion Lager*, concentration camp, in large letters on our right wrists. The needles were large and the procedure was painful. Though I didn't dare hint at my feelings, I felt violated.

As soon as I walked outside I began biting my wrist, and sucking out the ink and blood before spitting it into the dust. Since I acted quickly, this prevented any permanent marking. It was another typically rash move, because had I been spotted that would have been the end of me. There could be no more obvious sign of resistance – and no more predictable form of punishment than a bullet into the brain.

The pain was intense, and lingered for five or six days, until the swelling subsided and the bleeding stopped. It took years for the scar to fade into insignificance. In fact, it was only a vague memory when a man reached out to shake my hand on a recent visit to New York. I immediately noticed KL, tattooed on his wrist. It turned out that he, too, had survived Mielec.

What a small, brutal world.

I was more fortunate than him, in being mainly assigned to municipal projects in the city. Over the course of a month or so, we were sent out to various road-building or civic repair jobs and slept in schools, fire stations and sports halls. In some ways, we were the guilty secret of the local residents. They saw us, understood our plight, but looked the other way.

You might not have a uniform. You don't have to fire a gun, whip someone, or club them to the ground to be an oppressor. You simply do nothing to help a fellow human being. We were not behind electrified wire, but freedom was an illusion. Things that I once took for granted, like the sight of a roadside orchard on the way to a particular job, tempted and taunted me.

I hadn't seen an apple in a long, long time. These windfalls were small, and probably sour, but I craved the chance to taste them. My SS guard was less than fifteen metres away, and I knew he would not hesitate to shoot me if I stepped out of line. Instead, I waited until he came close, saluted, and asked, with great respect, if he would permit me to pick up a single piece of fruit.

His answer was to smash his rifle butt against my cheek.

Walking past, the following day, I noticed a bird sitting on a branch protruding from the orchard onto the verge. It was singing sweetly, as nature intended. Since reality was brutal, I decided to take refuge in fantasy, and proceeded to conduct an imaginary conversation with my newly found feathered friend.

'*I envy you,*' I told the bird, in my head at least. '*I wish I were free to sing and move as you do. How lucky you are. You are probably asking me for some food. If only I had some to give you. I would give it with pleasure. But let's reverse the situation. You can be a big help to me, by picking something up and bringing it to me. You could bring me food so that I will not starve.'*

All these years later, I realize now that episode seems childish, sad. Yet the bird was beautiful. I ended my imaginary monologue with a sense of peace. The moment of civility was a release.

It is hard not to despair at human nature, and impossible to ignore the unseen hand that guides us through life. I often wonder about the power of coincidence, and the significance of the message it sends. Years later, when I began to date my wonderful wife, Perla, I wanted to know her birthday, so that I could send flowers and arrange dinner. I was stunned when she announced it was 15 March, the date that had come into my mind when I first reported to Mielec.

I suppose the precise odds of that are 365–1 (or 366–1 in a leap year), but it felt much more unlikely than that. As I have said, I am a religious man, and believe nothing happens just because it happens. I cannot be angry at God because I live on His mercy, on His will. I pray to Him every day, beg His forgiveness, and thank Him for His gifts. Each of the trillions of blades of grass on this planet is under the supervision of Heaven; without that they would wither, and the world would ultimately die. In comparison, human beings are just specks of dust.

Oskar Schindler once told me a story about the random nature of survival. He was a familiar figure at Plaszow, though never in uniform. The doors of the boiler room were locked while I worked there, but I used to steal up onto the roof to watch him as he climbed the hill up to the infamous Red

House, where Goeth held drunken orgies and indulged his base instincts.

The world knows, largely through the film *Schindler's List*, but also through the novel *Schindler's Ark*, of the initiative, courage, persistence and pragmatism that allowed Oskar Schindler to help save the lives of 1,200 Jews by employing them in his enamelware and munitions factories. He shamelessly flattered and bribed the Nazis, and finally convinced Goeth to allow him to move his operation to Brünnlitz in the Sudetenland.

Schindler explained it was during this process that fate intervened on behalf of around 300 Jews under his control. They had been rejected as workers at a mine in Golleschau in southern Poland. Unwanted back at the local sub-camp of Auschwitz, they were herded into cattle cars and left to freeze to death in a siding – until Schindler demanded another consignment of workers.

Abandoning Jews to the certainty of a terrible, lonely death made economic sense to the SS, but one officer, remembering their decision, ordered that the prisoners be retrieved, and sent on to the Sudetenland. The boxcars were frozen shut when the officers arrived, forcing Schindler's wife, Emilie, to summon a factory engineer to open the doors using a soldering iron.

They found twelve people dead inside. The others, too weak and ill to work, were cared for in a makeshift hospital, and were liberated at the end of the war. I did not know of their story until Schindler told it to me, soon after I was liberated, but it brought home the fragility of the thread of life on which we all hang. Those survivors were protected by the angels.

My father, Symcha, was not so fortunate. He had vanished when I returned to Plaszow, where Goeth's reign of terror was at its height. I had no idea where he was, whether he was still alive or what had befallen him. Everyone was too preoccupied by their private agonies to offer sympathy or information. I prayed that he had not been a victim of the monster's whims.

It was not until after the war that, through the International Red Cross, I discovered my father was one of 30,000 Jews who had died from malnutrition, overwork or summary execution in the Flossenbürg concentration camp, a remote site in the Fichtel mountains in Bavaria, close to the German border with Czechoslovakia. There were no details of how he met his end.

He was just another slave, lost in the shadows of history. He had apparently spent time in Auschwitz before he died, on 10 August 1944, but I was haunted by unanswered questions, just as I had been with the loss of my mother and brothers. Why had I been spared? At that moment I wished I knew.

6

The Light of Life

I was seized by an orphan's grief, guilt and insecurity. I had never felt more alone. I missed my father's presence, his soothing words and wisdom, though I had not always heeded him when he was there. I knew I could not have saved him when he was effectively sent to his death, but that did not prevent me regretting that I was unable to share his final hours.

I lacked closure, to use the modern term that people refer to when personal loss is involved. Something deep inside told me his light had been snuffed out, but there was no confirmation of the methods or circumstances. That emptiness is dangerous, a pit that so many fall into, in so many ways and for so many reasons.

I craved detail, which was ironic, as ever since I have been more of a generalist in my personal and professional life. I'm naturally inquisitive and impatient. From my earliest days, when I studied Talmud, the holy record of generations of debate about law, philosophy and biblical interpretation, compiled between the third and eighth centuries, I was frustrated by the process of enlightenment.

The old rabbis loved to split hairs when discussing weighty matters of faith and principle. Those sages took time and much trouble to come to their conclusions. That's probably why they stand the test of time, but I'm not the type to wander the highways and byways in careful contemplation. I want to get straight to the point.

It has meant I have made big mistakes, but it is part of who I am, for better or worse.

I see many things that I resent and have done many things I regret, but I don't wish to waste time on pointless dispute. Why create friction by arguing about nothing? Heed someone's view but reach your own conclusion and trust you are following the right path. I was taught, through the terrible experience of those camps, that true strength comes from within.

I remember having conversations with God, saying, 'Help me, help me, because I am in trouble here. You are everything. Do whatever you can. See that I should have a piece of bread. Be with me so that I am not beaten up or killed.' The Almighty was the straw I clutched, the piece of driftwood I clung to when it seemed that I was about to drown.

There are puzzling contradictions. In my mind there was always hope, even though I saw none. I wanted to see the end of war but couldn't envisage peace being declared in time to rescue my people. I saw nothing but destruction. We had no say, no value. We had no homes, no families. Everything we once held dear had been taken from us. Logically there was nothing to live for.

Yet I refused to give up. I had to survive. I told myself to fight until my dying breath. I wanted to live so badly. Little else seemed to make sense. Who lived and died could not be explained rationally. Looking back, one of the main reasons I survived, apart from luck that bordered on the miraculous, was my ability to shut down mentally, to simply not think.

Some people pleaded with God to end their misery. They wanted Him to carry them away, to end their suffering. They could not take any more. Yet somehow, they prevailed. They survived. Others you thought were strong and resolute fell into despair. They looked into their future and saw only blackness. Their mood turned. They no longer believed in the idea of salvation, so they surrendered.

The light of life grew dim, flickered, and died.

You don't die because you want to die, because you want to get it all over with. You don't necessarily survive because you are desperate to remain alive. The six million Jews who were murdered during the Holocaust did not want to die. They wanted to live, to return to their homes, to watch their children grow and their families expand.

Yet they were wiped out. I have no answer to why their prayers were unanswered. I don't think anyone does.

Ask yourself this: what would you do if everything you cherished was ripped away from you? How would you cope if your carefree bubble suddenly burst? What qualities would enable you to be one of those left standing, famished and ragged, when evil was defeated, and rescuers arrived? There is a saying – money lost, nothing lost. Yet when your spirit is lost, everything is lost.

I am no psychologist, but I read somewhere that a lot of prisoners died around the time of Hanukkah, or Christmas. These are joyous occasions, times of celebration. They are festivals of faith in which families gather to give thanks and eat their fill. In Judaism, they are associated with light.

A quick history lesson, if I may. Hanukkah celebrates the reclamation of the Holy Temple in Jerusalem by a small group of poorly armed Jews, led by Judah the Maccabee. They defeated the mighty army of the Greek empire, whose king Antiochus IV Epiphanes had outlawed Jewish practice, slaughtered pigs in a sacred place, and installed an altar to Zeus.

According to a legend recounted in the Talmud, there was only enough oil to keep the Temple's menorah – a seven-branched candlestick holder that was one of its most important ritual objects – burning for one day. Miraculously, the flame stayed alight for eight days, until a new supply of oil could be produced in conditions of ritual purity.

That is why Hanukkah lasts eight days and is known as the Festival of Lights. I'm convinced the light of so many lives went out in the camps, at around that time of year, because prisoners lost hope that they would ever again experience such a satisfying and carefree occasion. They simply gave up, gave in.

The Nazis knew their history and understood the symbolic importance of our religion. That is why they belittled our values and defiled our traditions. A demon like Amon Goeth recognized the significance of our holiest days, and the grotesque pain he could inflict during them. He used them to make a point, to commit mass murder on a scale that catches the breath.

On Yom Kippur, our Day of Atonement, in October 1943, he ordered the SS, led by his deputy Edmund Zdrojewski, to round up fifty people from our barracks. We hid as best we could as the SS came in, running and screaming, attacking anyone within reach, before hauling the unlucky ones away to be shot. A day devoted to repentance, fasting and intensive prayer was awash with blood.

The monster mocked everything we held dear: 'God will not judge, but I will judge,' he told us.

That takes fear to unimaginable levels, but the outrage he committed a couple of weeks earlier on another of the Holy High Days, Rosh Hashanah, the Jewish New Year, was even more heinous. He selected 200 prisoners, assembled for roll call on the Appellplatz that morning, for execution. Our terror was total. Everyone desperately tried to blend into the background; I had never been as grateful to be small, at five foot three inches, or 1.6 metres.

We learned to be afraid of the madness of the moment, even if, to be honest, I rarely knew what day it was. Days merged into one, each as exhausting and horrendous as the next. Goeth was crazed one moment, calculating the next. He enjoyed ritual slaughter, almost as sport. That it helped him to impose discipline never seemed to be his main aim.

He had sixty people murdered on a work detail in Bonarka, another suburb of Krakow. Another sixteen slave labourers were killed on their way back to camp. His punishment of escape attempts was an obscene form of theatre. If anyone got away, he would order the entire group from which the escapee had come to line up in the parade ground.

Prisoners were then ordered to count to ten. The first man yelled 'one', the second 'two', and so on. The poor soul who was tenth had barely shouted 'ten' when Goeth shot him. As the pattern became obvious, the anguish of the man who realized he was tenth in a particular sequence was pitiful to behold. I pray he had time to pray.

I'm conscious that giving too many examples of depravity may dilute their impact, but some deaths, which came arbitrarily and suddenly, are too shocking to ignore. One poor soul was summarily shot by Goeth at morning roll call because he decided the man was too tall. As he lay dying, the beast urinated over him in a show of malice and contempt.

Friendships were a luxury in captivity, where the individual was made to feel insignificant, but they offered a degree of fleeting happiness and, occasionally, acute pain. I was unprepared for the depth of my despair when one of my closest friends, Shlomo Spielman, became a victim of more indiscriminate wickedness.

Such good people are hard to find. He was one of three brothers in the camp: the others, Chaim and Jacob, became lifelong allies and acquaintances. Our paths crossed during and after the war, firstly in various concentration camps and latterly in displaced persons' communities.

I was standing close to Shlomo on the Appellplatz one morning when Goeth strutted along the line. Our bodies were ravaged, but our hearts always beat faster whenever he was around. He was barely a couple of feet away when he ordered Shlomo to step forward and screamed, '*Ich kann es nicht ertragen, dass die Juden so gut aussehen.*'

I knew German but didn't truly understand the danger: 'I cannot take it that the Jews should look so handsome.' With that, he pulled out his revolver and shot my friend dead. Bang. For what? Ego? Jealousy? Fun? Pride? I felt sick and wanted desperately to cry out or bend down in a futile show of affinity and comradeship, but knew that any instinctive act would be my last.

The commandant paused for a moment, before walking away, his bloodlust temporarily satisfied. I still remember that scene, vividly. I cannot get it out of my mind. Words cannot adequately convey my feelings, the intensity of my disgust and the hatred I felt for my friend's murderer. It might have been an everyday episode, but we must never normalize it, nor forget its implications.

It was business as usual on that particular morning. No one dared pay Shlomo's body due attention as we were assigned our tasks for the day. As 1943 wore on, these tended to involve internal projects, created by the expansion of the camp. New roads had to be built, additional barracks erected, and a delousing area constructed. Thousands of tons of dirt had to be shifted and ground had to be levelled.

Goeth supervised another inhuman ghetto clearance in Tarnow in September, when 6,000 Jews were transported to Auschwitz. That meant room in Plaszow had to be made for another 2,000 or so slave labourers from the garment manufacturing factory owned by Julius Madritsch, an Austrian businessman who, like Oskar Schindler, did his best to save lives. He paid the SS for the food he gave his inmates and bravely argued against Goeth when he wanted to send elderly workers to their deaths.

By early 1944, when Plaszow had been reclassified as a concentration camp, we were denied relatively warm civilian clothing, and expected to wear the paper-thin blue striped uniforms that have become such symbols of the Holocaust experience. As time went on, and the atrocities continued unabated, these were taken from murdered prisoners and passed on to new inmates, without being washed.

I had never felt cold like it. We were used, in our thousands, to build a small-gauge railway and new sidings. We hauled huge wooden beams, filled and spread countless truckloads of gravel, and laid heavy iron rails that stretched for several kilometres. Punishment squads carried rocks across their shoulders, bowing under the weight and struggling in treacherous conditions. The SS guards cruised around, looking for any excuse to lay into us. They didn't care if we were ill, or under-nourished. They had the go-ahead to beat and kill if they thought we were slacking.

Even without the sub-zero temperatures, it was back-breaking work. Since our hands and feet were numb and our puny torsos were chilled to the bone, it was pitiless. We were standing in open fields. The snow was being driven by freezing winds, so strong they made us unsteady on our feet. It was as if an unseen hand wanted to carry us away on the storm, to our doom.

Every flake had the force of a pebble slung from a catapult. A warm drink? God forbid that we should gain respite from such a thing. Today, we would be able to huddle around the fire in such weather, and devour bowls of steaming soup. If we were forced to go outside, to do our chores, we would wear a thick, padded coat, a scarf, hat, gloves and boots. Back then, we had none of these, not even socks, and wore the equivalent of pyjamas made from tissue paper.

This was what Nazis meant when they referred to 'annihilation through work'. We developed an early warning system when the guards were approaching, and sped up our activities to avoid punishment, but nature tended to save the SS the job of finishing us off. I saw people collapse and never get up. We were not allowed to go to their aid. Life ebbed out of them, slowly and surely.

It is hard to describe something that is so unreal. A person was less than nothing.

It was just as bad in the summer. The opposite applied: the

sun baked us. We were denied the relief of a cold drink and instead of shivering uncontrollably we sweated until we felt faint. Our skin burned and was excruciating to touch. Our throats were parched, and our resistance was low. More men fell. More men died.

As a more experienced prisoner, I began to read the danger signs. Some were obvious: any sight of Goeth, even at long distance and especially when he emerged from the stable block on his favourite white horse with a rifle slung over his shoulder, had me looking for cover. The camp was now a mini-city, with its own road system, coal depot, gravel pit, warehouse complex and factory area. We were particularly wary of two no-go areas.

The first, the kitchens, were a magnet for those who allowed hunger to overcome reason. The occasional inmate, with the plumb job of cooking or distributing what passed for a meal, was brave enough to smuggle a morsel to friends. But those who begged too obviously for an extra scrap of food were easy pickings for the guards.

The second was the women's camp, situated on the eastern side of the Appellplatz. Crossing this divide was absolutely forbidden, yet captivity doesn't entirely wipe out traces of humanity. I had no reason to visit, but other men stole there, especially on Sundays, to grab a glimpse of their wives, sisters and daughters. Some even lingered, to share news or food, without regard for the risk.

The women were treated terribly, with less respect than the mules whose jobs they so often did. When we were building the railway, from the gravel pit to higher ground, they were harnessed to carriages filled with stones. They dragged these carriages uphill, bent double, often slipping because their wooden clogs either fell off or offered no grip. The mortality rates were criminal.

Their tormentor-in-chief was Alice Orlowski, whose official rank, *Kommandoführerin*, Work Detail Overseer, gave little hint of her degeneracy. Whispers followed her from two previous camps, Ravensbrück and Majdanek, where she had brutally supervised the loading of trucks, carrying women and children to the gas chambers.

She loved to whip women, especially across the eyes.

Forgive me, but anyone who can do that is unworthy of forgiveness. She evidently had the cunning of a cornered rat, and I'm with those who argue that she tried to come across as being humane, issuing water on the death march to Auschwitz-Birkenau in January 1945, because she sensed Germany's defeat and was preparing her defence for any war-crimes trial.

At that trial, in 1947, she was portrayed as a typical hard-faced SS woman, and sentenced to life imprisonment for crimes against humanity. I avoid bitterness, but the fact she served only ten years, and died of natural causes in 1976, at the age of seventy-two, while awaiting a retrial following her re-arrest in West Germany, rankles with me.

I have only learned in recent years of the special measures taken against females when Plaszow became a concentration camp and was subjected to a wide range of rules. Nazi bureaucrats were sticklers for detail, with a fiendish sense of order. One of their manuals issued to camp commandants was, for instance, devoted to the flogging of women.

What sort of callous man decides to create animosity between different nationalities by ordering that Polish women, for instance, are only beaten by Russian women? Or follows a similar principle by insisting that Slovak women must be thrashed by Czech women? And vice-versa in both cases? That was another unbelievable decision taken by the SS at Plaszow, way beyond the workings of any civilized mind.

Attempting to stay alive narrows the mind because everything is boiled down to the basics. I was not yet eighteen and had more immediate things to worry about than the increasing mass movements of people across war zones. Yet these events, like Goeth being told to make room for 10,000 Hungarian Jews in May 1944, had a direct influence on my life, and those around me.

Dignity had long since stopped being a consideration, but there was still something disturbing about the entire camp, both men and women, being ordered to parade naked in front of an inspection committee, led by the notorious SS doctor Max Blancke. This so-called Health Appel took several hours to complete.

Once again, our persecutors played God. The weak, the injured and those with any deformities were asked to step aside, and had their names taken. They were separated from us during a roll call a week later and taken away on wagons. No one knew where for certain, but no one expected to see them again. We didn't.

The fate of the children was worse because it was more public. Their mothers became hysterical when they saw them waving goodbye as they were being loaded into lorries along the main camp road. I heard the Nazis playing German lullabies and Polish nursery rhymes over the loudspeakers, which only made things worse.

Goeth reacted to the commotion by running around, waving his revolver, and threatening to shoot anyone who stepped out of line. That he didn't kill anyone in his rage was another sign that his powers were beginning to wane. He still organized mass whippings, and savage punishment details, but had to answer to superiors in Berlin, who controlled the machinery of murder.

The poor children were all dead by the following day, gassed at Auschwitz.

It had always been a numbers game, to an extent, but now, with more transportations to Plaszow from elsewhere in Galicia, the system was on overload. It was also being simultaneously geared to the erasure of crimes. I was a slave labourer, to be moved at the convenience of the planners, and had left the camp by the time bodies were exhumed from the mass graves at Hujowa Górka and incinerated.

Goeth had been arrested for embezzlement by the SS, a revealingly frightful 'achievement' in itself, by the time that gruesome task was completed in October. He had entered his own form of survival mode in the summer, making preparations for the card index of prisoners to be destroyed. He was as vicious to those who propped up his regime as he was to the thousands he killed.

Wilek Chilowicz, my unlikely savour, was another of his victims. As Goeth's favourite extortionist and executioner he knew too much. The extent of the betrayal was exposed at the war-crimes trial that I attended many years later. Even for someone like me, who had seen and heard far too much, the details were staggering.

Understandably, Goeth was afraid that Chilowicz might be transferred to another camp and reveal incriminating information. No one had more inside knowledge of the corrupt, murderous campaign waged against the innocent. When Plaszow was a lawless labour camp, the despatch of such a dangerous individual would have been the work of a single second.

Yet with the war starting to turn in favour of the Allies, and a new set of orders to follow, Goeth had to play a different game. He had to persuade Wilhelm Koppe, who was in overall charge of the SS and police in Nazi-occupied Poland, that Chilowicz was a traitor. To do so, he used a guard named Józef Sowiński to make a false report, suggesting that Chilowicz was secretly organizing a prisoners' uprising.

When Koppe, who was known as 'Little Himmler', gave permission for leaders of the fictitious revolt to be eliminated, a trap was laid. Goeth promised to allow Chilowicz and his family to escape, but when they arrived with the intention of fleeing on a Sunday morning, all were killed. Chilowicz's deputy, Mietek Finkelstein, who ran the Jewish police, was among five others shot in retribution.

Goeth could not resist the theatrical twist of laying their bodies on the main road through the camp, and ordering inmates to file past them. I was no longer there then. But if I had been, I would have shed no tears for a killer who was spoken of as 'a louse'.

This was not, you can be sure, the sort of thing central command in Berlin expected when it ordered that the camp be 'diluted'.

As a slave labourer I had no status. I had no papers and once the Plaszow files were erased, it was as if I didn't exist. I had no worth as a human being, no future. I was a non-person, a body to be used to fill a hole elsewhere in the system. With the camp at breaking point, and panic starting to spread at the approach of the front, I was loaded into a cattle car and sent on my way.

I travelled a little less than fifty miles, but only survived because so many died.

7

From Slave to Pilgrim

I do not want to remember, but I must. I share my suffering, because it is all I can do to warn the world and try to make it a better place. There are some things, like shivering in a thin, frayed and filthy uniform while working in sub-zero temperatures, that perhaps you can relate to. But other events, such as that journey from Plaszow to Auschwitz-Birkenau, are beyond human understanding.

Come with me, into the cattle car that served as a torture chamber and became a tomb. Prepare yourself for agony to be piled on agony. Try not to shy away from the truth, the images I am duty bound to create. This is what happens when human life is deemed so insignificant it becomes an inconvenience, an irrelevance.

I cannot say for sure what sort of carriage we were herded into. But, since most of the 'cargo' consisted of Hungarian Jews, it will probably have been of these dimensions, cited by Holocaust scholars as typical of the time. The average length was 8.2 metres, 26.9 feet. It would have been 2.2 metres (7.2 feet) wide and around 4.3 metres (14.1 feet) in height, from the bottom of the wheels.

Remember that the ceiling curved down from the middle. This compressed space even further, so that those standing at the centre had only around 2.2 metres between floor and ceiling. Those on the outer edges, whipped, kicked and pushed into the car when hardly any room was left, had even less.

To cram sixty people into such a space for a fifty-mile journey, without food or water on a hot early summer's day, would have been criminal, but there were 160 of us, squeezed somehow into that carriage. To abandon us in a siding, behind locked and bolted doors for two days and nights, when we had arrived at our destination, amounted to mass murder.

None of us knew what to expect. The route, through the towns of Skawina and Spytkowice, to the marshalling yard at Oświęcim, the site of Auschwitz, was a procession of long trains, carrying innocents to their death. Transporting so many Jews to the gas chambers presented a problem to the Nazis. They wanted as many of us as possible to die without the bother of having to kill us directly.

When you put so many people into such a small space it is immediately impossible to breathe normally. The movement of the train was terrible because it made us shudder and lurch and added to the pressure on our chests. There was the occasional cry of 'oy veh', the traditional Yiddish expression of dismay, but anything that passed as normal conversation soon stilled.

Everyone was concentrating on their own anguish, their next breath. Even before we arrived, the weak were beginning to buckle. They sighed and sagged as the air went out of them gradually, like a slow puncture in a tyre. Many were moaning, gently. Some began to gasp. Others uttered short, hopeless screams. The stranger holding onto me dropped slowly to the floor, never to rise again.

At the marshalling yard the train was taken over by a

shunting team, who rolled it to the railway ramp, just inside the camp in Birkenau. These transports travelled under armed guard, usually commanded by a Ukrainian SS officer, who did not allow anyone to approach. When we heard the locomotive being uncoupled at the gate, we gave silent thanks that our ordeal was about to end.

We were not to know it was just about to start in earnest.

Hours passed. No one came to our aid. Despair set in. Those who begged for mercy or a drink of water through the cracks in the wooden car, on hearing the scrunch of gravel by an unseen pair of boots beside the tracks, wasted precious energy. Our thirst was worse than our hunger because we were used to starvation's dull ache in our stomachs. Our mouths were desperately dry. Our tongues felt swollen and strangely sticky, like flypaper.

Nature's cooling system was breaking down. The more dehydrated we became, the less we sweated. Even when a scorching day gave way to relatively cool darkness, so much body heat, released in such an oppressive atmosphere, tormented us. Time stretched and snapped, so that it meant nothing. A minute felt like an hour, an hour like a day, a day like a year. But with every second that passed, without relief, it became easier to lose the will to live.

To the right and to the left of me, in front and behind, people collapsed. Some, in the final stages of distress, emptied their bowels. Somewhere, at the start of the journey, there had been a bucket, but there was little option but to urinate where we stood. The smell was unbearable. Gradually we realized we were standing, or occasionally sitting, on the bodies of our companions.

I did not want to admit they were dead, because that would

have been my fate, foretold. Many slipped away, like a drowning man dipping beneath the waves. Occasionally a body moved. A leg shifted. A hand or a finger twitched and rose an inch or so, as if saying farewell, or beckoning us to the afterlife.

We were all half dead. Deep down, I did not believe I would get out of that cattle car alive. Our torment was so great that death was not something to be afraid of. We knew it was coming, and the temptation to welcome it was immense. How did I remain a human being in that situation? To be honest I am not sure that I did.

As I have mentioned, I am a small man, five feet three inches tall (1.6 metres) tall. By the morning of the third day on that siding, the piles of bodies were so large my head was touching the roof. I could look out of a tiny window, with a mesh net, at the top of the carriage. The air was still foul. I resigned myself to the fact that my last glimpse of the world would be a blurred vision of tracks and fences.

Then, abruptly, a commotion. The doors, sealed from the outside, were opened. Light flooded in, so that those of us left alive flinched.

'*Raus. Raus.*'

'Out. Out.'

I am not exaggerating this. Truly I wish I were. But only twenty of us emerged and assembled unsteadily on the tracks. The SS men, indifferent to the bodies over which we had climbed or stumbled, screamed at us, and lashed out. Three or four other survivors were barely breathing and eventually got taken away on stretchers by inmates.

The smell of burning human flesh, one of the first things that struck me when we were left in the sidings, became overpowering. It was the stench of extermination. By that time the Nazis were two years into a building programme of massive crematoria and gas chambers they believed would enable them to kill and incinerate 1.6 million Jews a year.

The calculations of the *Zentralbauleitung*, the Central Construction Office of the Waffen-SS and Police in Auschwitz, were callous and precise. They reckoned they could burn 4,416 corpses a day, 1,440 in each of the two biggest crematoria, and 768 each in two others. These people might have been functionaries, engineers and planners, but they knew the nature of their role. They devised and delivered the mechanics of murder.

To this day I am very sensitive to barbecues. They remind me of bodies being burned, flesh being overwhelmed by the flames. The smoke from the grill brings back memories of the chimneys, belching out particles of Holocaust victims. I try not to show my discomfort, because I do not want to stop anyone enjoying a hearty meal, but that is my reality.

How many souls were taken away on the wind? History tells us that of the 1.3 million people sent to Auschwitz-Birkenau, 1.1 million were murdered. Some 960,000 of the victims were Jews. I am convinced I would have been among them had hundreds, even thousands, not died on that train, which stretched into the distance. There were simply too many bodies for the inmates, who usually cleaned out the cars before they returned to service, to cope with.

It is one thing to go into a cattle car and remove names, initials or last messages written on the walls by the doomed, and another entirely to unload countless corpses, day after day. The work details were used to scrubbing the marks clean, or painting over them with oil-based paint. They did not have the manpower to clean up death on an industrial scale.

As I said, we were all on the verge of succumbing when trapped inside. The pain had been so sustained, and the surroundings so terrible, that we were pushed beyond even our levels of endurance. Thankfully, the will to live is stronger than anything. I still had *emunah*, my belief. I renewed my trust in God. He was the one who could help. This is why I cherish my faith, fortify it whenever possible.

As we were marched away, the prospect of survival jolted us back into the land of the living. We knew better than to allow our faces to reveal our inner thoughts, but our minds raced: 'What are they going to do? What do they have in mind for us?' It turned out they realized they had a job for us. They could always kill us later.

We were going back to the scene of their great crime.

They forced us to undress and run the gauntlet of four SS men with sticks, which they pushed into our ears to see if we were hiding anything. They ordered us to open our mouths, and to lift our legs so they could examine our back passages. It was pointless since we had only the rags in which we travelled. As crazy as it is to say this today, these humiliations were routine, only to be expected.

Since Auschwitz was the only camp to tattoo its prisoners numerically, we lined up in front of a table, where a bored guard asked a few questions (I again made up answers on the spot) before roughly etching a number into the skin on our inner arm, just below the elbow. Later in the year, when masses of Hungarian deportees were being processed, they tended to tattoo them on the lower part of the outer arm.

As a slave labourer, sent around the system, I was then, to all intents and purposes, a number, 85314. I regret having it removed by a plastic surgeon, many years later in Colombia, but at the time, building a new post-war life in South America, where knowledge of the Holocaust was limited, I felt it was an embarrassment. I was asked continually about it, almost as if I was a criminal. I got it unwillingly and painfully, by force. The Nazis denigrated us by branding us like slaves, or cattle, but on reflection the number should have accompanied me to my grave.

There is still something that puzzles me. My prisoner's record from all the other camps is intact, transferred to an online database, but despite years of research I have never been able to find any documentation relating to my time in Auschwitz. I was there for somewhere between four and six weeks, before being moved on.

It is possible the records of my stay were destroyed, as many were in the face of the Russian advance. It is equally possible that, due to the chaotic nature of my arrival, and the relative proximity of Plaszow, I was simply overlooked, a victim of a clerical error. That's easy to imagine, since survivors of Amon Goeth's murderous regime were being sent, apparently randomly, across the system to other camps such as Freiberg, Buchenwald and Gross-Rosen.

All I know is that it felt all too real when we returned to the cattle cars, to complete the grim task that kept us alive. The mind switches off in such moments. You become unemotional, aloof, indifferent. You may keep a prayer alive in your heart, but you become a machine. Do this. Do that. Go here. Go there. Total obedience is the only option. No matter how bad or bitter the orders are, you do as you are told.

The bodies were stiff and cold, skin and bone. We carried them on wheelbarrows and loaded them into trucks. Once outside the crematoria, they were tipped onto the ground and ferried towards the ovens. We were forced to undress them, while the guards screamed and their dogs howled. The SS saw only potential for profit, jewels or money hidden in rags. To them, a Jewish human being was nothing.

Memories are the price I pay for my miracles.

There were times those memories threatened to overwhelm me on my return to Auschwitz-Birkenau. The contrast between what I was seeing with my eyes and what I was replaying in my brain was so stark that I found myself breathing a little faster, slightly shallower. I saw normality and simplicity that verged on beauty while being reminded of abnormality and destruction.

On the drive in, I noticed a newly built bungalow close to the camp site. It had a smart tiled roof and seemed freshly painted. A child's slide and swing were in the garden, alongside a playhouse. It took my breath away. How could people live there, among these ghosts? I looked at trees and flowers, and wondered how they could bloom and grow, in the ashes of so many Jewish victims.

This ground contains terrible secrets. Bones that did not burn completely in the furnaces were ground to powder with pestles and then used as landfill in marshy or uneven areas. They were scattered in nearby ponds and rivers, or across the fields, as fertilizer. Farmhouses, just outside the Birkenau camp, were requisitioned, had their windows concreted over, and became gas chambers.

We had just passed a modern shopping mall, with packed

car parks and families scurrying hither and thither. So many people were nicely dressed. They carried their purchases without an apparent care in the world. Yet I could not forget what this place was, what it represented. It was the site of an unimaginable disaster for my people.

Perhaps this explains why I have tried to protect some members of my miraculous family, particularly my younger grandchildren, from the full force of my experiences. I am moved by their playfulness, openness and innocence. Why jeopardize such precious things by telling them of death and destruction, cruelty and terror?

They have time to know the truth. Let them be carefree, so they can concentrate on their dreams. They will grow up and have a great Jewish education. They will be told, and begin to understand, what happened to their ancestors. Maybe their tomorrows will be enriched by my yesterdays. Pray God, they may even pass this book on to their children, and their children's children.

If I have one wish, it is that they are taught life is meaningful.

Future generations have their own stories to write, their own worlds to create, but I took heart from the passion of so many visitors I met. I sang the old songs, just inside the gate at Birkenau, with a French tour group, who wore T-shirts which proclaimed 'Voyage de la Mémoire'. I'm afraid I was a little croaky, since I was dry and my vocal chords have aged with the rest of me.

I walked through the gates at Auschwitz, which infamously proclaim the Great Lie, 'Arbeit Macht Frei' or 'Work Makes You Free', and turned instinctively towards the watchtower, where I visualized four, or even eight, SS men, facing different directions with the identical intent of shooting anyone driven mad by desperation, attempting to escape.

I could not avoid the small, square signs with a black skull and crossbones, ordering long-dead men to '*Stoj!*', halt in Polish, yet the contrasts were everywhere. Lilacs were in bloom beside the administrative buildings, made of weathered brick, pitted by time. They smelled so good, so sweet, so strange despite this once having been a dangerous, fearful place.

It took me back to scary mornings, waiting in eight or ten rows, formed on the grey, dusty cobbles, to learn my fate for the day. We were afraid from the moment the siren sounded to call us to order. We were surrounded by murderous faces. They looked at us with such hate and contempt. It was here that they selected us, in groups of five or ten. We never saw some of these groups again. The relief at being given a job, however grotesque, was powerful but momentary.

'*Umzug. Schnellere, schmutzige Juden.*'

'Move. Faster, dirty Jews.'

It did not matter that they yelled and spat at us. We had heard their insults day after day, so that they lost their meaning. Words didn't sting, or make us bleed, so we could ignore them. So long as they didn't shoot us, hang us, or send us to the gas chambers in Birkenau, we were content. We praised Heaven for the smallest of mercies.

We were generally used to collect bodies but were also marched to the northern edge of Birkenau, where the final construction phase was being completed. On other occasions we were used for menial maintenance work or ordered to clean the camp. It seemed the main aim was to keep us busy, exhausted and downtrodden. The pointlessness of such heavy labour was often obvious, and never mentioned.

Jolted back into the present, I found myself living out my own story. I hope this does not come across as arrogance, but due to my background I could never be just another tourist, one of the 2.3 million who flock to the site each year. Yet I still pulled out my mobile phone and took photographs of the presentational displays that served to put our historic plight into perspective.

These photographs were placed where they were originally taken, so they had a rare emotional power. I welled up, focusing on an image of women and children waiting, unknowingly, for their final solution. A small boy crouched beside the line, head bowed, playing with a stone. Another had a pristine white rucksack, slung across his back. He was on his toes. They probably had minutes to live.

I could not stop myself exclaiming, 'That was me, that was me!' to no one in particular, when I came across a photograph of a work party digging ditches just outside Birkenau. I didn't physically see myself; I meant it was a representation of my job, in the latter stages of my imprisonment there. I recognized the bridge, with thin metal railings, which still leads visitors into the camp.

Those steeply sided ditches, approximately three metres deep, ran for thirteen kilometres around the camp. They helped to drain the water away from marshy areas, where long-stemmed grass still flourishes. We were watched by sour SS men, with bayoneted rifles, as we prepared the ground, and laid pipes. Kapos were ready to whip us if they sensed we were slacking, or if they simply wanted to impress their lords and masters.

It took nearly eighty years for me to turn from a slave to a pilgrim.

There were two things I most wanted to do on my return. The first involved the most painful ritual, a search for the place to which we transported the bodies from the train. It seemed as if some of the camp layout had changed, but I was looking for a specific landmark, a low, single-storey building. It was exactly as I remembered it.

It had an aura of menace and regret. The external wall was covered in a form of grey cement, which had come away close to a heavy door, exposing the original brickwork. We used to carry naked bodies into this bunker-type building on wheelbarrows, before loading them into rudimentary wooden carriages which ran on short rails up to the ovens. One of us would usually hold the dead man's head, the other his legs. It was left to prisoners who formed the dreaded *Sonderkommando* units to incinerate them.

This place, apparently a pre-war ammunition store, was temporarily pressed back into service after originally being closed in the summer of 1943. It contained three furnaces. When I was there, in the summer of 1944, they were required to deal with the surge in demand, caused by the daily arrival of 12,000 Hungarian Jews. Corpses were scattered across the floor of a room at the back, which acted as a makeshift morgue. Elsewhere on the site, piles of bodies were being thrown into external incineration pits, a case of desperation leading to degradation.

I was left alone with my thoughts in a place that felt like a

110

cross between a prison and a crypt. A burst of light from a small window created a patch of brightness on the floor, but the shadows cast from four bare bulbs hanging from the ceiling set a dark, brooding mood. I felt chilled to my bones. Today's notices ask visitors to remain silent, to protect the dignity of the dead, but I was compelled to speak. My voice had a hollow echo, as I recalled a line from a sign outside which read, 'Remember their suffering.'

I remembered my suffering . . .

I also could not forget the anguish of those whose journey ended there. I sought out the symbolic box car, which remains in the sidings, with the so-called Gate of Death in the distance. Appropriately enough, it had the air of a grave. Stones of varying shapes and sizes had been placed on the footholds, ramps, and along the rods which drove the wheels of the train.

This gesture of mourning is consistent with one of the great traditions of Judaism, in which stones are placed on an individual's final resting place. Cut flowers, used in other faiths and cultures, are like life: they flourish, fade and die. Stones endure; they are associated with the consistency of remembrance. Stone is also frequently used in the Torah as a metaphor for the Almighty.

It took me several attempts to light a candle, and place it on the track, underneath the car. It was only a gentle breeze, so, in my more imaginative moments, I wonder if that signalled the presence of the last breaths of so many lost souls. I was determined to pay my respects, closed my eyes, and prayed for their deliverance.

My deliverance, of a sort, came in the second week of August 1944, when I was told my usefulness at Auschwitz-Birkenau had been exhausted. My work was done and I was, at least for the moment, being spared. My next destination was a concentration camp called Mauthausen, to the east of Linz, in Austria. It seemed a blessed relief because conditions there, on a hill overlooking a market town, surely had to be an improvement.

How wrong could I have been?

8

The Stairway of Death

What is a man? It is one of life's great questions. A philosopher will give you one answer, a physician another. A man of faith, a rabbi, priest, or imam, will concentrate on the spiritual aspects of humanity. I've always tended to their view, that someone's soul is more central to their being than skin and bone, muscle and sinew.

As I have grown older, I have sometimes felt I am studying another person, who exists in historical archives. These documents, occasionally blurred and strangely mundane, chart my life in captivity, which could have been extinguished for any reason, at any time, in any number of places. They are incomplete and contain inaccuracies, but they shed light on the bureaucracy of persecution.

They tell me I was one of 4,590 Jews who arrived at Mauthausen, one of the war's most notorious concentration camps, on 10 August 1944. I was officially registered as a *Lehrling*, an apprentice. My *Häftlings-Personal-Karte*, or Prisoner's Personal Card, names me as Josef. I was the 1,014th prisoner to be accepted that day: on that piece of paperwork, marked number 21, I was known as Jozek.

My *Personenbeschreibung*, my personal description, describes my *gestalt*, my shape, as *schlank*, slim. This is unsurprising since at that time I was perpetually hungry and weighed fewer than forty kilogrammes. My *haare*, hair, is *dunkel*, dark. My *augen*, eyes, are *blau*, blue. My *gesicht*, face, is *schmal*, narrow.

I don't know whether this was the clerk's slip (the word is typed between the lines) but my *nase*, nose, is supposedly *rude*. The best translation I can come up with for that is brusque. I'm not sure that's accurate, and it definitely doesn't feel like a compliment. Thankfully, everything else about me is described as *norm*, standard.

Today's memorial at Mauthausen describes it as:

> ... a former crime scene, a place of memory, a cemetery for the mortal remains of thousands of those murdered here and, increasingly, a site of political and historical education. Its task is to ensure public awareness of the history of the Mauthausen concentration camp and its subcamps, the memory of its victims, and the responsibility borne by the perpetrators and onlookers.

I was one of 190,000 people, from more than forty different nations, imprisoned here. It was the only Grade-III camp, the worst category, in the Nazi system. Our suffering is symbolized by a series of striking statues from such countries as Albania, Belgium, the Czech Republic, Denmark, France, Greece, Great Britain, Hungary, Ukraine, Russia, Spain and Poland. The memorial to Slovenian victims is an unforgettable sculpture of a screaming, skeletal man reaching up at the sky as if pleading for freedom.

The memorial to a Russian general, Lieutenant General Dmitry Mikhailovich Karbyshev, beside the entrance to the camp, depicts him encased in a slab of ice. Depending on the source, he either drowned, after having a hose pushed down his throat in the showers, or froze to death, when he was forced to stand outside in the depths of winter, with water being poured over him.

I was moved to tears after standing underneath Israel's contribution, made in the name of all Jewish victims. It is a huge angular version of a menorah, a sacred candelabrum with seven branches used in the ancient temple in Jerusalem. Piles of local granite, which cost many thousands of enslaved prisoners their lives, are in compartments around its base.

The menorah has great significance in my faith. The branches represent human knowledge. Six lean in towards the central lamp, which symbolizes the light of God. The object also signifies His creation of the world in seven days. My life is shaped by such beliefs, but it is not the reason why I was overwhelmed by the experience.

My senses were overloaded.

I leaned on the protective fence and looked out across the valley, in which that murderous quarry was situated. Again, pastoral beauty triggered painful memories. The Austrian countryside had a charming simplicity. The trees were mature and full-leaved. There was a newly ploughed field, almost a question mark in shape, next to a white-walled farmhouse on the hill on the far side.

I walked further along the line of the cliff, to another brutal, oversized monument, depicting the barbed wire which once confined us. This was donated by the East German regime before its fall in 1990. On its right sits a statue of a woman, with a quotation, written in 1933 by the German poet and playwright Bertolt Brecht, on the wall behind her. The English translation is:

O Germany, pale Mother,
How your sons have hurt you.
So you are sitting among the nations,
A thing of scorn and fear.

I paused, reflected on the remorse, and could not contain myself when I came to a final fence, which blocked the path that led to the top of the Stairway of Death. I had spent only six days, struggling up those 186 steps with blocks of granite across my back, but I saw enough suffering and barbarity to last a lifetime.

Flashbacks ambushed me, and I leaned into the embrace of my companion, Rabbi Naftali Schiff. He tried to lighten my mood, by pointing out that he, as a boy, would not have been allowed by his mother to wear my short-sleeved striped shirt, because it resembled the uniforms in which concentration camp prisoners lived, and often died.

My sadness and grief had been replaced by anger by the time we descended into the valley and reached the foot of the stairs by a circular route. I looked up at the thirty-one-metre-high staircase, which curved to the right, and impulsively threw a stone at it, as hard as I could. It might not have made much sense, but I wanted to retaliate, to punish it for what it did to us.

Perhaps returning, as a free man, meant more to me than I realized. I learned from bad people not to be bad. Do the opposite of what your persecutor does. A wise man never loses sight of who he is. That's why I could never kill, even to avenge the many wrongs done to me, and my race. It is not me. It is not who I am.

In Mauthausen, prisoners were systematically worked to

death. Rations were the worst in the concentration camp system, a slither of daily bread being accompanied by weed soup. We first had to prise off blocks of stone with an iron pick, or explosives. I learned quickly, under the supervision of a civilian foreman.

Like a climber seeking handholds, I looked for crevices and fissures that made the process of splitting the rock relatively pain free. The agony would come soon enough, when others took our place at the rock face, and we became human mules, to be used and abused. The granite was sharp and bored a hole in our shoulders.

The average load was calculated at around fifty kilogrammes, but I would try to find the smallest possible piece before lining up, in lines eight abreast. We had to walk up the steep incline, one behind the other, and do our best to avoid the whips of the SS men, situated every few metres or so. This went on, non-stop, for eleven hours each day.

It was chaos, with people attempting to come down against the tide of humanity. We were all exhausted, and when someone collapsed, he usually fell on the man behind him. This created a domino effect, all the way to the foot of the stairs. Heads were cracked, bones were broken. Can you imagine how we felt? Dead. How did I keep going? Through Heaven's will. I was not using my strength. It came from elsewhere.

These guards were not merely following orders. They seemed to take a sadistic pride in creating panic, by forcing us to run up the stairs to shouts of 'Härter arbeiten!' ('Work harder!') That was physically impossible, given the traffic jam created by sweating, swaying, struggling bodies in front of us. Yet it was preferable to what awaited us at the end of the climb, when the stones were placed in piles that would be used to build SS quarters.

Certain groups, usually singled out due to a note in their prisoner file that read RU, an abbreviation of 'Rückkehr unerwünscht', or 'Return undesirable', would be placed at the edge of the cliff, known by the guards as Fallschirmspring-erwand, 'The Sky Diving Wall'. Each prisoner, at gunpoint, was then given the option of being shot, or pushing the inmate in front of him off the cliff, to his death.

I thank God I did not face such a moral dilemma. Who among us would make the ultimate sacrifice, and take a bullet for a stranger who was, in any case, probably doomed anyway? Annihilation was unavoidable for many. For some, like a contingent of Dutch Jews who arrived during my time, as part of a transport of 8,000, it was unspeakably cruel.

They had a heart-breaking dignity, entering the camp carrying their best shoes in boxes and with their suits arranged neatly on hangers. Their fate was to be marched to the top of the cliff, to be met by sneering SS guards and Kapos who asked who, among them, would volunteer as parachutists. Confused and petrified, most agreed.

They were immediately shoved off the edge, their bodies bouncing off the cliff face on a descent of around a hundred feet. Some were dismembered before they hit the ground; others fell into a pond at the bottom. When, many years later, I walked past that pond, the water was still, yet somehow sinister. I could not stop myself wondering how many human remains it contained.

Their deaths were recorded in official camp documents as 'Selbstmord durch Springen' ('Suicide by jumping').

The bestiality was confirmed at the Nuremberg International Tribunal by Lieutenant Commander Jack Taylor, a US Navy commando who had been captured after being parachuted into Austria to collect intelligence and establish contact with partisan groups. He was twice scheduled for execution at Mauthausen. His first reprieve came when a sympathetic clerk in the camp's political office burned his papers, the second when the camp was liberated by the 11th Armoured Division of the US Army in May 1945.

Celebrated as the first commando to operate over air, land and sea, Taylor gave a famous eyewitness account to an American film crew, which accompanied the liberators. At the trial, which led to the conviction of all sixty-one defendants from the camp, he was asked by the prosecutor to outline how many ways the SS had to kill. His answer still sends a shiver down my spine:

Gassing, hanging, shooting, beating. There was one particular group of Dutch Jews who were beaten until they jumped over the cliff into the stone quarry. Some that were not killed on the first fall were taken back up and thrown over to be sure. Then there was exposure. Any new transport coming in was forced to stand out in the open, regardless of the time of the year, practically naked.

Other forms of killing included clubbing to death with axes or hammers and so forth, tearing to pieces by dogs specially trained for the purpose, injections into the heart and veins with magnesium chloride or benzene, whippings with a cow-tail to tear the flesh away, mashing in a concrete mixer, forcing them to drink a great quantity of water and jumping on the stomach while the prisoner was lying

119

on his back, freezing half-naked in sub-zero temperatures, buried alive, red-hot poker down the throat.

Take all that in, and then consider this: the perpetrators considered themselves normal human beings. Georg Bach-mayer, the SS captain in charge of the quarry, who oversaw the massacre of 300 deportees with axes and had two blood-hounds he regularly set on inmates, was, by all accounts, a huge football fan. The SS football team entered the local league. Newspapers carried their match reports.

German citizens were invited to watch them play on a pitch next to the camp infirmary, in which thousands died. The local population knew the scale of imprisonment, since all new arrivals were marched four kilometres, through the centre of the town, to the camp. They simply turned a blind eye and, in one infamous incident, known as *Hasenjagd*, the 'Hare Hunt', helped track down hundreds of Soviet escapees. Only eleven survived.

How and why did this happen? In later years, as a busi-nessman, I learned to follow the money. The Nazis had rented the quarry from the City of Vienna as early as 1938, when the SS leadership founded *Deutsche Erd- und Steinwerke GmbH*, the German Earth and Stone Works Company, as part of its expansion into the building materials industry.

Hitler hated Vienna, where he had become homeless after twice failing to enter the Academy of Fine Art. He associated it with rejection and his own shortcomings. Mauthausen's gran-ite, originally used to pave its streets, was diverted to huge construction projects in what he considered to be his home town, Linz. He named Linz as a *Führerstadt*, the 'Führer city', and envisioned it as the main cultural centre of the Third Reich.

Death was considered an occupational hazard, an acceptable business expense. Labour costs were zero since workers were enslaved. Board and lodgings were minimal. Up to 400 of us slept as best we could, head to tail, on the floor of a large room, which led out into the assembly square. Food consisted of bits of bread, washed down by stinging-nettle soup or a white, semolina-style liquid.

We were unwitting economic assets: those prisoners with gold teeth were very specifically recorded on arrival, so that they would be easier to find and their teeth extracted in the event of death. No wonder that, once the camp had been established, Granitwerke Mauthausen was the biggest, most productive, and most profitable branch of the SS building system.

The money to build and expand the camp was stolen from the prisoners, or the German Red Cross. It was also loaned from compliant banks in Dresden and Prague. It was a monstrous form of capitalism, without moral scruple or official oversight. By 1944 Mauthausen was making an annual profit of more than 11 million Reichsmarks, the modern equivalent of around 80 million Euros.

Local businesses needed more slave labourers, because increasing numbers of Austrian workers were being drafted into the Wehrmacht. Prisoners in Mauthausen and three of the sub-camps to which I was later assigned, Melk, Amstetten and Ebensee, were rented out to work on local farms, road-building programmes and residential construction projects.

Work details also repaired and strengthened the banks of the Danube, and supported a nearby archaeological dig in a ruined twelfth-century castle. They hacked tunnels through limestone in the Loiblpass in the Southern Alps, which linked

Austria with Slovenia. In total, forty-five companies, ranging from drug companies to battery producers, exploited our helplessness.

Most, inevitably, were linked to the war effort. A section of the quarry was converted into an assembly plant for Mauser machine pistols. Panzer tanks were made from locally produced steel. Though inmates received special cigarette tokens for building an underground factory for the Steyr Daimler Puch AG company, many attempts were made to sabotage production lines manufacturing rifles and military vehicles.

I do not wish to appear critical, since the memorials and museum are deeply affecting, well presented, and do not shy away from the role of the local population in, at the very least, tolerating our suffering, but Mauthausen is still contributing to the local economy, through the number of visitors it attracts. On balance that is a good thing, because our agonies are acknowledged, and respected.

When I walked through the gates and into the courtyard, I was struck by a simple plaque that had recently been placed on the forbidding stone walls. It featured the famous statement by Simon Wiesenthal, of blessed memory: 'Hope lives when people remember.' I choose also to dwell on another timeless truth, expressed by the former Mauthausen prisoner who devoted his life to bringing Nazis to justice: 'Freedom is not a gift from heaven, it must be earned every day.'

Franz Ziereis, the camp commander, was promoted to the rank of SS *Standartenführer*, Regiment Leader, because he was so successful in denying us that freedom. His recognition for 'outstanding service' was quickly followed by the award of the *Deutsche Kreuz*, the German Cross, a swastika encircled by gold laurel leaves, introduced by Hitler for 'repeated exceptional acts of troop leadership'.

Ziereis was the puppet master of Mauthausen, deciding where and when we would be sent out to work elsewhere. By the end of the war he was in overall charge of forty-nine *Aussenlager*, external or sub-camps, one of the biggest of which was Melk, where I was transported on 16 August 1944. Mortality rates there were around 45 per cent.

Ziereis at least paid for his crimes. Having fled Mauthausen with his wife, two days before its liberation, he was discovered hiding in his hunting lodge in the mountains and arrested by a US army unit. He was shot while trying to escape, suffering mortal wounds to his stomach, lungs and back, and, following a confession extracted during eight hours of questioning by US officers and civilians, died in a US Army field hospital set up in another of his fiefdoms, Gusen.

He was denied the dignity in death he denied others. Polish and Russian former prisoners hung his body on to the same electrified barbed-wire fence at Mauthausen on which the Kapos under his control used to throw inmates. It was naked, apart from a bandage covering a gunshot wound on the left arm, and had anti-Nazi slogans painted on its back. It was only removed, on the orders of a US army officer, when it began to decompose.

Those who wish to rewrite history suggest that his confession was an invention, and that he was already dead by the time photographs were taken of him apparently answering questions from US army personnel, clustered around his deathbed. They even deny that he was in the hospital, a ludicrous claim easily answered by the official logbook, which is in the US National Archives.

I only wish that these conspiracy theorists could have followed me to Melk and endured the hardest of winters alongside inmates drawn from twenty-six countries. At its height, the camp contained 10,000 prisoners, crammed into eighteen barracks built within the Freiherr von Birago military training base. More than 200 of them died each week from exposure in late 1944 and early 1945.

This is not so surprising, since our uniforms were rags, covered mainly by thin, specially marked civilian clothing left by murdered inmates. They offered no protection against the wind, rain and snow. We were reduced to stuffing our shirts and wooden clogs with paper, torn from cement sacks, to find a slither of warmth. Cement dust settled at the back of the throat and, if you were unlucky, filtered into the lungs.

Sores on unprotected feet lingered for weeks because our bodies were so weak. The sores carried the threat of deadly blood poisoning. I was too cautious, but some inmates were prepared to risk summary execution for sabotage by cutting pieces of rubber from the production lines, smuggling them past the guards into the camp, and inserting them into the clogs.

We were effectively sold to the highest bidder. Depending on the auction price, or the whim of our masters, we would be told to pour concrete, prepare munitions, lay pipes, prepare timber, or simply build houses for SS officers or senior members of the Luftwaffe contingent assigned to the camp.

Countless prisoners were buried alive in a variety of tunnelling projects in the surrounding hills, which were originally intended to establish underground factories, producing ball bearings, aircraft engines and other military hardware. Six gigantic caverns, several hundred metres long, were gouged out, but cave-ins were inevitable, since the ground, which consisted of fine sand and quartz, was unstable.

My work detail slept on sacks of straw and worked around the clock for Wayss & Freytag, a German civil engineering company whose wartime activity included the construction of Hitler's reinforced bunker in the Wolf's Lair, the command centre for the Eastern Front that was the site of an unsuccessful assassination attempt on the Führer in July 1944.

The company still operates international tunnelling projects and has a current annual turnover of approximately €300 million. According to its publicity, it has a 'highly motivated workforce' and 'works in compliance with the applicable standards for quality management and environmental protection and always strives for the highest possible standard of safety at work'.

Things have certainly changed.

Despite the ever-present dangers, we lacked proper equipment, and were often expected to dig with our bare hands. Since the caverns were designed to hide munitions at a time of increasing air-raid activity by the Allies, we were eventually given picks, hammers and chisels to build wooden shelves, attached to the rock walls.

As usual, since I was so small, my job was to fasten the highest shelves from a rickety scaffold. On one occasion it collapsed, leaving me hanging by my crotch. I was in agony, and had to work myself loose before falling to the ground. I could not move because of the pain but was hauled to my feet by my fellow workers.

If the guards had realized the extent of my plight, that would have been the end of me. I would have been deemed *arbeitsunfähig*, disabled, or unfit for work, and sent back to

Mauthausen for extermination, either by chemical injection or at a local euthanasia centre. This was the fate of 1,400 prisoners, more unfortunate than I was. Treatment in the camp infirmary was an impossibility; designed to house 100 patients, it contained 2,000 seriously ill or injured prisoners in the depth of winter.

None of this could have come as any surprise to the soldiers and civilians who witnessed our plight on a daily basis. Link roads looked down onto the camp, where one of the main Wehrmacht thoroughfares faced straight onto the entrance to the crematorium, which had an extremely tall, relatively thin chimney. The stench was appalling, so the extent of the atrocities was unavoidable.

Death was not quite as public as it was under Amon Goeth in Plaszow, but it was equally random. The order, '*Komm, Komm. Doch Heraus, Jude!*' ('Come, come. Get out, Jew!'), often led to people being taken out of the tunnel, savagely beaten, or shot for no apparent reason. I consider myself fortunate, though I still suffer from excruciating pain in my lower back from the injuries I was forced to conceal in Melk. It took years for an associated hernia to clear up.

My life is full of contrasts and contradictions. Evil men helped to keep me alive, against the odds. I testified at the war-crimes trial of one Melk camp commander, Julius Ludolf. He was duly, and rightly, hanged, since he was a murderous ogre, but without his impulsive decision to allow me into his house, I probably would not have survived.

9

The Limits of Kindness

The day began like any other, with a bell that sounded at 4 a.m. We knew we could not linger, because each minute was allocated and carried the threat of punishment if it was wasted. We were barely awake but created an illusion of order and normality by rearranging the lice-ridden straw sacks on our bunks through force of habit.

That done, we lined up for a brief wash, or a visit to the toilet block. The Kapos prowled around, yelling '*Beeil dich. Mach schnell!*' ('Hurry up. Make it fast!') as we did our business as best we could. That involved squatting over holes, back-to-back with the inmate on the other side of the row. We simply got used to the smell, and the indignity.

I recently met a lady who asked me whether we were provided with toilet paper. When I said 'no' she asked me what I did to clean myself, and how we coped. I understood her confusion, because the process was understandably beyond her comprehension, and merely answered: 'Madam, I leave that to your imagination.'

There was no hygiene. When people became sick, there was no doctor to examine them, or provide medication. They either continued working, and gradually recovered, or died. Degradation was official Nazi policy, part of a package that made people succumb, when they could so easily have been cured. Let them collapse. Let them die. That's what they are here for.

Most of us took the precaution of only relieving ourselves twice a day, first thing in the morning and last thing at night. I would not wish the desperate feeling of having to hang on for hours at a time on anyone, but the alternative, of being beaten up for taking the briefest break from work to empty your bowels or bladder, was frightening.

Rations at Melk were reduced in the winter of 1944–5, so that we were expected to exist on one-sixteenth of a loaf a day. We lined up for so-called 'morning coffee', which had to sustain us until a form of soup was served at midday, before assembling, block by block, on the Appellplatz for roll call. This could last for hours, as the SS checked for escapees, and was the most dangerous time of our day.

This was where floggings were administered, for the slightest offence. Anyone showing signs of weakness or inattention was prey to the arbitrary mood of the guards, who beat their victims to the ground before kicking them in the kidneys or spine, so that many never got up again. Since we were arranged in height, from the smallest to the tallest, I was always in the front row, and most vulnerable.

Some SS men loved to intimidate by leaning forward, so close to your face you could smell their stale breath. You never knew what they might do, or how their warped minds worked. If you made a nervous movement, while waiting for your work detail for the day, they would shoot you as soon as look at you.

The stakes were raised when the commandant, Julius Ludolf, made his inspection. He was a haughty man, with a high forehead and a large, angular nose, who trailed an entourage of three or four lieutenants. He came to Melk in May 1944, after being promoted from several smaller sub-camps, and was full of his own importance.

When he passed you on parade without registering your presence, you heaved a sigh of relief. On this particular morning, he suddenly stopped in front of me, and stared intently into my eyes without saying a word. I was terrified, almost hypnotized by his grim, angry face. It is amazing how many thoughts race through your mind, in that split second which could decide your fate.

I heard my father's voice again: 'If they beat you, do not fight back. Bow your head down and take it. Quieten your enemy by your obedience.' His image faded, to be replaced by that of Wilek Chilowicz, the collaborator who had saved my life by beating me up at Plaszow before Amon Goeth could shoot me. Ludolf would not have bothered saving me had I not become his shoeshine boy. It was almost as if my father's ghost was telling me to trust in the power of flattery.

I took a terrible chance, that Ludolf would be as intrigued by my naïve response as Chilowicz was, back in Plaszow. I clicked the heels of my wooden clogs together, saluted extravagantly with my right hand, and shouted, '*Hochgeschätzter Herr Lagerkommandant*' ('Dear Sir, Camp Commandant'), '*Ich werde Ihre Stiefel polieren, damit sie wie die Sonne strahlen*' ('I will shine your boots so they shine like the sun').

It wasn't original, but after a couple of agonizing seconds it proved to be effective. I thought I saw a smile start to form at the side of Ludolf's mouth as he turned to face his entourage. He had a gruff, deep voice, and, though I could not hear what he said, he made what I assumed was a disparaging remark before bursting out laughing. I took that as a positive sign. Finally, before walking on, he called the camp administrator to him, and issued his order:

'OK. *Lass ihn machen.*'

'OK. Let him do it.'

The fear kicked in again, immediately an SS officer pulled me, roughly, out of the line. He waved his bayoneted rifle in my direction, and barked contemptuously, '*Komm, folge mir.*' I did as he ordered and followed him out of the camp gates, and up a steep grassy incline towards Ludolf's villa, at the top of the hill.

As my escort moved behind me, to cover my back, my mind raced. I was scared but tried to convince myself that if the commandant had wanted to kill me, I would already have been dead. We had heard awful rumours about what went on in that villa; drunken parties, debauched behaviour, and people who simply disappeared. I had passed the point of no return.

The soldier opened a door, ushered me in, and left me sitting, alone, to deal with my imagination. What did I have to lose? I had seen my friends die, and my family taken away to be murdered. I had been treated as Untermensch, sub-human. How much more pain and humiliation could they inflict upon me?

I froze inside when Ludolf arrived from his round, but saluted him once more, and pandered to his ego by referring to him as SS-*Hauptsturmführer*, which was Amon Goeth's title at Plaszow. It was a higher rank than Ludolf's real one, SS-*Obersturmführer*, or senior assault leader. The 'mistake' seemed to please him.

He rarely used complete sentences, preferring to communicate through grunts and gestures, but after studying me suspiciously, as if to work out my intent, he referred to me as *'Putzer Jude'* ('Cleaner Jew') and directed me towards a cabinet which contained cleaning creams and brushes, and a closet, which housed several pairs of shoes and an array of calf-length leather boots.

I scoured and polished those boots as if there were no tomorrow, which arguably would have been the case if my efforts had disappointed him. I had finished when he returned; he nodded in satisfaction and asked my name. Taking advantage of my childhood instruction in German, I took my chance to ask him, in return, what else he wished of me.

He led me into the garden, a place of wonder and opportunity. There were deer in a fenced-off enclosure, monkeys on the roof, and chickens running free. Plump pigeons pecked at remnants of their grain. Ludolf, though, ushered me towards a long, large cage at the bottom of the garden. It was full of rabbits. He told me my job was to ensure they were fed every day and pointed at a pail of carrots kept nearby.

Every. Day. Two words with such meaning.

My joy was well disguised, but unconfined. That meant he intended me to live, for the time being at least. As he turned, and walked away towards the house, leaving me to my new chores, I resolved to be the first rabbit to be fed. I knew the dangers, but bit deep into a carrot. The flavour exploded in my mouth as I chewed it.

It was delicious, a dream. It tasted like redemption. It was my happiest moment since I was separated from my mother and brothers. I knew, at that instant, that my prayers had been heard. The villa was my place of work, my refuge, my chance.

I was disappointed not to find that building when I returned many years later to Melk, which has been a Federal Austrian army barracks since 1956. Part of a 1,150-metre motor-racing track, the Wachauring, occupies the site. At least, then, I was welcomed in peace, instead of being among sheep, led into the slaughterhouse. I took great pleasure in having the freedom to share my story with the current commanding officer.

Ludolf had not changed. He was still capable of monstrous cruelty. He took apparent pleasure in publicly pummelling prisoners, beating some to death. Though I did not see this personally, the post-war trial at Dachau, in which I testified, heard that he ordered a group of Russian and Polish inmates to be thrown against the electrified fences, with gruesome and fatal consequences.

The camp doctor, Josef Sora, was from the Luftwaffe, whose guards were in general more forgiving. He was a good man, who passed on snippets of news from the BBC in the final months of the war. He was also a brave man, ignoring Ludolf's command that fifty tuberculosis patients should be starved to death. His testimony at the war-crimes trial was influential because it captured the corruption of absolute power:

Especially at night these people did some things that frightened me because of the things I saw,' Sora told the court. 'At midnight he [Ludolf] had the prisoners brought out from their barracks by floodlight. He had them form up and when they stood there at attention, all lined up, one of the prisoners stood by with a pail of water while another prisoner held a towel.

He would then select a prisoner at random and beat him extremely hard with his fists until blood flowed. Then he would wash his hands in a ceremonial fashion, and had the towel handed him, whereupon he would select yet another prisoner and beat him so thoroughly that he drove him into the electric fence by kicking him constantly.

I could not afford to think of such inhumanity, even though I remembered it well. My responsibility was to concentrate on the additional responsibility that Ludolf gave me. I had to feed the chickens and fatten up ducks and turkeys brought into camp by SS officers. Needless to say, I shared their grain, and, when I knew the way was clear, began surreptitiously picking through the garbage for morsels of food.

There was plenty to eat, because Ludolf had dinner guests every day, and demanded that meals be lavish. Occasionally, he ordered me to clean out the cellar, which contained racks of wine, potatoes, onions, and other vegetables. The store included fruit and baking materials, used to create a range of cakes and desserts.

Little did I know that he stole the best food from the kitchens, serving both soldiers and inmates. He sold spare meat, and a large percentage of the prisoners' cigarette rations, to local civilians. He was a greedy braggart, a nondescript former barber and taxi driver who became used to being fawned over by those who feared his displeasure.

I thought of the starving men in the barracks I left each morning. Instead of lining up for roll call, I would be walked up the hill to the villa by one of the soldiers. A plan began to form in my mind, but first I had to continue to gain and retain

Ludolf's confidence. I didn't care that I was being treated rather like his household pet.

Eventually, after a couple of weeks, he gave orders that I should be allowed to walk, unaccompanied, to my work. I was even given a set of keys to let myself in to his house. The gates at the back of the camp opened, as if by magic, as I approached. I was smart enough to realize that I was not as free as it appeared.

I was tracked up and down the hill, by unseen eyes from the observation tower. If I had been foolish enough to make a break for it, I would have been swiftly apprehended, and executed as an example to others. Ludolf wanted a willing slave. I duly shined his boots, scrubbed the toilets, cleaned the floors, and prepared laundry to be sent out to the town.

I made up the fire, hauling coal and wood in from an outside store. An endless supply of women, four or five different ones a night, worked in the kitchen. I turned down the beds, and closed the window blinds, for the overnight guests, who tended to be female, since he was a great womanizer. My job was to see nothing, and to ask no questions.

I stayed out of the main rooms, unless summoned. The guests tended to fall silent when I came in, to serve vodka and other drinks, but I knew when they began singing and laughing that secrets would begin to slip out. They would talk loudly about the war, celebrating German victories and lamenting their defeats, which always made me smile. My final act, before descending to my barracks at night, was to make hot drinks for the household.

Some visitors were off-limits. I hid in a cupboard when Ludolf entertained Heinrich Himmler, and several generals. I knew that if the main architect of the Holocaust spotted me, at the very least he would have reprimanded the commandant for allowing a Jew in his household. I hid not to protect Ludolf from criticism, or me from potential punishment, but because others were starting to rely on me.

I was conscious of the possibility of being lured into a trap. I inadvertently found a huge amount of foreign currency, stolen jewellery and gold coins while cleaning the upstairs rooms but dared not touch it, in case it was left there as a test of my honesty. It was of no value to me, in any case. Bread was more important than baubles or banknotes.

Ludolf probably realized I was scavenging from the leftovers. I calculated that so long as I was not too obvious, and he thought I was looking after myself without making him look weak, I would be able to put my plan into operation and smuggle scraps into the camp. I knew my job was precious and didn't want to jeopardize it, so began by storing small slices of chicken and rabbit in the hems of my clothes.

As time went on, and I was not being checked, I became bolder. I found a piece of string, which I wrapped around my pants to create a sort of bag. I hid food underneath my shirt and in my coat pockets. I knew the risk I was taking, but, through my solidarity with my fellow prisoners, I had the chance to make a difference between their life or death.

Deep friendships were difficult to sustain, for obvious reasons. I barely had time to know someone's name before he was either transferred to another camp or despatched to the gas chambers. That made me defensive, cautious, because I did not want to be hurt unnecessarily. The Spielman brothers, Chaim and Jacob, were exceptions to the rule.

They survived, with God's grace, and we remained close until they passed away. Jacob was the best man at my marriage to Perla in Colombia in March 1954, and I shared several happy holidays with Chaim, who eventually lived in New York.

They followed me through the camp system, from Plaszow to Auschwitz and Mauthausen. Since our bunks were close, I waited until darkness to transfer slithers of food over to them. It was, of course, impossible to keep my exploits a secret between the three of us. That is when I began to understand the limits of kindness.

Food leads men to do desperate things. It was so scarce in Melk that the rations of the recently dead were quickly shared, usually by workers in the sick bay in return for cigarettes. Sometimes callousness took over. 'Musselmen', a slang term for inmates in the final stages of suffering from starvation, exhaustion, or listlessness, found that their food was taken, and given to those who needed a little extra to survive. No one cared since their end was imminent.

Inmates were literally in a food chain. Senior prisoners, serving in the kitchens, would take bribes, again usually in the form of cigarettes, to dig deeper into their vat of soup, where beans, and other rare items of substance like dehydrated cabbage, could be found.

Those unable to buy their favour were left to watch in despair, as their inadequate portion of precious liquid was scooped from just beneath the surface, and resembled, at best, a weak broth. Fights often broke out when promises were broken, which gave the guards the opportunity to break heads.

The *Barackenältester*, a German criminal trusted to oversee the 200 or so men in our barracks, was at the top of that food chain. He picked up whispers of my exploits and, on my return from the villa one night, pulled me aside and threatened to denounce me to the Nazis. We needed to come to an arrangement. That meant getting whatever he asked for.

He wanted me to bring specific items from the villa, such as soap or schnapps. This was possible, in small quantities, provided I was careful. He also demanded a pair of shoes, to replace his wooden clogs. That would be difficult. I kept him sweet by bribing the inmate in charge of the clothing store, who, in turn, used my 'present' of food and cigarettes to buy himself a favour.

A hungry Russian gave me a five-zloty coin, which I passed on to a Chinese prisoner, a silversmith in his former life. In return for a little food, and a promise that he should 'keep close' when I returned from the villa, he produced a pendant that I hung around my neck with a wire. I was able to keep it safe since searches were becoming less frequent.

One side of the flattened coin featured my number, 85314, and the name of the main camp, Mauthausen. The back was dominated by my initials, JL, in swirling letters. The inscription, in Chinese script, read: 'May a lucky star accompany you on your way, always.' A thing of beauty, it remains a family heirloom.

I quickly found myself at the centre of a web of conflicting interests, bartering and petty corruption, which we called 'organizing'. I formed a business relationship with the camp administrator, giving him items in return for better jobs for my allies. I had power but lived on the edge. I never knew what those around me would do out of sheer desperation.

On one level, I was treated as a hero by the twenty or so inmates I was able to help. Despite our tribulations, we sustained our faith by reminding ourselves of the lessons of the Torah, so I became known as 'the Joseph in Egypt' after the passage in the Book of Genesis where my namesake was appointed by the Pharaoh to manage the food crisis.

I took the comparison as a huge compliment. The Bible records Joseph as an unselfish man, who thought of others rather than taking personal advantage of his new position at the head of the royal court. He regarded wisdom and powers of judgement as gifts from God, and thanked Him for offering comfort in moments of emotional distress.

My smuggled food gave people hope and, in many cases, kept them alive. Most of my friends in Melk survived: I regard that as one of the greatest achievements of my life. Yet it made me enemies because I could not help everyone in the barracks. They surrounded me, cursing and begging, asking for things I could not give. I was hated by them and lived in fear of betrayal.

Had Ludolf been informed of my activities, my friends would have been saying Kaddish prayers for me.

I carefully and gradually wore him down. Initially, he would slap me if I asked for permission to eat some scraps, or a slice of stale bread. My strategy was to bow to his authority and do as he pleased. When I asked what he wanted to do with several old loaves on the kitchen counter, he told me to throw them out.

I did, after a fashion of course. I tore the bread into pieces and carried it downhill. One day, I had the chutzpah to ask him for permission to eat a little of a torte, which had remained on the kitchen table for several days. To my great surprise, he nodded, and told me to put the rest in the bin. Since that was my private food bank, I gratefully followed his command. That torte kept us going for a month.

I felt safe in the villa, though Otto Striegel, the SS sergeant in charge of the kitchens and food transports, was a sinister presence. He loved to toy with me, ordering me to stand in the corner with my mouth wide open. He used my mouth as a target as he threw stones at me, but often missed and hit me in the face. He enjoyed my discomfort as I winced in pain and he revelled in my helplessness.

Striegel had lost all his arrogance when I testified against him during a six-week trial at Dachau. He was just another grey, sad man with a number, in his case 53, on a piece of card hung around his neck. He was a serial sadist; I used to see him beat prisoners with a rubber truncheon, often for hours. He denied everything, suggested he had been confused with Karl Striegel, an unrelated guard at Mauthausen, and told the court that the stone-throwing was a prank, during which apparently we had both laughed.

I was one of seven prosecution witnesses in Striegel's case. Others outlined his role in the execution of twenty-eight Dutch prisoners and testified that he would kick and punch seriously ill inmates, as they were tossed into evacuation lorries that took them to Mauthausen's gas chambers, or an external euthanasia centre. Following his wife's unsuccessful appeal for clemency, he was hanged on 20 June 1947, aged thirty.

Ludolf was another of the fifty-eight Nazis sentenced to death in the Dachau trial (the other three defendants received terms of life imprisonment). He was one of many who turned pale when his fate was read out. I didn't appreciate it at the time, because my mind was whirling, but it was ironic that, for most of his trial, he too was referred to as a number, in his case 38. Perhaps Ludolf knew then how we felt when we were branded.

He told the court he had been good to me and claimed he had not fired a shot in anger for the duration of the war. He denied throwing prisoners against the electrified fence, despite being shown the camp Death Book, which recorded twenty-four 'suicides' during his time in charge, several from electrocution. He insisted there had been a solitary execution at Melk but was not believed.

I was in a group of five or six former Melk inmates who discovered him, close to the camp at Ebensee, three days after our liberation. He was trying to pass himself off as a peasant farmer, but none of us could forget his sour face or his gruff voice. I felt extremely privileged, elevated, that I survived to see him reduced in this way. The big man had become a little sheep.

As powerful and as pitiless as they once were, these Nazis were nothing. They all tried to pin the blame on higher authorities. They all insisted they were only following orders and had no choice in the way they behaved. We jostled and punched Ludolf before taking him to the US Army HQ, at the local hotel, but it was his sense of humiliation that gave me the greatest pleasure.

I felt around in his pockets and, much to my surprise since I thought it would have been the first thing he would have thrown away, I found a red arm band with a white circle enclosing a swastika. He refused to put in on, but when he weakened, and started to do so, I wrenched it out of his hand, threw it on the ground and stamped on it. I then forced him to make a 'Heil Hitler' salute against his will. He cried as I forced his hand upwards, above his head. That was all the revenge I required.

I gave my evidence against him at Dachau from a wooden

chair, on a small, square raised platform. When asked to identify him by the prosecutor, I walked across the court towards
him, made sure I maintained eye contact, and pointed my finger at him, inches from his face. 'This is him,' I said. 'The
filthy murderer.'

US Major General Fay Prickett, head of a military tribunal
that included eight judges, told him: 'The Court, in closed
session, at least two thirds of the members present at the time
the vote was taken concurring, sentences you to death by
hanging at such time and place as higher authority may direct.' He was executed in Landsberg prison on 28 May 1947,
aged fifty-three.

Justice was served, and history will record Melk as another
example of man's inhumanity to man. Yet I cannot also forget
the few isolated acts of kindness by those empowered to make
our lives Hell. One came about a month after we entered the
camp, when I was on a work detail assigned to lay rails.

An older man, with a very weak voice, suddenly said: 'Hey
brothers, Jews, do you know what day it is today?' As one
day was very much like the rest, and we had little conception
of time apart from Sundays, which meant the distribution of
two cigarettes each, we shook our heads and kept working.
The old man explained it was Yom Kippur, our sacred and
revered Day of Atonement. Lolo, the Kapo on duty, noticed
the stir.

'Hey, Joe,' he asked, 'what's happening?' I explained the
significance of the Holiest of days, on which we fasted, rested
and dedicated ourselves to God. I must admit to momentary
fear, since I recalled that, at Plaszow the previous year, Amon
Goeth marked Yom Kippur with mass murder. People came
from other camps with tales of SS guards taunting prisoners

141

with offers of special foods on High Holy Days, tempting them to go against their religious beliefs.

Lolo, though, was different. 'Are you allowed to work?' he asked. When I explained that Jewish law permitted us to do so, only when our lives were in danger, he thought quickly and called us to order. 'Put down your shovels,' he said firmly but carefully, since he did not want to draw the attention of the SS men, wandering up and down the line of workers. 'Put down your picks and lie on the ground. Today you will rest.'

He pointed at a nearby pile of gravel. 'I will stand on top and watch out for you. When I see the SS approaching, I will shout "*Geschrie zek*" [Code Six]. Pick up your tools and start working. I will scream and yell at you to work harder, and flick a few of you with my whip. Once the Germans pass by, out of sight, you can go back to your rest.'

He was wonderful, as good as his word. He allowed us the grace to pray, and make Teshuva, repentance. The literal Hebrew translation is 'return', which refers to turning back to a way of life from which you have strayed. In our case this was inevitable in captivity, but the chance to purify ourselves by praising the Almighty gave us the strength we did not think we had.

We felt closer not only to God, but to one another. Our souls soared. It was a brief respite, but Lolo gave us the chance to reconnect with who we were before our lives were shattered by war. For that alone, I resolved never to forget him. As things turned out, we would meet again, at our moment of liberation.

10

Freedom

I was eighteen. I had seen too much of death, and too little of life. I had lost nearly six years of study and innocent enjoyment. The closest I got to a normal young man's rite of passage was to wake up with my first hangover, underneath a wagon pulled by a train caught up in an Allied air raid. I realize that might require some explanation, so bear with me.

I never knew where I was being sent, or what awaited me, but was relieved to leave Melk. I arrived in Amstetten, a hastily assembled sub-camp of Mauthausen that operated for less than a month, on 2 April 1945. I was part of a *Bahnbau* railway construction detachment billeted in a deserted military barracks known as the *Panzerlager* after its former use as a tank camp.

There was hardly any food, and sanitary conditions were disgusting, but it felt like a reprieve until we discovered the reason for our emergency arrival. The war was accelerating to a close. As the site of a strategically important railway hub on the main line between Vienna and Linz, Amstetten was a primary target for Allied bombers. We were expendable.

Countless prisoners had been killed a fortnight previously, when the Eisenreichdornach neighbourhood bore the brunt of the assault. They were not allowed into civilian shelters and fled into the forest to the east of the town, which was heavily hit. At least thirty-four female prisoners died. Local records spoke of trucks carrying corpses: 'layered between straw hung their hands, feet and heads'.

Our task, during shifts that lasted for up to fourteen hours, was to repair air-raid trenches and clean up the area around the bombed-out station, which was a surreal sight. I had never seen such destruction. Heavy iron tracks were buckled into strange shapes, like crumpled paper straws. Locomotives, bombed and upended while pulling open carriages, had been left, looking like a dog on its haunches.

My detail was assigned to clearing away the wreckage from a set of wagons, propelled off the tracks by the force of explosions. One had a circular tank, from which a clear liquid dripped. When the guards, mainly Austrian criminals who were more concerned with their own welfare, were not looking, a couple of brave souls dipped their fingers into the fractures.

Their eyes widened suddenly. The liquid was some form of spirit, most probably vodka. Like many, I surreptitiously gathered some in the dish that hung from my waist and took a sip. I was a stranger to alcohol but found to my surprise that I liked the taste. The next thing I knew I woke up the following morning underneath a nearby wagon, which had remained intact.

I did not know where I was, or why I felt so sick, but that was the least of my problems. I realized the rest of my work detail had been sober enough to get back to the barracks overnight, while I had crawled away to sleep. I lay as flat as possible and tried to work out what was going on by looking out at the passing sets of legs. Clogs worn by prisoners signalled safety; the occasional jackboot warned that the SS were in the vicinity.

When the Germans were out of my line of sight, I waited for a minute or so, then sneaked out on all fours. By some miracle, I shuffled straight into a group of inmates, who disguised their surprise and made sure I was not noticed. The task was hopeless, and increasingly pointless, because more and more of our oppressors were distracted. Chaos was in the air.

I was among the prisoners taken to the Ebensee sub-camp by 15 April, as part of the wider evacuation of bigger camps in the face of Allied advances. We heard rumours, later confirmed, that a contingent of thirty prisoners at Amstetten, so weak they were unable to walk, were murdered on the spot by a few remaining Nazi fanatics.

History had not finished with the town. Its infamy was renewed in 2009 when a local man, Josef Fritzl, was found to have kidnapped, raped and imprisoned his daughter Elisabeth for twenty-four years in the basement of the family home, which had once been a fallout shelter. During the global media controversy, it emerged that Amstetten's civic records still listed Adolf Hitler as an honorary citizen.

Hitler, of course, committed suicide in his bunker on 30 April 1945, when I still had a week in captivity to survive. It proved a close-run thing because Ebensee was a hellhole. As the end of the war came closer, the daily death rate exceeded 350. The crematorium operated around the clock but was unable to cope. Naked bodies were stacked up outside our barracks, each of which held 750 prisoners despite being designed for just 100.

The Nazis were so desperate they ordered inmates to dig a

ditch outside the camp. Bodies were tossed in and covered with quicklime. I did not see this, but rumours circulated that some of the bodies were still twitching. Another story, that four sick prisoners had been buried alive to free up space in the infirmary, also carried the ring of truth.

The stench of death was inescapable and unbearable.

Food was so scarce we ate grass. There were also outbreaks of cannibalism. Lolo, the friendly Kapo who had followed us from Melk to Ebensee, came across a group of Russians roasting the backside of a young man who had recently died. Despite his urging, I could not bear to look. What had we become? The sub-humans Hitler had decreed us to be?

The official record of our American liberators, the 3rd Cavalry Reconnaissance Squadron, summed up our plight:

Abuse and disease were rampant. The prisoners lived in the vilest filth imaginable. The stench from the camp was nauseating. Many of them had been reduced to the point of eating their own dead. The camp was in the same class as the more notorious ones at Belsen and Buchenwald.

Like many survivors, I have a complicated relationship with food. Appreciation is laced with guilt. Back then, when the main midday meal was three-quarters of a litre of water, flavoured by potato peelings, I couldn't think about anything else. Bread was so treasured I could barely bring myself to eat it. In a peaceful, normal world, that seems incredible.

My wife Perla was a great cook, a wonderful baker who created her own recipes. I never cooked for myself, because I was too busy, working to ensure we had the best possible life, but she taught our children the basics. I can still remember their pride in showing me the bread and cakes they had made. Our kitchen smelled of home.

Today, living on my own in Jerusalem, I have individual meals delivered. Friends and neighbours bring me fresh fruit and succulent cheesecakes. My TV dinners are simple but flavourful. They include a piece of fish or meat and some vegetables, but I throw away, unopened, the section containing potatoes, rice or couscous.

That hurts me so much. Every time I do so, I think back to the days when such a portion would have sustained me for several weeks. How could I do such a thing? I now have the privilege of an old man's caution, not to mention vanity, stimulated by his great-granddaughter.

On my last visit to New York, she looked at me in a puzzled manner. 'Are you going to have a baby?' she asked me, with that innocence young children express so naturally. 'Why?' I asked. 'Well, when my mummy had a stomach like you, she had a baby.'

A big compliment . . .

I want to look after myself as best I can. I occasionally use a wheelchair, for very long distances, and don't want it to be too hard for me to walk as, God willing, I get older. I've tried to keep mentally active, but I'm still dealing with some of the injuries I suffered in the camps. I hurt my back badly in the tunnels: those at Ebensee were originally designed as an underground rocket factory and became a weapons dump.

When I was younger, I neglected the damage inflicted on me in captivity, which also included a perforated eardrum, caused by a beating. Perla and I visited spas in Slovakia for treatment, but when she passed away, I had no desire to go on my own. The Israeli army organized medical insurance, which provided for a short course of hydrotherapy, and I try to visit the Dead Sea each summer, to take advantage of the healing properties of the mud.

Those indulgences were as far as possible from my mind in the days before US troops, part of the 80th Infantry Division of the 3rd Army, arrived to guarantee our freedom. Given our experiences at Amstetten, we gained great heart when, one afternoon early in May, the sky darkened. We looked up to see hundreds of Allied aircraft on their way to complete the job of pounding the Germans into submission.

After agonizing days, weeks, months and years, things moved quickly. On 4 May, when US troops entered Austria from Germany and headed south towards us, the camp became eerily quiet. We were not sent out to work and were unaware that around half the guards had fled. Instead, without warning, the camp's final commandant, Anton Ganz, ordered us all to assemble on the Appellplatz.

He had succeeded the deranged Otto Riemer, who went on drunken rampages, personally beating, torturing and shooting prisoners. Riemer would offer cigarettes and additional leave to the guards who killed the most. Those who had not fulfilled their quota used to knock a prisoner's cap off and throw it into a forbidden zone. When the inmate attempted to retrieve it, he would be shot dead.

Ganz, a former nightclub bouncer, was a sadist who oversaw thousands of deaths, so when he announced he wanted to keep us safe, by hiding us in the tunnels, no one in their right mind was inclined to trust him. He insisted, through a loudspeaker and in several languages, that the Americans planned to bomb the camp as a military installation.

We reckoned there was a good chance that if we did as he

said, we would never re-emerge. After all, he had plenty to hide, since it turned out he had buried more than 2,000 inmates in two mass graves. Rumours were already circulating that the underground complex had been rigged with explosives. Sure enough, it was a trap: those explosives were packed in a loco-motive driven into the mouth of the cave, and later detonated.

This was no time for the obedience that usually went some way to saving your life in captivity. There was a lot of yelling and shouting. Out of the din, the entire camp set up a chant, in unison: '*Nein, Nein, Nein . . .*' Ganz, who appeared shaken by our defiance, took the coward's way out and vanished overnight.

He was hidden by an Austrian farmer immediately after the war, but lived openly as a construction worker in Ger-many, under his real name, from 1949 until his retirement and subsequent arrest in November 1967. He served seven months on remand before paying a bail of 20,000 marks. Though sentenced to life imprisonment for four token mur-der charges, he was released on compassionate grounds and died of cancer in 1973.

In his case, as with so many other SS escapees, like Riemer, whose fate is unknown, the punishment did not fit the crime.

Madness descended the following morning, 5 May.

The SS contingent had fled so quickly that they did not bother to cover their tracks by destroying the weapons stored in the caves. There was no law, no order. More than fifty of the cruellest Kapos were lynched almost immediately, includ-ing 'Tyshan' Hartmann, an illiterate German gypsy who killed indiscriminately while in charge of one of the twenty-five bar-rack buildings. He was dragged back into the camp, and burned alive in the crematorium. Starving inmates started fighting among themselves, after breaking into the storage rooms, and carrying away whatever they could reach. Many were unwittingly signing their own death warrants: several hundred died through what modern doctors refer to as refeeding syndrome.

In other words, when starving people gorge on food, and take in too much fluid too quickly, their digestive system cannot cope, often with fatal consequences. This is not new – the first-century Roman historian Flavius Josephus described such symptoms among survivors of the siege of Jerusalem – but it is surely the cruellest of ironies.

People were wandering around in a daze as if trapped between life and death. Many did not dare to think the nightmare was over. Others cried with joy, but I was among those who needed greater reassurance. That came when Lolo and I ran across the yard towards the fences. We saw an elderly German, a member of the Volkssturm – former Wehrmacht soldiers pressed into service towards the end of the conflict – walking between the two sets of wires.

He carried an old-fashioned, standard-issue rifle over his shoulder, but showed no signs of wanting to use it. Lolo walked up to him and asked where the SS men were. The soldier shook his head slowly. He did not know. He explained he was following their final set of orders, issued before they disappeared. 'They told us to patrol here,' he said. 'They did not elaborate.'

Since the inner wire was electrified, the soldier was given a simple test. 'Touch it,' Lolo ordered. He did so without hesitation, and without harm. Lolo followed his example and then, to make sure, took two rocks and severed the wires, again without a deadly shower of sparks. I looked on, astonished. That was the moment I realized it was all over.

I had survived.

I didn't react as you might imagine, after such a long and painful ordeal. I had fantasized about freedom, but couldn't whoop in celebration, nor shout in exultation. That happened the following day, on 6 May, when the US troops arrived. My senses were scrambled, and my feelings were mixed. Could this be real? Had the impossible happened? Had my prayers been answered? At that moment of release, I realized I had temporarily forgotten how to think for myself.

Primal impulses took over. We broke through the fence and flooded out onto the surrounding grassland and small roads which headed north into town, and the Traun Lake. The area was strewn with backpacks, clothing, uniforms, weapon, and valuables, discarded by SS troops in their rush to escape.

I bent down, picked up a revolver, and clumsily pulled the trigger. Much to my surprise, it was loaded. I didn't have a clue how to use it, but reckoned that, with so much uncertainty, it would at least offer me a little protection. The chaos in the camp, where the dying were being ignored as they writhed in their final agonies on the floor, had shaken me badly.

I felt a powerful compulsion to rid myself of my striped prisoner's uniform, which was a stained, stinking ball of rags. I tore it off my body, spat and stamped on it, before pulling on some unwanted civilian clothing. I regret that decision today: I should have kept the uniform for future generations as a *zecher l'churban*; in very simple terms, a symbolic reminder of life's tragedies

One of the most moving aspects of putting my life down on paper is the way memory and history link together. War is a terrible, unforgettable phenomenon that unites us, through a common humanity, and occasional inhumanity. I have recently been so struck by the testimony of one of our first liberators, Staff Sergeant Robert B. Persinger.

An M24 tank commander from Illinois, he was only twenty-one when he arrived at the gates of Ebensee in the early afternoon of 6 May. Two elderly German guards gladly surrendered their rifles, which he made a show of smashing on his tank's turret. The gates were opened to pandemonium, and his vehicle, together with another tank, rolled onto the Appellplatz.

He saw 'dead, torn bodies' and 'starved, half dead human beings', and took the precaution of imposing order, and commanding attention, by firing well above the heads of the thousands who rushed towards his men. The place was in uproar. Different nationalities sang their own anthems; Jewish prisoners sang 'Ha Tikvah', the anthem written in 1886, sixty-two years before Israel became a nation state.

I managed to scramble onto the other tank, where one of the American soldiers identified himself as being Jewish. He gave me a piece of chocolate, which took me back to my childhood, and several pieces of chewing gum, which I swallowed whole. I was still desperately hungry, but help was on its way: at precisely 4.52 p.m. the US Army requisitioned all food from local bakeries, shops and houses.

Persinger was deeply affected by his immediate tour of the camp. 'I knew that what I saw that afternoon I would remember for the rest of my life,' he told Mary Cook and Nita Howton, American interviewers, in April 1994:

I'd seen death before, by being in a combat unit across Europe, but this was a different type of death.

The prisoners were skin and bone. They had hollow eyes and a deep piercing stare you could not forget. They were overjoyed that the war was over, but I don't know how they must have felt when they were taken prisoner. I wonder just how in the world anybody can do that to other people.

Max Garcia, a Jew from Amsterdam who quickly became his translator, began by showing Persinger's men the stacks of bodies near the crematorium. Persinger was normally a non-smoker, but as he paused, to take in the scene, he compulsively lit up a Lucky Strike cigarette. When he returned to his army base, at the Hotel Post in town, that evening, he threw his combat boots away, because they stank of death.

He returned the next day, 7 May, with two senior officers, Lieutenant Colonel Marshall Wallach and Colonel James H. Polk, who immediately ordered fifteen truckloads of food and organized medical facilities. Polk, Persinger's commanding officer, sent the following signal to the Allied headquarters: 'Conditions are indescribable. There is no, repeat no, food in this area. Medic assistance and administration vitally necessary.'

A full field hospital was established by 9 May, but the ordeal was far from over, because American doctors, who had worked around the clock from the initial stage of liberation, had to choose who to treat first. Those inmates on the verge of death were passed over, in favour of those with a greater chance of survival.

There was an edge, a distinct sense of ugliness, in the air. Thoughts of revenge stirred among many of the inmates who headed into town. In such circumstances, Julius Ludolf, the Melk camp commander whose arrest by former prisoners near the camp in Ebensee I participated in (and described in the last chapter), was very fortunate to avoid being lynched.

Persinger sensed the fearfulness of the local population but felt an abiding contempt for them as he helped ensure that they, too, toured the camp, so they could be confronted by the horrors it contained. 'They said nothing as they were shown around, but I had no sorrow for them,' he admitted. 'They could have tried to prevent it but didn't.'

We were strangers, yet somehow brothers. Persinger was a good man; he returned to Illinois and the town of Marengo, where he met and married Arlene, his wife of sixty-six years. Like myself, he was reluctant to share his wartime experiences with his family and found it easier to speak to fellow veterans. It was not until later in life that he felt able to tell his story more widely, to students and civic organizations.

'We did what we needed to do,' he explained. 'It's now up to history to take over.' He had three children and six grandchildren, and passed away on Monday, 19 November 2018, aged ninety-five. The family wished that, instead of flowers at his funeral, donations be made to the Illinois Holocaust Museum and Education Centre. May his memory be a blessing.

His military colleagues shared his disdain for the citizens of Ebensee. The squadron's official record reads: 'No man in the third Cavalry will forget that concentration camp. They will not soon forget the dainty Frauleins and sedate Burghers who comprised the progressive, educated, "nice" German people, and lived so close to the camp yet pretended ignorance of its existence.'

Was anything learned? Residential homes were built on the site of the camp with indecent haste, in 1946. I tend to agree with Persinger, who said: 'I can't understand how anyone could live over that.' A cemetery containing the remains of 4,000 victims was relocated nearby in 1952, but the camp remained a secret that dared not speak its name.

Ebensee even elected a mayor with an SS background in the 1960s, without comment. It was not until the mid-1990s that attitudes changed and the tunnels were reopened for visitors, with suitable acknowledgement of the suffering they represented. A museum was established in a former schoolhouse in 2001, and annual commemorative services are now held.

What can we do, in such circumstances, but hold fast to our own principles? I have learned that life cannot function normally without a modicum of trust in human nature, but those lessons have been harsh and occasionally troubling. The headstrong young man liberated, all those years ago, required time to adjust to the realities of freedom.

I felt helpless as I considered what to do, and where to go. I had become used to looking into the deepest, darkest recesses of my soul to survive, and now I needed to live again, and rediscover what was truly important to me. In short, it was my family.

The surviving Spielman brothers, Chaim and Jacob, who answered to the name of Yutshe, had been with me most of the way. They were my surrogate family and, like me, had questions to answer. As we tried to decide what to do and where to go, Lolo, the friendly Kapo who had become our talisman, took a far-reaching decision on our behalf.

'Come on,' he said, with a firmness that revealed his comfort with authority. 'We're going to my home in Vienna.'

11

Betrayal

Lolo quickly returned to his trade, as a professional thief. Freed from the jeopardy of the job, which had condemned him to the camps as a common criminal, he simply went into local houses and took whatever he fancied. He was on a mission and thought nothing of threatening people with the gun he had picked up on the roadside.

I was uneasy, trapped between morality and necessity. I knew what we were doing was wrong, in normal circumstances, but the situation was completely abnormal. We were coming to terms with a world that had been tipped on its axis and were prepared to use force to get what we wanted. Peace brought anarchy, confusion – and opportunity.

The way householders looked at us, with a mixture of fear, guilt and contempt, reflected extraordinary times. Most, worried about retribution for their earlier indifference to our plight, were submissive. Anyone who resisted was slapped or punched. I didn't get involved in direct violence, but I went along with the intimidation.

Lolo announced the best way to get to Vienna was by boat, so naturally he stole one that had been moored on Lake Traun, by cutting through the padlocks. We 'borrowed' fuel and loaded on as much food as we could carry. Round cheeses and hunks of smoked meats, found drying in attics, were taken, along with the remnants of the winter stores. We reckoned if supplies ran low, we could fish for pike or tench.

The Danube flows through ten countries from the Black Forest in Germany to the Black Sea: Vienna is one of the biggest cities on its route. Our plan was to go down the River Traun, which flows into the Danube near Linz. It was a good plan, on paper, but quickly fell apart because of lawlessness and post-war politics, which divided up Europe into bite-sized chunks.

Trouble loomed when we sailed, unwittingly, out of the American zone. The weather had been good, pleasantly warm and still, but the sense of calm was shattered by sudden shouts in Russian. We had been spotted from the shore by troops who were convinced we were Nazis, fleeing the scene of their crimes.

We tried to ignore their screams for us to stop, and moved downstream as fast as we could, but when we came under gunfire there was no alternative but to do as they demanded. Though no one was hurt, the boat was holed, so we were forced to make landfall. As the Russians ran menacingly towards us, I quickly called out 'I am a Jew' in Yiddish, to see if it would curry favour for us.

It worked, to an extent. A Russian officer replied, in terribly accented Yiddish, '*Yich a Yid.*' That at least gave me a point of contact to work with. I explained our story, again in Yiddish. I described the horrors of the camps, and the desolation that had forced us to look for our families. I told them of the compassion and concern of the US soldiers who liberated us, and of our respect for the role of the Red Army in our rescue.

The officer listened attentively and seemed sympathetic. Not sympathetic enough, it turned out, to allow us on our way, unmolested. This was a new dog-eat-dog world, in which everyone was out for themselves. The Russians stole our food and fled, leaving us with little more than a couple of loaves of bread.

Plan B involved abandoning the boat, and hitch-hiking in the general direction of Vienna. It took more than a week, but fortunately some of the troops in the Russian convoys were more considerate than their bandit colleagues. We arrived on the outskirts of the capital on the back of a lorry, with no papers, and no protection, other than the force of our story.

Vienna was occupied by all four Allied forces, who took security in their individual zones seriously. That meant we were stopped constantly and asked to explain our presence and our intentions. There were a lot of refugees around, so it was a familiar ritual, and we must have been convincing because we were always allowed on our way without any trouble.

War had broken the back of the city. Around a quarter of the housing stock and many of the bridges were destroyed. There were countless bomb craters and open sewers. Water and gas pipes were severely damaged. Lolo was, however, as good as his word. He welcomed me and the Spielman brothers into his family home, which was in a relatively unscathed district.

There were shortages of food, but he looked after us well. Never one to allow the grass to grow underneath his feet, he brought his niece over one evening, and introduced us. When she had gone, he suggested I marry her. I tactfully explained that, though she was beautiful, I thought he was being a little premature, and that I had other priorities. I had my *yichus*, my bloodline, to take into consideration.

Lolo had friends and knew how to influence people. He

managed to get his hands on a few coins for us; though, to be perfectly honest, that made little difference to our lives. We had become used to scavenging and if we had no money we refused to pay. No one challenged us when we travelled by bus or train without tickets.

It did not take long to integrate into the local Jewish community. We met many former prisoners, who had been released by the Russians six months earlier than us. This led to an invitation from the Schreiber family, who were prominent descendants of Rabbi Moshe Schreiber, leader of the Orthodox community in the Austro-Hungarian empire during the first third of the nineteenth century.

He operated from Pressburg, which is now Bratislava in Slovakia, and was known as the *Chatam Sofer*, which means 'Sign of the Scribe'. A brilliant Torah scholar, who gave learned explanations and judgements on almost every area of Jewish law, he influenced generations of rabbis and civic leaders across Central Europe.

The Schreibers, who had become very wealthy, took their *yichus* extremely seriously. We were invited to their beautifully furnished apartment one evening, when they held a special meeting to determine what could be done to help Holocaust survivors, within their own community. I suppose, in modern terms, it was a networking event.

Everyone, it seemed, was attempting to piece together their previous lives, and work out the way forward. We met a variety of individuals, Jews who had come from as far afield as England and Palestine. This led to further invitations to meetings with leaders of religious Zionist organizations, who found places for us to stay, and formed contacts for future discussions.

I was reminded of the lessons of my childhood, on the streets and in the stores. This was an extension of the way business was done publicly, based on trust and mutual interest. Personal relationships were paramount, and despite being let down occasionally, I have never lost my faith in people.

Every survivor had his or her own journey to complete. As a group, we tended to be obsessed with finding our own flesh and blood. Any clue, or contact point, was followed up. So it was that I followed the Spielman brothers to northern Hungary, after they heard that an old business acquaintance, an importer of animal skins named Fuchs, had also survived the camps.

We travelled to his home city, Miskolc, Mishkoltz in Yiddish, by hitching rides on trains, buses and lorries, and were welcomed by the Fuchs family with open arms. We identified with one another because our wartime experiences were so similar, in tone if not in timing. More than 14,000 Jewish adults and children from Miskolc had been sent by cattle car to Auschwitz in June 1944. Most were gassed on arrival.

History has so many echoes. In November of that year approximately 100,000 Jews were driven to walk roughly the opposite way to the route we had taken after liberation, from Hungary to Austria. Around a quarter perished on the way. Like us, Holocaust survivors returned home to Miskolc, a centre of heavy industry, to find family, reclaim land and possessions, and to renew their lives.

We were not to know this at the time, but more than a hundred local Jews would later be rounded up on their return, by neighbours who still followed the Nazi-supporting Arrow Cross Party. Their murder is commemorated in the Jewish cemetery, set on a hill overlooking the city. The memorial includes the ten commandments, carved in stone. All are written in Hebrew except 'Thou shalt not kill', which is written in Hungarian.

Perhaps it was as well that I was unprepared for the betrayal that awaited. The pull of returning to Poland proved irresistible, and so, temporarily at least, the Spielman brothers and I parted ways. It was hugely emotional, since we had gone through so much together, but each of us had to follow our own path.

Chaim and Jacob set off for their home town, Skawina, to the south-west of Krakow, while I headed fractionally northeast of the city, for Dzialoszyce. It was an adventure to get there since I had no papers or passports, but I managed to bluff my way across the border by using my liberation paper from Mauthausen as a form of ID.

It proved to be one of the most painful experiences of my life, a trauma revived by my return, more than seventy years later. Our old apartment building remained, though the masonry was crumbling, exposing original brickwork. The front window in which father had lit the menorah needed a lick of paint. New roads and houses had been established on old dirt tracks, but I recognized my father's mill among them.

Sadness flooded over me as I touched the recess, beside the heavy wooden front door, that had once housed the Mezuzah, a decorative case containing a small sample of scripture, installed at an angle in the doorway of every Jewish home. Three elderly ladies in the street, sensing my discomfort, offered pungent purple flowers from a nearby bush, but I could not bring myself to enter the building.

Memories of my arrival there, in the summer of 1945, were all too vivid. I had wanted so badly to walk into a fairy-tale reunion with my nearest and dearest, but the realization that everything had changed, and no one had returned, was crushing.

When I summoned the courage to knock on that old wooden door, it was opened by Pani Szymanska, the building's janitor. She recognized me immediately, gestured me in, and offered the respite of a glass of cold water on what was a boiling hot day. This was a moment I had imagined, in a whole range of ways. I could not contain myself, and blurted out all the questions that had been taunting me:

'Has anyone come back? My mother or father? Any of my brothers? My uncle, maybe? My grandparents or cousins? Anyone at all?' She looked at me sadly and shook her head slowly. 'No,' she said. 'No one has come back. You are the first and only one.' Her words had the force of an SS beating. I knew if anyone was left alive, this would have been their first port of call.

The janitor had lived in the basement before the war, but it quickly became clear that she had appropriated our apartment when we were deported. As we talked, I noticed the bedroom door was open. My eyes were drawn to the needlepoint on the wall. It was my mother's masterpiece, a portrait of Adam and Eve in paradise, with the tree of knowledge, the tree of life, and the snake.

She might as well have been standing in that doorway, beckoning me towards her.

That picture had not moved an inch during our years of Hell. It was a time capsule, a terrible reminder of a lost life. To this day, I continue to look for something of similar quality. I have never found it, though I have come to appreciate art from different cultures and antique European furniture.

163

I couldn't help myself, pointing at the needlework, the result of so many hours devotion. 'I recognize that,' I said, as the temperature in the room suddenly plummeted. Pani ignored me. If she felt guilty at the way she had taken advantage of my family's misfortune, she was determined not to show it. I felt very uncomfortable, so got up and left, empty-handed.

This wasn't about material things. Even if I had been able to retrieve some keepsakes I had nowhere to put them. I was interested in people, rather than possessions, however precious. I couldn't stop thinking about all those who had been denied another chance at life. I had never felt so lonely, even in my worst moments in the camps. I was in utter despair.

Family was everything to me. It was beyond value. To try and explain that, I ask you to consider which person truly considers a dollar, a pound, or a shekel to be vital to their very existence. The answer is obvious: it is the one who does not have one, because if they are hungry, and need a loaf of bread, what can they do but beg or steal? Money is suddenly all important.

My family was all important because now I didn't have one.

People tell me I come across as a very independent person, but to be honest I have had no alternative. Living on my wits became second nature, and, after leaving our old apartment on that hot summer's day, I picked up word that the small Jewish community had organized a place of refuge for people in my position.

That gave me time to breathe, and to plan. I could not survive on fresh air and charity, and was suddenly struck by a hazy childhood memory, of hearing my father and uncle whispering about hiding valuables in the cellar. I had the vague impression of them saying something like 'two bricks from the side and four bricks from the top'.

This was, of course, when Jews were forbidden to possess anything of note. Parents were careful not to let their children know where items of value were stored, because they feared if they saw them being beaten up, or worse, by the Gestapo, they would reveal the location of the hiding place to protect them.

I resolved to be a cross between a burglar and a detective. I waited in the bushes near my old home a couple of evenings later, watching for one of the residents to go down to the cellar, where, in a pre-refrigerator era, food was stored in relatively cool conditions. Eventually, a man I did not recognize unlocked the padlock on the iron gate and entered.

I stole in behind him, unnoticed, and, once again giving thanks for being so short, managed to lose myself in the shadows. When the man left with his food, locking the gate, I was alone. It was eerily quiet and quickly became disconcertingly dark. The only things I had taken with me were a flashlight, a small hammer and chisel, and a bar of chocolate.

For once, I had run out of miracles. I started slowly and quietly dislodging bricks, in roughly the area I reckoned related to my memories, but found nothing. It was a predictable outcome to a desperate gamble, and it was all I could do to endure the cold until morning, when I was alerted to the faint noise of a key being inserted in a lock.

Surprise was my only weapon, so I ran at the resident, barged him out of the way, and fled. I figured it all happened so quickly, and so early in the morning, that I was a blur. The man was certainly too shocked to give chase. I took the precaution of waiting for a few days before, hoping against hope that the janitor would have good news, I returned.

Once again, she shook her head when I asked if any of my family had shown up. She invited me inside, to sit with her and her two sons, tall and strong young men who began peppering me with questions. I didn't need to be that perceptive to work out that they were not thrilled by my presence.

I was lifted, momentarily, from my darkest thoughts by the sound of music. I turned to look, and it was coming from our old family radio, in a carved wooden box. It was another example of petty betrayal, which pierced my heart. I looked around, and saw other personal items, and felt a wave of sadness, anger and suspicion.

My doubts were well founded. According to the testimony of Sally Bass, who was hidden from the Germans behind a false wall by local schoolteachers during the war after the rest of her family were murdered in Belzec, fifteen other Jewish survivors returned to Dzialoszyce just before me, in June 1945, to recover their homes and property.

They made the fatal mistake of calculating that they would be safe if they stayed in the same house before making their individual initiatives, to reclaim their birthright. Polish residents of the town attacked the house, killing four of them. Many such scenes were being enacted across the country: the legacy of war was envy, resentment and sustained violence.

Some of us, like the Spielman brothers, were more fortunate, at least in terms of their property. Their parents had taken the risk of telling them where they had hidden the family treasures before the war. While in Skawina they recovered an antique candelabra, a silver becher (a large drinking mug), and other precious items.

166

Ultimately, though, it didn't really matter. Personal profit seemed so empty, given what we had gone through together. When the Spielman brothers emigrated to the United States, and settled in New York, they gave everything to the Bobover Rebbe, so the Jewish community could benefit from their heritage. It was a beautiful gesture.

My experience was different, and like many survivors I was suspicious of strangers. So, when a Polish couple called out to me from behind their gate, as I passed on the opposite side of the street, I stared at them, and made to move on. They seemed uneasy, and were constantly looking around, but dropped to their knees and crossed themselves as if making a sign that they meant no harm.

I was scared and did not know them but decided on an impulse to trust them. As I moved closer, they called me by my Polish name, and spoke quickly and quietly. 'We heard that you are the only survivor, that none of your family came back,' they said. 'We want you to know that your father and mother were always so very good to us.

'Whenever we needed help or needed to buy something they always helped us. They were such nice people. And who knows? Maybe they are not coming back. But there is one thing you need to know. We hear that when you went back into your home you recognized some personal belongings. We must warn you: we overheard the sons, and they are planning something against you. Please, please be careful.'

I saw the concern in their eyes and heard it in their voices. My mind was made up. I was an outcast, and in dire danger. I had to get away. Instead of turning left towards our old apartment, as I had planned, I turned right, and retraced my steps. I never saw the janitor, her sons, or the couple again.

What could I do?

I was liberated but not free, to quote Abraham Klausner, a Jewish chaplain in the United States Army who arrived at the Dachau concentration camp soon after its liberation on 29 April 1945. He was one of the great post-war heroes, a rabbi who was so moved by the desperation of survivors to reunite with their families that he made it his life's work to help them. To aid their search, he compiled and circulated lists of more than 30,000 survivors.

Roughly two-thirds of us discovered we were the only family member to survive. I was feeling, with great force, the paradox of being a Jew, because opening the gates of a camp, or tearing down its barbed-wire fences, does not bring closure. I had to learn to live with what I had seen, and who I had lost. I was left wondering what fate had in store for me.

In many ways it was natural to try to put the war behind you by recreating the family you had lost. Many younger survivors quickly married and had children. The birth rate in the displaced persons' camps between 1946 and 1948 was the highest in the world, with up to 700 babies being born each month. The Jewish community set up clinics and counselling services for young mothers.

I understood why, since happiness had been such an alien emotion, but was still too young to consider settling down. It would have been easier to shut down the memory banks and seek domestic bliss, as so many did, but I was driven by deeper desires. I wanted to honour the memory of my family.

The best way I could do so, it seemed to me, was to bring Nazis to justice. My involvement in the citizens' arrest of Julius Ludolf might have involved a random element of chance, but it brought me into contact with the American authorities. I had nothing to lose by returning to the Ebensee area, to try to convince them of my usefulness.

One of the lessons of my business life is to offer practical solutions to a customer's problems. I quickly discovered there were real problems in the newly established Steinkogel displaced persons' camp in the American zone. It consisted of four wooden barracks, in which roughly 500 Jews were outnumbered by Polish inmates.

Tensions were high between the two cultures, with Jews being understandably resentful of their lack of representation in the camp administration. They felt they were, once again, being discriminated against, and the United Nations Relief and Rehabilitation Association, tasked with the welfare of refugees and camp survivors, were concerned about the potential for violence.

The situation was serious enough to attract the attention of Judah Nadich, the rabbi who was the first adviser on Jewish Affairs to General Dwight Eisenhower, commander of the US forces in Europe. Through the UNRRA, I suggested to the Americans that I could help in two areas, administration and enforcement.

I had a good command of German, was learning English, and knew enough Russian to get by, so I argued I would be useful to them, in translating documents and dealing with the relevant authorities. As a survivor, I also understood the resentment of the Jewish inmates. What I needed from the Americans was the authority to help bring things under control.

They had little to lose, so agreed, gave me a uniform, some basic training, and set me up as a camp policeman. Things were moving quickly – after all, three months previously I'd been a feral creature released from captivity – and in my direction. I like to think I proved myself, by helping to keep a lid on things while Rabbi Nadich arranged the transfer of the Jewish inmates to a separate DP camp, established in Bad Gastein, in the mountains south of Salzburg.

That was when the next stage of my plan went into operation. I would do similar police work while based at a DP camp in Bad Ischl, another spa town east of Salzburg, but wanted to make my business personal. I presented the Americans with a short list of names of SS men who had made me suffer in the camps and, to my great surprise, they supplied me with their list of known Nazis.

Some names overlapped. In other cases, I could easily add to their knowledge base. We had a common cause in finding the worst and most senior SS men possible, and knew time was of the essence, since they had already scattered. I had witnessed their bestial behaviour. I knew their faces, their voices, their demeanour, their history, their crimes. I was desperate to help bring them to justice.

I must have been persuasive because the Americans gave me a motorcycle so that I could begin travelling around Austria and Germany. They included me in their operations and promised to oversee co-operation with local police forces. I had another uniform, that of a military policeman. I was a little guy with a big white hat.

There was one man at the top of my list.

Amon Goeth.

12

Beginning of the End

Translation of Sworn Statement of Josef Lewkowicz

Before me, CHARLES B DEIBEL, 1ˢᵗ LT. MAC, being
authorised to administer oaths, personally appeared JOSEF
LEWKOWICZ, who, being by me first duly sworn in
GERMAN, made and subscribed the following statement in
his own handwriting:

I, the former prisoner No 85314 Josef LEWKOWICZ, born
15 March 1928 at Krakau, 'Poland', was arrested in 1940
because I was a Jew. I was sent to a compulsory labor camp,
to Liszki near Krakau, and remained there rather one year.
One day all the sub-camps of the surroundings of Krakau
were dissolved. I was taken to the Krakau-Plaszow camp. It
was not so good as subcamp Liszki. At that time SS T/Sgt
MULLER was the camp commander and M/Sgt
STROJEWSKI was his representative. They beat the
prisoners and impelled them to work.

In 1942 a new camp commander arrived. When he came
into the camp he introduced himself as follows: he is that
man who killed all Jews in Lublin, Poland. His name was
Amon Goeth, SS 2ⁿᵈ Lt. Then he began to introduce terrible

things in the camp. He impelled the prisoners to their work with whips. He ordered SS men who guarded the prisoners while working in the camp, and all had to make running paces with wheelbarrow filled with sand or to drag stones in double-time march.

The SS men were very great murderers. They had an order of the commander that they had to shoot those prisoners who did not work diligently; and they did so, too. The names of those SS men in the camp who were known as the greatest beaters and murderers are the following: SS Pfc GROSS, SS Cpls KUMKE and WILLY, T/Sgts STROJEWSKI and CHUJAR.

The commander Goeth immediately carried out a selection of sick and old people in the camp who could no longer endure hard work, and of all children up to 13 years. All of them were shot by Goeth with his officers and NCOs and buried in great mass graves. And then he inspected the camp. When he walked through the camp it sometimes cost the life of 100 men, who were shot by Goeth himself with his pistol.

Goeth had installed workshops in the camp. The skilled workers among the prisoners came into these workshops. The workshops were working for the Deutsche Ausrüstungswerke, DAW (German Equipment Works). Goeth ran around with his two dogs – 1) 'Rolf' 2) 'Rex': they were as dangerous as he himself. When he caught a prisoner smoking a cigarette he said to him: 'you pig-Jew, now you have to work and not to smoke. You have caused the war, you cursed dogs!' And then he took him out of the workshop and shot him.

During the working hours one was not allowed to go out to the toilet. If GOETH caught a prisoner he was shot by Goeth in the toilet.

In the year the transfer of Jews from the Krakau Ghetto to the Krakau-Plaszow Concentration Camp began, Goeth made the selections. He issued the order that he wished to see no children and no old people with him in the camp, also no sick people and no people unfit for working. By order of SS Lt Gen KRIEGER, SS Gen Maj SCHERMER all people unfit for work were transferred to Ghetto B, those fit for work went to Ghetto A. They were taken into the camp to their workplaces from Ghetto A.

Many people were carried away by motor cars from Ghetto B, and one does not know until today where they had been transferred. All others were taken to the camp not as workers but for extermination. They were driven by trucks into the camp where great mass graves were already prepared. The people were brought before by tens and shot with machine pistols by GOETH, GLASER, JANIEK, STROJEWSKI and others.

Then the children were brought in from Ghetto B and were thrown alive into the mass graves and then shot with machine pistols. GOETH performed the selection. The earth still moved because not all children were dead. Capt. BLANKE, camp physician, participated in the most selections, too. I myself had to fill up the mass graves with earth. After many days the earth was still moving because the children were not shot through because they lay in the ditch. The children were half a year or one year old; they were all such little children.

One of my acquaintances tried to escape one day. After some days he was caught and taken to the camp. GOETH gave the order to hang him at the roll call place and all prisoners had to look at it.

The next case which I experienced was that of two Jewish girls who had also been caught while escaping. GOETH gave the order to hang them at the roll call place. The camp prisoners were ordered to look on. They tore themselves twice from the gallows. Then they were hung again and shot by GOETH. I also know that case where he hung one prisoner because he had sung a Russian song.

GOETH deprived the prisoners of their last chances for rescue as well as of gold, brilliants, golden watches and common watches, money, several other foreign exchanges, all things being in the possession of the prisoners, so that one was not able to buy a piece of bread while working in the town.

I saw one case of GOETH: when he came to the roll call place one morning he approached a young man and said 'why do you look so angry to me?' He took his pistol and beat him until he was unconscious and then he shot him. His name was SPIELMAN, Szlama. There are two brothers of SPIELMAN at Bad Ischl who can confirm it by oath.

GOETH also participated in selections at Tarnow and Bochrina. I know one Mr GRUNBERG, Izak, whose wife and two children he shot.

The next case is how he shot the sister of LOHAJ, Chaim, with her child with one bullet. He said: 'concerning a Jewish woman every bullet is too good.' That mother had to take her child to her breast and they were shot by one bullet.

One prisoner named OLMER was bitten by GOETH's two dogs. When the dogs had bitten him, GOETH shot him, left the dead lying on the street and went on. Then he shot a prisoner because he did not take off his cap before him.

After their day work the prisoners had to go to working to the quarry by night which was in the camp area itself and to street construction in the camp. The chief of the quarry was SS 2nd Lt SCHEIDT. How he killed and shot prisoners! He beat my own head with his pistol and wanted to shoot me at that time because I had not the strength to work diligently but he went fast to another prisoner who did not work diligently, too, and shot him and forgot me totally.

All that I have written down is the full truth and I can confirm it by my oath. The people who survived all that are the following:

GRUNBERG, Izak, living at Bad Ischl, Hotel Goldenes Kreuz.

BREUER, Simcha ' ' ' ' ' '

LOHAJ, Chaim ' ' Linz, Bindermichl Jewish Camp

SPIELMAN, Jakob ' ' Bad Ischl, Hotel Goldenes Kreuz

I can state myself under oath that he executed my whole family in the Ghetto and at Krakau-Plaszow. GOETH was one of the most outstanding sadists of the camp. I saw all that what I wrote down with my own eyes.

I sign: LEWKOWICZ, Josef, born in Poland, now living in Bad Ischl, Hotel Goldenes Kreuz.

This declaration was written by me on four pages in my own handwriting, at Dachau, Germany, on 6 April 1946 at 11.00 hours, voluntarily and without compulsion. I swear by God Almighty that I speak nothing but the pure truth, that I have not kept anything secret nor added anything.

Subscribed and sworn to before me at Dachau, Germany, this sixth day of April, 1946. CHARLES B DEIBEL, 1st Lt M.A.C. Investigating Officer.

There have been moments in my life when time has appeared to stand still. One such moment occurred in my apartment in Jerusalem on a hot afternoon in early June 2022, when I leaned forward, across the dining-room table, to study an archive copy of that typewritten document on the screen of a small laptop computer.

As the deposition was read to me by Michael, my collaborator on this book, I found myself fighting powerful emotions and terrible images. I remembered making the statement, soon after discovering Amon Goeth, skulking in the dirt in a prisoner-of-war camp in Dachau, but this was the first time I had seen it in more than seventy-eight years.

Those poor babies. That tragic woman. Those horrific scenes. That monster, who I found trying to pass himself off as a faceless, nameless Wehrmacht soldier. All frozen in time and offering a troubling form of immortality. I had never felt more closely connected to, or distant from, the young man who had seen too much, but felt obliged to share his experiences in the name of justice.

The document, the first formal witness statement against Goeth, is franked and stamped, but, for me, its authenticity is assured by the inaccuracies it contains. That is why I wished to reproduce the statement in full, unedited. It gives the clearest indication of how I was affected by the fallout from the war, and how trauma can distort experiences without altering their basic truth.

Some errors, such as the year of my birth being recorded as 1928, instead of 1926, are the result of mistranslation. The precise date given, 15 March, was an invention. Other inconsistencies are due to confusion. Time lost its formality in captivity; days merged, so the calendar lost its meaning. I suspect the arrest I refer to as being 'in 1940 because I was a Jew' was a more general reference to the restrictions of occupation, rather than a specific instance of partisan activity, like helping to blow up that bridge in Dzialoszyce.

I clearly overestimated the time I spent at Liszki. I'm not perfect. My memory can be extremely sharp, but it is not photographic. I need the help of individuals and institutions, brilliantly qualified in their particular areas of expertise, to help put my life and experiences into the proper perspective.

So many pieces in the jigsaw of Goeth's life and death have been put together by Jonathan Kalmus, a London-based journalist and film-maker who works alongside Rabbi Naftali Schiff for the JRoots charity. The diligence of his research, over several years, has been remarkable, and, interspersed with my reminiscence, helps to solve some of the riddles surrounding such a notorious killer.

Goeth was initially arrested by the SS on 13 September 1944, primarily for the embezzlement of Jewish property worth millions. His crime was to keep it for himself, rather than for the German state, which owned it under Nazi regulations. There were some suggestions he was suffering from a form of mental illness, and he was sent to a sanatorium in Bad Tölz, in Bavaria.

Proceedings against him were never followed up, as defeat by the Allies loomed, and were only officially quashed by German police in 1946, in the build-up to his war-crimes trial in Poland. Goeth claimed he was released in April 1945, to join an anti-aircraft replacement battalion in the Munich suburb of Freimann, yet he was arrested by the US 7th Army in Bad Tölz at 3 p.m. on 4 May, probably following a tip-off from an informer. He was detained in Ludwigsburg, in

Internee Camp No. 71, the following day, when US Special Agent O.J. Paquette Jr. described him as a farmer.

It helps to put this in context. The task of finding war criminals, holding them, and confirming their identities and actions, was immense. Many evaded prosecution and were mistakenly released, due to the sheer volume of Nazis captured by the Americans. There are historic reports of them being freed, or simply walking out of huge US prisoner-of-war camps, before investigators could understand their importance.

Searching for the truth, several generations later, involves reconciling different, occasionally contradictory, or divergent, documents. Goeth was found with an SS ID, and his official detention report states he 'admitted to being Haupstamfurher in Waffen SS and director of Plaschow-Krakow'. This was a rank common to concentration-camp commandants, but apart from giving the reason for arrest as 'SS Dachau – War Crimes' it appears the Americans did not grasp its significance.

The arrest documents produced at his war-crimes trial were different, handwritten and lacking in detail. This suggests information about him was either excluded in error, lost, or misunderstood. A document logged on 8 May, which recorded that he was arrested in Dachau, an hour away from Bad Tölz, might be a red herring.

The fact it took nearly three weeks for the local branch of the US Army's Counter-Intelligence Corps to process Goeth (a CIC stamp on the documents says 'RECEIVED 24.5.45') does not suggest any great urgency. There is no further reference to him in the files until 29 August, when he is photographed by the US military, most probably in Ludwigsburg, just north of Stuttgart. He was moved to Internee Camp 78 there on 10 October.

Those files reveal a massive, deeply hidden, irony. US Army doctors effectively saved Goeth's life in August, when they treated him for typhus in Ludwigsburg's camp hospital, following an inoculation for what they termed 'Fleckfeiber', or Spotted Fever.

In a letter to his mistress Ruth Kalder on 17 December, discovered by the distinguished Austrian academic Johannes Sachslehner, Goeth wrote that 'I hope to see you in a few months.' He asked her to send a monthly package: 'I need underpants, a singlet, a pair of socks, two tissues, a shaving brush, a pencil, two exercise books, some cigarette paper. If father can, can he also provide groceries and some tobacco.'

He signed himself off with his pet name, 'Mony'.

On 21 January 1946, when the US authorities made a so-called Retention of Prisoner request to keep Goeth in Ludwigsburg, it became clearer that he had somehow managed to remain under the radar. Described as being on the staff of General Friedrich-Wilhelm Krüger, one of the key figures in genocide in Poland, Goeth was also linked to the SS-Wirtschafts-Verwaltungshauptamt (SS Economics and Administration Office), which was responsible for running Plaszow as a concentration camp.

He was associated loosely with events in Krakow, but the dots had not been joined. An undated request, written by Lieutenant Colonel Marian Muszkat, the Polish government's head of War Crimes Liaison, asking the Americans to keep looking out for him, adds to the sense that Goeth could so easily have slipped through the cracks of the post-war system.

While this was going on, I was sourcing and following up leads, and methodically working through the most likely sites or refuges for someone of his military status. I had moved to live in the displaced persons camp in Bad Ischl, from which I travelled on my motorcycle, if I was working on my own, or by jeep, if I was liaising with two or three US investigators.

Transport was key, since I had long distances to travel, so I told a whopping white lie when the Americans offered me a personal jeep and asked, as an afterthought, whether I could drive. 'Yes,' I replied, without hesitation. This was not strictly true: I had learned, from being a passenger, how to change gear, and where to find the gas pedal, but had never been behind the wheel.

To cut a long story short, I succumbed to panic, couldn't locate the brake in time, and ploughed into a building situated at the fork between two roads. My three passengers were shocked, but unhurt. I reported an 'accident' with as little detail as I could get away with, and was soon back on the road, building a picture of the personality, habits and networks of our subjects.

It was a painstaking business. We were regularly lied to by family members and had to hope that seemingly innocuous enquiries about the units in which suspects had served, and the identity of the superiors under whom they had operated, bore fruit. We were also dependent on one of the most basic human emotions, jealousy.

The SS generated a lot of resentment because they had everything in abundance during the war, when food, and other essential items, were scarce for civilians. Travelling around shattered villages and towns, trying to pick the brains of potential enemies outside immediate families, a familiar pattern of complaint emerged: they had everything, we had nothing.

It wasn't expressed loudly, or openly, but people were bitter about being expected to struggle. Life was difficult, and some were prepared to gossip about their neighbours. Their information wasn't startling, but every morsel of knowledge was important. By piecing together details of individual soldiers, Nazi divisions, and linking them to combat records, we began to realize the huge POW camps would be fruitful places to look.

A Yiddish saying, *getapt in de finster*, refers to 'tapping at the window' or reaching for something indistinct in the dark. There was a sense that a breakthrough of sorts was close, but we had no clear vision when and where that would be. The sheer scale of the search was intimidating, and ensured any progress was slow.

Meanwhile, the records suggest Goeth was moved to Dachau in early February 1946. He gave a sworn statement at 4 p.m. on the 20th of that month, in which he admitted his Nazi background, dating back to 1930, and confirmed his arrival at Plaszow, which he described as 'a supply dump for the Eastern divisions', as commandant in March 1943.

Again, my blood ran cold when Michael read out his words to me. Goeth insisted, in typically curt, self-justifying tones:

Accommodation in barracks was furnished. Food was good, appropriate to work, a little less good in the beginning. By a generous handling of classification as heavy workers etc, improvements could currently be made.

The following was issued per head, per week: 6kg of potatoes, 25kg of vegetables, 300g of meat, about 120g of fat, barley, groats, cereal, jam and a quarter of a loaf of bread each day. Instead of meat, eggs or cheese could be issued. The camp was equipped with a large kitchen, five

181

medical barracks, a large bath with delousing installations, so that all sorts of epidemics did not occur.

An obscene fantasy, of course.
But he went on:

In a few cases executions were ordered because of establishment of communication with partisans' organizations or sabotage, and looting of army property respectively, as well as shootings because of unauthorized possession of arms, explosives or ammunition, under martial law. Otherwise, the camp as a matter of principle detailed execution squads only for the execution of court martial sentences on soldiers.

Frequently the Secret State Police would bring executed bodies for burial or would bring prisoners for execution. This, however, was done by the Secret State Police with own personnel; it was not announced what persons might have been concerned, but it is to be presumed that they might have been partisans.

A bundle of recently declassified US documents contains a short-form note from an investigator, reporting that 'subject lied continually during his interrogation and may be hiding certain facts'. However, he chose to highlight Goeth's informal insistence that he was arrested by the SS because he refused to shoot Jews, rather than digging deeper into suspicions of what the German was hiding.

Logically, the Americans must have had convincing evidence against him, for Goeth to voluntarily admit to being a commandant. Yet on 5 March, as the US 7th Army was in the process of transferring remaining German prisoners to Dachau prior to its withdrawal from Europe, a US intelligence report, outlining Goeth's crimes, insisted his 'whereabouts are unknown. Believed to be at large.'

Most of the Germans in the POW camps were still wearing military uniform, without badges or other insignia, though some had civilian clothing. Their air of superiority had vanished, along with their freedom. They had the sullen, downcast look of prisoners as they squatted on the floor. I must admit it was very satisfying to see them so careworn, and forlorn. So much for their master race.

Dachau, which housed around 30,000 Germans, was an obvious place for us to look, but the size of the compound, the way in which it was associated with the horrors of the former concentration camp on the site, and the huge numbers involved were intimidating. We needed to be rational rather than emotional and follow the process.

This began almost randomly, asking individuals where they had served, whether their entire battalion had been captured, and if officers were mingling with ordinary soldiers in the compound. If so, I asked them to point them out. We followed up by asking whether they had seen any strangers, attempting to insinuate themselves into their group.

Our aim was to find SS men who acted as guards and persecutors in the camps. We took down the name and rank of each man interviewed, and cross-checked them with our colleagues in the CIC, American intelligence, which operated alongside the JAG War Crimes Corps. It was slow, deliberate work, done on the understanding that anyone involved with the SS would lie out of their back teeth.

There was one simple test, which involved ordering them

to remove their shirts. The blood group tattoo, applied to all Waffen SS members, was small, etched in black ink, and located on the underside of the left arm. Designed as a potential life saver, to identify a casualty in need of battlefield treatment, it turned out to be our most reliable clue to a prisoner's background.

Every SS volunteer in Dachau was automatically regarded as a war criminal and not subject to the Geneva Convention, because the SS was designated by the Allies as a criminal organization even before post-war trials began. Similar rules applied to any member of the Nazi Party, or anyone who had an official job within it.

This was the Allied concept of participating in a so-called 'common plan', as laid out in Article II, paragraph 2, of Law Order No. 10. The Germans might not have committed an atrocity themselves but were automatically regarded as being guilty by association and did not deserve to be treated as traditional prisoners of war.

Not all, of course, were ruthless killers. It was our responsibility to carry the burden of truth, and to identify those linked to the more heinous crimes. As badly as I wanted to uncover them, it wasn't easy. We plodded on with the leg work, mainly among ordinary Wehrmacht soldiers, while increasing the pressure on those we had identified.

Some had the SS mark in other places, such as the back of the arm or the rib cage, but all were wary of our follow-up questioning, which was designed to give us a pattern of their movements during the war. Once we worked out where they had been, we had an inkling of what they did. I didn't believe them when they denied being in a specific place, at a specific moment. They were too obviously trying not to incriminate themselves.

The basic rules of interrogation applied. Ask the same questions, over and over, and look for inconsistencies. I would see individuals every three or four days, to go through the ritual of determining their functions, and on what front or in which section they had served. Their explanations changed subtly, so that each time they revealed a little more than they intended.

Seeing them, at such close quarters, reminded me what paradoxical lives they must have led. They presumably loved their wives and children, yet they surrendered their humanity during 'working' hours. I wondered how they could live with themselves, but who but the Almighty can see into the darkest corners of a man's soul?

Like any policeman, seeking to solve a crime, I needed a slice of luck to reward my perseverance. It came about three weeks or so into our spell at Dachau, when I approached yet another group of Wehrmacht soldiers. One, identified as an officer by his men, was willing to engage with me.

'Are all of your soldiers here?' I asked him.

'Most, but not all of them,' he replied.

'Are there any strangers here that are not from your group, your battalion, or your division? Is there anyone here that you do not know?'

'There is someone, a stranger who wasn't with us. We do not know him.'

'Where is he?'

'There.'

He was pointing at a hunched, rather pitiful, figure squatting on the ground like a beggar, about twenty paces away. As I came closer, I let out a scream and began running towards him. He was dressed in a scruffy Wehrmacht uniform that was several sizes too small, and tried not to react, but I would have recognized him anywhere.

It was Amon Goeth.

He was haggard, and had lost a lot of weight, but I knew that cruel face anywhere. It was the last thing that so many people in Plaszow had seen before they met their end. I was boiling inside, and lost control, kicking and punching him in a flurry of rage. I screamed: *'Steh auf du Sauhund! Sauhund, verfluchter Scheiss!'* ('Get up you bastard! You bastard, damn shit!')

He did so eventually but showed no sign of comprehending who I was. That was understandable, since the military policeman spitting in his face wore a white helmet and was well fed. The last time we had been in close contact, I was just another emaciated victim of his brutality, unworthy of individual recognition. He did not need to know me. In fact, I was probably repulsive to him.

Now, though, things were different. He had lost the power of life and death. I screamed, *'Sie werden dafür bezahlen, unschuldiges Blut zu vergießen!'* ('You will pay for spilling innocent blood!') *'Warum hast du das getan?'* ('Why did you do it?') I was so angry I was saying the first thing that came into my head: *'Du warst bereit, mich zu ermorden!'* ('You were ready to murder me!')

He tried to protect himself from my kicks and punches but did not say a single word. It was as if he had primed himself for just such a moment. Interacting with me would have somehow made me worthy of his attention, almost an equal. The monster might have been cornered and captured, but it lived on.

Yes, I know what I said about being rational rather than emotional, but what would you have done in my position?

The two CIC men with me didn't try to restrain me, but shock registered across their faces. I tried to explain who Goeth was, and what he was responsible for, but I was probably not making that much sense. My only memory of logical thought was an inner determination not to kill him. I could have easily done so, and taken pleasure in his death, but I reasoned that, by sparing him to meet his fate, his suffering would be prolonged.

People ask me why I didn't shoot him on the spot, such was the enormity of his crimes. That would have been like giving him a gold medal for his deeds. I am not proud of this, and regret saying it at his trial, because it was a little childish, but I would have loved to have paid him back by taking a butcher's knife, cutting him, and putting salt on the wound. I would have returned the next day, and the next, doing so continually until this beast lost the will to live.

Once I had reported my discovery to the US commander at Dachau, a major if I remember correctly, Goeth was placed in solitary confinement. I went into his cell, alone, and sat beside him on a low bench. Once again, I lost my temper. I demanded to know why he was so violent, malicious and unfeeling. I asked him to explain what had turned him into such a sadist.

I finished with a small, impassioned speech in German: '*Wenn du ein netter Mensch gewesen wärst, wärst du Welt berühmt. Du wärst ein Held. Die ganze Welt würde über dich reden und schreiben. Du wärst Multimillionär. Die Leute würden dir alles geben. Aber du warst ein Biest und du wirst dafür mit deinem Leben bezahlen.*'

Roughly translated, that meant: 'If you had been a nice person, you would be world famous. You would be a hero.

187

The whole world would talk about and write about you. You would be a multi-millionaire. People would give you everything. But you were a beast, and you are going to pay for it with your life.'

I might as well have been talking to the stone wall of his cell. Once again, he did not utter a word.

The CIC took a dim view of me assaulting a prisoner and reprimanded me. As impulsive as ever, I talked back to my superior: 'If you would have been there, and seen what he did, you would have cut pieces off him.' I was eager for Goeth to face justice, but something within me changed that day.

Word of my discovery evidently reached Lieutenant Colonel Marian Muszkat very quickly. Even before I could make my official deposition, he wrote to the Americans, in a letter addressed to Prisoner of War Enclosure 29, Dachau, citing Goeth as the 'leader of the liquidation' of Jews in southern Poland. He held him accountable for thousands of deaths.

This was significant, because Muszkat had immense political power, as a direct representative of Poland's new Stalinist Ministry of Justice. A specialist in international public law, he chaired the Polish delegation to the Nuremberg trials, and was deputy in Najwyższy Sąd Wojskowy, their highest military court. He would eventually settle in Israel, where the Yad Vashem Institute chose Muszkat as co-ordinator and adviser to the Adolf Eichmann trial.

It was the beginning of Goeth's end.

13

Crime and Punishment

Oskar Schindler was a troubled man. Beset by money problems, he was lonely and fearful of his past. Some former Nazis wanted to kill him. Other enemies saw him as a collaborator. He made a special 300-kilometre journey, from his post-war home in Regensburg, north of Munich, to the displaced persons' camp at Bad Ischl in Austria, to convince me of his good intentions.

It was 19 April 1946, only thirteen days after I had made the first prosecution statement by a Plaszow survivor against Amon Goeth, in Dachau. I know this because Schindler included the date in an inscription on the back of a photographic portrait, which he produced with a flourish from a small satchel. This captured him in film-star mode, years before his story became Hollywood legend.

There was a hint of a smile as he leaned forward and made eyes at the camera. The inscription, in German and in bold, almost artistic handwriting, has faded over time. It reads: 'To My Most Dear Friend, Yosef Lewkowicz, forever lasting remembrance. From your friend, always, Oskar Schindler.' I gave the original to the Yad Vashem Museum in Jerusalem because of his historical significance.

Why was he seeking my approval? He was a natural

opportunist. He had heard of my work in helping to hunt down Goeth, and of my courtroom testimony against Julius Ludolf, in his Dachau trial the previous week. He knew I had been in Plaszow and had seen him regularly in Goeth's entourage. He wanted me to know that such behaviour had been a means to an end.

'I am a nice man,' he told me. 'I am not a war criminal.' I put my arm on his shoulder. 'Don't worry,' I said. 'If the court comes for you, I will vouch for you. I will tell you why you are not a war criminal. You didn't shoot anybody. You didn't hang anybody. You didn't beat your people. You gave them more food than anyone in the concentration camps. They mostly survived. You might not be the nicest, because you took things, but the Nazis would have taken them anyway.'

Schindler gave me a long, puzzled look, as if he was trying to work out whether to trust me. He struck me as a man ill at ease with himself. The Jews he helped to save were elsewhere, trying to reconnect with former lives, or build new ones. Though they never divorced, his wife was deeply affected by his womanizing. She had thrown him out of the family home.

He was proud of how he had been the saviour of so many Jews, but gratitude didn't pay his bills. He was being supported by several Jewish organizations, but his business ventures were struggling. He gave me the photograph because it was the only thing he could afford to give. In return, I suppose, I could help to spread the word about him, within the community.

I introduced him to Rabbi Hirsch, whom we had employed as spiritual leader of the 300 or so survivors assembled at the Hotel Goldenes Kreuz. I outlined Schindler's background and invited him to a kosher supper. It was a happy occasion: we buzzed with new ideas, old stories, and grand plans. This seemed to tranquillize him and provide temporary relief from his worries.

He could not hide his problems, and though I could not bring myself to do business with a German, he had been an ally, and was a friend in need. He was, at heart, a profiteer, who worked his political contacts in the Nazi regime, but could have committed crimes against our people and chose not to do so.

Schindler had asked me to find him a bottle of liquor, preferably Schnapps, which he seemed desperate for. This was difficult, since even the black market had limitations, but I persevered because it was as if he couldn't live without alcohol. I also noticed his shirt was frayed and managed to get him a couple of new ones from local contacts. When his visit was over, and we said farewell, he kissed me.

I wondered how he would fare, and it turned out that his life would not be easy, despite the support of his 'children' scattered around the world. Some of them followed him to Buenos Aires when he emigrated to Argentina in 1949, after being refused entry to the United States because of his Nazi past. He tried farming without any luck and was made bankrupt after returning to Germany in 1958.

After dying of liver failure in 1974, one of Schindler's final wishes, that he be buried in Jerusalem, was granted. At a time in which it is too easy to forget, it is heartening that his grave in the Roman Catholic section of Mount Zion cemetery is still popular with tourists. He was honoured by the State of Israel, in 1993, as Righteous Among the Nations, an award reserved for those non-Jews who had helped save Jews during the Holocaust.

Though I never asked him, it was probably not a coincidence that he turned up in Bad Ischl after the American investigators, led by Captain Hugo Romero, who had taken Goeth's original statement, took out newspaper advertisements, asking for witnesses to atrocities associated with him. I was determined to do anything I could to assist their cause.

Just as Schindler was relying on the tightness of the bonds between survivors, I tried to turn that to my advantage, in seeking justice for the many thousands who Goeth had murdered. I knew a group of young Jews, originally from Dzialoszyce, in another displaced persons' camp, Centre Number 7 in Deggendorf. On 7 April 1946, the day after I had made my prosecution statement, they came forward and offered to testify. That was quickly taken up by Lieutenant Colonel L.S. Storey of the CIC.

More than twenty witnesses were ready to give evidence. The Szlamowitsch brothers, Natek and Chaim, who would later change his name to Henry Slamovich, were among those who hired a bus and drove to Dachau, where they identified Goeth in person. They, and other acquaintances from our original shtetl, such as Monek Huppert, Bezek Jurysta, Ryba Szaja, Moniek Sarna, Aba Balicki and Moric Zelmanowitsch, gave witness statements to American investigators, who visited Deggendorf on 16 and 17 May.

They all backed up my recollections. Chaim described Strauss waltzes being played as 'children were being loaded on to trucks and taken away to be destroyed'. Natek remembered being at the camp garage and seeing Goeth shoot a woman for not cleaning his car window properly. When he realized she was still alive, he ordered a guard, Janiz, to 'give the Jewess two more shots'.

Ryba Szaja spoke of being forced to bury fifty inmates, murdered after being pulled out of a work detail. Moniek Sarna, the young man who had recruited me to help the

192

partisans prior to the liquidation of Dzialoszyce, detailed a night-long killing spree; in the morning he had to bury the body of his cousin.

Chaim Spielman, who had become president of the displaced persons' camp in Bad Ischl, had followed me in giving a statement in Dachau on 24 April 1946. He recalled being forced to walk past the body of his brother Shlomo, and the agony of seeing his mother selected for transportation from Plaszow to the gas chambers at Auschwitz.

Another group of seven Plaszow survivors, from the Landsberg DP camp, identified Goeth in person, and gave statements on 10 May. One, Josef Kempler, said that Goeth 'made a very big fortune from robbing the dead'. He reported that four men committed suicide, by slitting their wrists, during a four-day journey from Plaszow to Mauthausen in a heavily overcrowded cattle car.

Another Landsberg resident, Fryda Korczyn, said something to which I really related: 'Goeth's greatest pleasure was the sight of fresh human blood, and he didn't abstain from such a pleasure during my time in the camp.'

The main investigation examiners, First Lieutenants Henry M.W. Winchester Jr., Harvey Szanger and Alan D. Cameron, were already convinced of the gravity of Goeth's offences. I believe the Americans planned to put Goeth on trial in Dachau, but momentum was shifting. Politicians were starting to call the shots. The Poles, through Marian Muszkat, were pressing for him to be extradited, since his crimes had been committed on their soil.

This was a matter of national honour. A Commission for the Investigation of German Crimes in Poland had been set up on 10 November 1945. Regional teams were created, to collect documentation, but it was not until May and June 1946 that they interviewed the majority of the thirty-one witnesses who contributed to Goeth's trial. His extradition was set for 28 June.

I had moved on from the CIC long before then, very soon after giving my statement. I was alienated by the reprimand I received for beating Goeth, which served to highlight my wider resentment of US conduct during the war. They knew the extent of the atrocities being committed against the Jewish people but lacked the will to take decisive action.

Why didn't the US president, Franklin D. Roosevelt, the great liberal democrat, do more when millions of Jews, young and old, were being murdered? Where was his love of humanity? Why did he not act when so many young people with great hopes and dreams were being extinguished? Where were the Americans when we were being slaughtered and needed help?

If they had bombed the concentration camps, they would have saved hundreds of thousands, if not millions, of lives. What were they afraid of? Retaliation? Killing innocent civilians, innocent people who were going to be killed anyway? As someone who would have been in the line of fire, I would have been happy to take my chances.

I put these points to General Mark Clark, the Commander in Chief of US Forces of Occupation in Austria, when he visited the US War Crimes Court in Dachau in 1946. I knew he was extremely close to Dwight D. Eisenhower, the future US president who had made him the war's youngest four-star general in 1945. He was a key figure in post-war negotiations with the communists, but I reasoned I had the right to challenge him because of what I had been through.

General Clark shook my hand warmly when an aide introduced us, and listened to me in respectful silence. I was equally respectful, reassured him I would do everything in my power to assist the legal process, and hoped he would understand my need for answers. My views did not lessen my gratitude towards the American soldiers who had liberated me from Ebensee.

I began by relaying the story of looking up during the final days before liberation and seeing hundreds of Allied aircraft on their way to attack German targets. 'General,' I said, 'that sight gave us such joy. You knew that there were concentration camps, you knew that there were gas chambers, so why didn't you bombard them? I know the Nazis would have rebuilt them but between destroying and rebuilding you could have saved tens of thousands of people.'

He was impassive. 'We were after military targets,' he said. 'Concentration camps were not military targets.' His tone suggested he was not open for debate. I have subsequently discussed these matters with many American Jews, who admit to a sense of shame that more was not done, but I knew, at that moment, that I had to move on.

I was as good as my word with regards to Goeth and was proud that my evidence against him was singled out, from thirty-one witness statements, by Tadeusz Cyprian, Prosecutor for the Supreme National Tribunal. As he said in his opening remarks to the court:

These present proceedings are the first in the world where the accused is directly charged with mass murder, which apparently became the German customary mode of behaviour in the extermination plan they were following.

In the framework of the activities of the accused Goeth in particular, his personal and direct involvement in mass murder, however clear, is only but a fragment of the whole matter. In order to recognize fully, understand and appraise the activities of the accused Goeth, it is our duty as prosecutors in this Tribunal, to introduce to you the whole system of murder, thought out and introduced by the Germans, into the life of our country.

The full might of these cruel German measures were directed against the Jewish population. No other nation has been subjected to such crimes, so clearly and directly, as the Jewish nation. The accused Goeth planned the layout of the camp in Plaszow, in such a way to screen the activities within the camp from the outside. All barracks were positioned in order to block the view.

It was common knowledge in the vicinity of the camp, that the murder of the entire population of southern Poland was the prime objective of the Nazi SS. The Germans were justifying these activities, of progressive oppression and murder of Jews, for no other reason, than because they were Jews, and as such, had no right to live.

The Nazis had, of course, plans for the murder of other people as well. These plans were never put into action, in anywhere near the proportions that have been reached in the measures against the Jewish population. The extermination program of the Jewish population was executed thoroughly, and swiftly, all over Europe, and it befell upon Poland, to be the recipient of all the corpses followed by the ashes of the victims that have perished. It is the task of the prosecution to present to the Tribunal the complete mechanism of the murderous machine in action.

I must however, emphasise, that in this case, as the accusing victims, the Polish nation stands side by side, with the Jewish nation, to see that justice be done. Not only because there were countless Polish victims in Plaszow, not only because, with the exception of a few transports of Jews from outside of Poland, who whilst indeed being practising Jews, were nevertheless in every way, rightful citizens of the Polish state, its culture and its traditions.

They were powerful words. To this day, they touch a chord, deep within me.

Someone once said to me that when I found Goeth, I had the world in my pocket. I could have shot him on the spot. It would have been the easiest thing just to get rid of him. Yet, to my way of thinking, that is crazy. Number one, I couldn't shoot a human being like a dog. Why take away someone's life? It would have made me no better than him.

When I looked around the court, at Nazi defendants, I felt pity for them. I could not forget the atrocities they had committed, but I looked at them and knew they were going to have a terrible death, to be hanged. They had families, loved ones, but they had worked towards that death. They had earned it.

I choose not to dwell on the details of Goeth's trial, which lasted from 27 August to 5 September 1946, but cannot ignore the appropriate irony of his end. He was hanged, on 13 September, at the Montelupich prison in Krakow, close to the site of the Plaszow camp. His remains were cremated, and the ashes thrown in the Vistula River.

That will not bring back the many thousands he killed, or rebalance history, but his actions, in liquidating the ghettos, had an influence in the next great change of direction in my life. I wanted to make that second chance at life worth something. I felt I had to do something bigger than myself. An idea, formed in the earliest days of freedom, came to fruition.

One of the great characteristics of our community is its ability to help itself. There is an interdependence to Jewish life that manifests itself in times of trial and tribulation. I benefited from that through the support of the Schreiber family in Vienna, and the contacts they provided. It was there that I began to realize the extent of the opportunity we had to rescue Jewish orphans and give them a new chance in life.

Oh, how the little ones suffered! It pierces my heart to think of it. Goeth killed countless children in cold blood during those inhumane operations in the ghettos. During the early days at Plaszow, I often overheard my father talking about babies given away by desperate parents, who knew the fate which awaited them in the camps.

The babies were hidden in monasteries, convents and churches. They were left in farmyards and stable blocks, on doorsteps and street corners. Many were taken in by Christian families, some of whom were paid for the privilege. They survived, unlike so many whose final resting place was a mass grave. We had to try and find them, even if there was only the slimmest chance that they could be reunited with their natural families and reacquainted with their faith.

This was a huge undertaking, beyond the capabilities of one man, or a single group. It needed influential allies, people who could bend the system, or shape official policy. My first thought was to mention this to Rabbi Eliezer Silver, who came to visit us in Bad Ischl. He was one of the foremost Orthodox Jewish leaders in North America, who saved thousands during the war. Representatives of his organization,

Vaad Hatzalah, even negotiated directly with the SS, ransoming concentration camp prisoners for cash and tractors.

A short man with a long white beard, Rabbi Silver arrived wearing the uniform of an American colonel, as a mark of the respect in which he was held by the occupying forces. He asked how he could help, and readily agreed to get us some kosher products, which duly arrived in boxes a couple of weeks later. But before I could bring up the plight of the orphans, he was bundled away by his aides.

My idea was by no means unique. Others were thinking on similar lines. I wasn't immediately aware of this, but the so-called Zionist Coordinatsia for the Redemption of Children in Poland had been set up in January 1946. This eventually included nine separate organizations which worked for the common cause of discovering, and reintegrating, lost children.

It was clear that, to help others, we had to learn to help ourselves. To do so, we organized a meeting of Jewish community groups in Krakow, Lodz and Warsaw, led respectively by three presidents, Finkelstein, Minsk and Jacobovitz, whose given names I am afraid I cannot recall. This led to the formation of a committee, which began the drawn-out process of piecing together clues to the children's whereabouts.

Lists included their names and ages, the identity of families who were thought to have adopted them, and the villages and towns in which, logically, they could be found. It was well intentioned, but imperfect. Some of the information was little more than unsubstantiated hearsay. Again, it required greater powers of detection and enforcement.

There was a central problem: since Poland was a communist satellite, the concept of Jewishness was rejected by the state. We could not be obvious about the specific nature of our aim, to reunite kids with the Jewish faith and, ideally, practising families. That's why we operated under the slogan of 'uniting families that the Nazis had separated'.

I had not stretched myself intellectually in captivity because I had to force everything of consequence out of my mind just to get from one day to the next. I was preoccupied by staying alive and, in any case, lacked the life experience to grasp big issues or complicated problems. Now, from consciously not thinking about anything, as a self-defence mechanism, I suddenly had to think about everything. To do so, the fog in my brain had to clear.

A deeply hidden memory surfaced. It was of a man, a fellow Jew named Daniusz Goubart. He had been a communist agitator in Poland before the war, when he was viewed as a threat to the state and was in and out of jail. He was married to Anka, a distant cousin of my mother. They had a daughter, Stefanka.

The family struggled financially and socially when he was imprisoned, and Anka never forgot my mother's kindness in their time of need. Mother used to send me to their house in Krakow, a couple of streets away from ours, with a parcel of food before the Sabbath and on Yom Tov, our festival dates. She also invited Anka and Stefanka to stay with us, whenever they found themselves alone.

When war broke out, the doors to the jails sprang open. Daniusz was spirited to Moscow by the Soviets. His family followed, and he was groomed as an influential apparatchik. With Poland under Soviet occupation, he returned as a communist leader, a key member of the Politburo. He had the sort of power we needed if we were to have the authority to act.

I mentioned our family links to Mr Finkelstein, who galvanized his contacts in the Krakow area to look for Daniusz.

'This is a gift from Heaven,' Finkelstein told me. 'If you are related you must get to him.' It wasn't that simple, of course, since Daniusz had changed his name, to Daniek Danusz, in order to sound less Jewish and more Polish.

He operated mainly from an office in Warsaw, but was quickly traced to a large villa, on a huge plot on the outskirts of Krakow. His home was heavily fortified, and patrolled by soldiers, so I was instantly challenged when I drew near. I was sent away several times by increasingly irritated plain-clothes policemen, whose patience was notoriously thin.

I reported back to the community leaders that Daniusz was apparently unreachable to anyone but his political cohorts. They advised that I return and ask to speak to the head of the compound. I should explain my status as a Holocaust survivor, the fact that our families had been close, and that Daniusz's wife was probably my only relative left alive.

The plan didn't work immediately, but eventually a Polish officer came to see me at the entrance to the driveway leading to the villa. I played Daniusz at his own game and introduced myself by using the Polish version of my name, Jozek Lewkowich. The officer carefully took notes on a slip of paper as I explained my links to the family, before sternly instructing me to stay where I was. I could hardly disobey.

Within a couple of minutes he returned with Anka. She was weeping and wildly emotional, hugging me tightly as she exclaimed that her prayers had been answered. She, too, had lost everyone during the war. Although only distantly related, I was the first person associated with her family to make contact. 'You are not going anywhere,' she said, leading me into her home by the hand.

The rest of the day flew by in mutual reminiscence. Anka

was saddened by the fate which had befallen my parents and brothers. Their thoughtfulness, she said, would never be forgotten. I knew I had to be delicate when discussing her family's flight to the Soviet Union, and her husband's political advancement. Daniusz, it seemed, was a distant figure, who was rarely at home.

Who knows whether this was a result of loneliness, relief, or gratitude, but when I got up to leave she insisted I stay. She showed me to a room and invited me to be her house guest for as long as I wished. She would arrange fresh clothing and anything else I needed. Given my ulterior motives, I had little option but to accept.

It was a strange situation. Daniusz was seldom around; when we were introduced, he was polite, but preoccupied. I glimpsed him infrequently, and it was not until a couple of weeks after my arrival that he settled down to the dinner table with us. This was my chance, and I had planned exactly what I would say.

'Daniusz,' I began, trying to put him at ease by choosing the name I knew from my childhood, 'I have a big problem.'

'Oh,' he replied, as if he expected a favour to be asked. 'Is it your problem?'

'No, it's not personal, but a communal problem that must be solved. There was a great injustice done by the Nazis when they occupied Poland. The Germans separated many families during the war.'

'I know, but what about it? What's the big problem you wanted to speak about?'

'We want to reunite those families.'

'How do you plan to do that?'

'With your help it can and will be done. We know how to

do it. We have done the necessary research. What we really need is the authority to do the job. To succeed we must have the backing of the security forces.'

'You say "we". Who is "we"?'

'My team. I would like that team to be empowered by the authorities to find these lost children and take them back to their parents. They were abandoned by necessity. We need to locate them and return them to their real families. We will also be searching for those families. You can give us this power. You can help us succeed in our mission.'

He smiled slyly. His mask was slipping to reveal the selfish, calculating politician who started out as an idealistic activist, willing to suffer for his beliefs. He could disguise his ruthlessness with charm, if necessary, but was used to wielding power, and understood its effect on people. My plea probably stimulated his ego.

He wasn't the only communist of Jewish descent who chose to play down his heritage. Jakub Berman, who also escaped to Moscow during the war, and trained displaced Polish activists on behalf of the Soviet-sponsored Polish Workers' Party, oversaw state security. He courted public opinion by propagating the myth that as many non-Jewish Poles, three million, died in the war as Poles of Jewish descent.

It all went to prove that under a communist regime some people are more equal than others. If you judge the book by its cover, Engels, Marx, equality, opportunity, and promises of an end to oppression, it looks good. But ideology places a weight on people. It changes them, destroys their minds. Daniusz, and his kind, cared about little but themselves.

'You should see Bielecki,' he said, waiting to gauge the impact of the name.

Jan Ludwik Frey-Bielecki, head of the secret police, the UB, in Krakow, was one of the most feared men in the city. He, too, came from a family of Jewish descent, but had just brutally suppressed protests in support of an independent nation. He had personally driven an armoured car into the demonstration and ordered his men to open fire.

The UB was responsible for imprisoning, torturing and murdering thousands of political opponents, many of whom disappeared without trace after being taken to Mokotów prison, the site of an infamous Nazi massacre in the early stages of the Warsaw uprising. Bielecki oversaw the arrest of more than a thousand people, including 800 students, in the aftermath of the demonstration. He was promoted to lieutenant colonel.

Daniusz had made his point. He laughed when I asked if this was possible. 'Leave it with me,' he said, getting up from the table. It would be the last I saw of him for about a fortnight. The longer I waited for word, the more worried the Jewish community leaders became. The committee had been given a former spa building in the town of Rabka-Zdrój, which was being renovated in anticipation of the arrival of the first contingent of children.

I tried to reassure them but could do nothing except wait. Anka, a very fine lady who did not deserve to be so neglected, continued to be the perfect host. Eventually, at around 11.30 one night, there was a knock on my bedroom door. I was in my pyjamas, and about to try to sleep. I opened the door to find a smiling Daniusz.

'Get your pants on and come to the boardroom immediately,' he said, knowing it was an offer I could not refuse.

14

Save the Children

The boardroom was dimly lit and wreathed in cigar and cigarette smoke. It stank of power, deal-making and entitlement. An acidic tang of stale breath, laced with vodka and whisky, lingered in the air. As my eyes adjusted to the murkiness, I became aware of Russian marshals and Polish generals, their braid and medals somehow glinting in the gloom.

I had dressed quickly, with a mixture of anxiety and curiosity. I reasoned that Daniusz Goubart, as I still knew him, would not have invited me into the regime's inner circle for nothing. He had no reason to kill me or inflict harm. Perhaps it was simply payback for the old days, different times. Whatever his motivation, I had to confront a new truth: to do good, I had to rely on bad people.

The uniformed officer who had opened the door guided me forward with an unseen hand in the small of my back. Daniusz, sitting at the head of a large table, beckoned me over, and rose to greet me when I was a couple of paces away. He was in his element. 'Bielecki,' he said. 'This is the man I was telling you about. He needs something important from us. Do whatever you can to help him. Joe, tell him what you want.'

I froze momentarily as I recognized the man sitting at a side table, surrounded by high-ranking officers and civilian officials, who looked at me as if I was something they needed to scrape off the soles of their shoes. As the local head of the UB, in charge of the shadowy figures who did the Soviets' dirty work, Jan Ludwik Frey-Bielecki was someone you really didn't want to know.

He was surprisingly young, around thirty. He had quite a long face, a sandy-coloured moustache, and a high forehead, but my eyes were drawn to his. They were deep set and shone with a strange intensity. He looked like a fox in human form. 'Please,' he said, gesturing towards an empty seat, which had suddenly appeared beside him. 'Tell me everything.'

This was my moment. I knew I had little time to get my message across, since the hum of conversation in the background signalled that a variety of big decisions needed to be made, on what was probably going to be a long night. My points had to be brief, and precise. Thankfully, I had committed them to heart.

I knew I could not mention Jews, or Judaism. I had to concentrate on a common enemy, the Nazis. It was our duty, as we saw it, to reunite the families they had destroyed. Children he would never see, strangers he would never meet, needed his help. We had the building, in which to house them, but needed the might to do what was right.

Those hypnotic eyes narrowed. 'Who is we?' he asked. 'What are you? How many of you are there? How will you do what you want to do?' I went through the list of targets, churches, monasteries, orphanages, private homes, organizations, societies. I mentioned that Moniek Sarna, the friend who recruited me for anti-Nazi activity as a boy, would be my right-hand man.

Bielecki thought for a moment that seemed like a month.

'That is a major operation,' he said. 'You will need a lot of force to do that, a lot more than two people. Come to UB headquarters in Warsaw tomorrow. When you get to the entrance ask to speak to the person in charge. I will give you a code, that you will pass on.

'You will be taken to see Pulkownik [Colonel] Kowalski. He will know what to do – I will give him the order. You will be given twenty people in plain clothes, and twenty in uniform. They are extremely brave and heroic fighters, but they need to be told what to do. You will have to be their chief.'

This took me by surprise, and I stuttered over my reply. Bielecki grinned and continued, on the assumption I agreed. He spoke about the dangers of the mission, and the attacks we would face from the Armia Krajowa (AK), the so-called Home Army. Although officially disbanded in January 1945, after staging underground resistance to the Nazis, elements remained loyal to the Polish government in exile. The Soviets saw them as the enemy within.

The UB men would be fully armed. He promised to provide a tank, and a range of automatic weapons, rifles, mortars and cannons. I would receive documents, issued with his blessing, giving me complete authority to conduct our operations undisturbed by any other security officials. We had the power to temporarily enlist local police officers as we saw fit.

'The AK are attacking everything we do,' he said. 'So, they will come at you as well, out of the forests. You will have the means to defend yourselves. Put the machine gun on the roof when you get these children to your places. They will come at night. Don't worry. The men I will give you know how to fight.'

My audience was at an end. To tell the truth, I was scared,

but was in too deep to walk away. I had to act quickly, and barely slept that night. I roused members of the Jewish committee from their beds and explained what had occurred. They were astonished, but excited, and promised to fund my trip to Warsaw, and any other provisions I needed.

The UB, *Urząd Bezpieczeństwa*, or Department of Security, had its headquarters on Koszykowa Street in central Warsaw. This was the nerve centre of their secret war against dissidents, which involved thousands of informers. They were responsible for counter-intelligence, surveillance and enforcement, which led to thousands being sent to gulags in Siberia.

Bielecki's code was a jumble of words, which I now cannot remember. Sure enough, it led to me being ushered into the presence of Colonel Kowalski, who turned out to be his deputy. He, too, needed reassurance about the scope of our intentions, and our readiness to complete the task. He also highlighted the opposition we would face.

'Many will try to hurt you and sabotage your plans,' he warned. 'You are the one who has to run this operation. The men we will give you will not know what you want them to do. It is up to you to tell them. They are career officers and very well trained with weaponry. They are exceptionally capable people and very trustworthy. Without a doubt, they will be loyal to the mission.'

Again, I swallowed hard. There I was, barely twenty years old, given command of battle-hardened men. Apart from that revolver, clumsily discharged into the dirt outside Ebensee concentration camp, soon after liberation, I had never handled a gun. When I admitted that, Kowalski didn't bat an eyelid. He simply summoned an officer to take me into a nearby shooting ground. There, for an hour, he gave me rudimentary training in weapons handling.

Kowalski organized a pistol for me and promised a machine gun. He then signed and sealed the UB identification documents, written in Polish and Russian. He entrusted us with the power to seize and search which, come to think of it, was a remarkable testament to the influence of Daniusz. Any debt owed to my absent family had been repaid.

These people will not be judged kindly by history. Daniusz left his wife and child and disappeared into the Soviet Union with his mistress in the early 1950s. His fate is uncertain, but it is most likely that he became a victim of one of the many Stalinist purges.

Bielecki was more cunning. He organized a transfer to the army, with the rank of lieutenant colonel, in October that year. He used political contacts to gain a place at the Soviet Military Aviation Academy in Monino, a suburb of Moscow, and eventually became Commander of the Polish air force. He was buried with full military honours on his death, aged seventy-seven, in June 1994.

I was, of course, playing the role of an eager, communist-supporting youth leader. In fact, I loathed everything the Soviet regime stood for. My respect was reserved for the Red Army, for their sacrifices as they fought and defeated the Nazis during the war. Their advances on the battlefield had led to the evacuation of some of the most notorious concentration camps, like Plaszow and Mauthausen.

The UB men assigned to me were as good as the word of their superiors. They were great with me, understanding my inexperience and literally covering my back during the search operations, which spanned the country. They soon picked up on the Jewish connection but remained loyal because they saw the way the children were cared for. Our job, to find, protect and take those abandoned children back into our community, aroused powerful emotions. I became used to being hated.

A pattern emerged. Whenever we arrived in a new town, or village, our first port of call was the police station. We let the local commander know who we were, by sharing our UB identification documents, but did not tell him, or his men, what we wanted to accomplish. We did not trust them and did not want to take the risk of them alerting families who had the missing children.

Only when we had confirmed the facts, by speaking to neighbours, who often volunteered additional leads, or to relevant nuns and priests, did we ask for the specific support of local police. They gave us extra security when we confronted the foster families with our suspicions and intentions. I take no pride in admitting I was very tough with them. I had to be, otherwise we could not have succeeded.

I developed an instinct for tell-tale differences. It seemed that some fostered children were singled out for manual work. Around 90 per cent were girls. At one house I watched a girl, no more than eight or nine years old, struggle back from the well with two large, extremely heavy pails of water. Her dress, several sizes too big, was worn and grubby. At another I discovered a girl of similar age who slept on a bed of straw in the kitchen, beside the range.

There were obvious physical clues. The child had different facial features to the foster parents. The hair was a different colour. Even mannerisms were different. Yet in most cases they didn't want to part from their Polish families, even when they had obviously been poorly treated. Many were so young when they were fostered, they had no memories of former lives.

They had been smuggled out of the ghettos, in many cases minutes before their natural parents were deported to the death camps. They had been hidden in stairways, attics and ditches. Many of those old enough to understand their situation had lived in fear of capture. Most now had a Christian identity, at odds with their Jewish heritage.

Taking them away was often extremely distressing. I began with beautiful words, praising the foster parents for their goodness in saving a life. Some asked for money, which I could not give. Many became stubborn and refused to co-operate. That gave me no alternative but to use the power at my disposal.

It was heart-breaking to see the anguish and confusion of the children. They cried as those they had lived with during the war claimed they had officially adopted them but were unable to prove it. The adults questioned our authority and were not satisfied with the official papers we carried. Occasionally, they were supported by local police, who tended to shut up when told to take up their complaints with Bielecki and the UB.

We could not tell them where we were going, other than to promise they would be well looked after. One man threw himself on our jeep as we tried to leave with a child in the back. He was pushed off when we reached the edge of the village, and we accelerated away. Others threw rocks at us, attacked us with anything they could lay their hands on. Some started shooting, but we could not afford a gun battle, and so retreated as quickly as possible.

Looking back, it was an extreme case of being cruel to be kind.

The refuge in Rabka-Zdrój, at a former spa that had treated tuberculosis patients before the war due to the healing qualities of the mineral waters, was spread across three or four separate buildings, but centred on a former hotel. Nurses and psychologists had been recruited to look after the children, who found it difficult to adjust to a new environment and needed time to build trust.

Kindly ladies came in to do their hair. Others made them clothes, cooked them meals. Teachers, funded by underground Zionist organizations, set up classes. Though I was not involved in the administration, and rarely had time to concentrate on anything other than pursuing potential cases of child reintegration, or protecting the HQ, I loved quiet moments with the children.

I started to teach them the Jewish alphabet, and such basic Jewish prayers as the Modeh, which is said before rising each morning: 'I offer thanks to You, God, for You have restored my soul within me; You, God, are awesome.' I felt sad that the children had been forced to endure so much in their short lives but believed we could give them a better future.

Sadly, almost all of them proved to be orphans. I remember only one child who was successfully reunited with her mother. She was called Malinki, a name with a Russian influence, if memory serves. She didn't recognize her mother, and refused to leave with her at first, so we allowed the distressed woman to stay with us so she could rebuild her relationship with her daughter.

Slowly, the girl grew in confidence. She began asking her mother, who was committed to her Jewish faith, to take her to church, which she had obviously become used to with her foster family. She quickly grew tired of daily excuses as to why this was not possible. 'Mammie,' she eventually exclaimed, a breakthrough in itself, 'I know why you don't want to take me to church.'

'Why?'

'Because you are very stingy. When the priest goes around with the plate to collect money, you are lazy, and look away. You don't want to put a few *groshen* into the collection.'

This was something, however, on which a connection could be established. I often wonder what happened to them; that girl would now be in her late eighties. I doubt they stayed in Poland, since there were many emigration schemes available. It was a delicate, extremely difficult situation, but we believed we were doing the right thing, in offering the children a new life in the Jewish community.

I had other onerous responsibilities because the world was still a dangerous place. One morning in early July 1946 we were directed to the city of Kielce, where an anti-Jewish pogrom was in progress. I left a strong guard behind at Rabka-Zdrój, in case of associated attacks. When we arrived in Kielce, in the UB's tank, the main street was filled by a mob armed with axes, sickles, metal bars and shovels.

As so often in these circumstances, hate had overwhelmed reason. Rumours had spread that a young Christian boy, Henryk Blaszczyk, had been abducted and killed by Jews, who had used his blood in the making of Matzah, our unleavened bread, for Passover. This is what is popularly known as a 'blood libel'.

The boy had, in fact, become lost in the local forest. Instead of admitting his mistake when he was found two days later, he pointed out a man from the local displaced persons' camp, in a small street in the centre of town, and accused him, through his father, of imprisoning him in the basement.

Even though there was no basement in that building, which housed around 160 Jews, that triggered a massacre which left forty-two people, including women and children, dead. They were buried in a mass grave three days later. Nine attackers were quickly sentenced to death by Polish courts, but our job was to maintain an uneasy calm, while claims and counter-claims, about the blame attached to soldiers, militia and civilians, were investigated.

Retaliation, on our part, would have led to more deaths. As it was, the Kielce pogrom had such a huge impact on an already traumatized community that 100,000 Jews fled Eastern Europe in the following three months.

We were targets, as predicted. Our jeep came under fire from a rooftop sniper on more than one occasion in Rabka-Zdrój, where we also had to fight off night-time raids. This had already taken a toll on Lena Küchler, a wonderful teacher and psychologist who worked with abandoned children aged between three and fifteen, found at the Jewish Committee Centre in Krakow, where survivors could obtain food, water, clothing and temporary shelter.

Her bravery could not be questioned. She used an alias and posed as a Roman Catholic nanny during the war, after escaping transportation to Belzec following the liquidation of her home town, Wieliczka, where I had endured forced labour in the salt mine.

Her most famous act of compassion and defiance involved discovering a living baby lying on top of the corpse of her mother. She hid the baby under her coat, smuggled it out of the ghetto, and found refuge in a monastery, despite the monks initially refusing to take in a circumcized child.

After the war, she quickly transferred her children to a house forty kilometres south, in Zakopane. When that, too, came under attack from anti-Semitic villagers, in March 1946, she moved the group, which had grown to around a hundred, to Czechoslovakia, Germany, France, and finally, in 1949, to a kibbutz in Israel. She lived in Tel Aviv and kept in touch with her surrogate family until she passed away, aged seventy-seven, in 1987.

I was more familiar with the work of Yeshayahu Drucker, a chaplain in the Polish Army, who ran a similar rescue model to ours in Zabrze, in southern Poland, near Katowice, and visited Rabka-Zdrój on several occasions. We had similar beliefs, and belonged to the Mizrachi, a religious Zionist organization. He also understood the power of military associations and wore a major's uniform in all his dealings.

He was a thoughtful, quietly passionate man in his early thirties, who located and oversaw the care of around 700 children between 1945 and 1948. I looked up to him immensely. I was too young to handle both sides of my job – a cross between being a security guard and a social worker – and I valued his practical advice about the educational and organizational challenges we faced.

He also liaised with the Koordynacja, which matched the efforts of nine Zionist organizations and looked after approximately a thousand children in four homes, two in Lodz and two in Silesia, until June 1949, when there was political upheaval in Poland. They also assisted Jewish minors taken to Soviet Russia during the war.

We both knew the Chief Rabbi of the Polish Army, David

215

Kahane, through our links to the Mizrachi. His parents had been murdered in Belzec and he survived the war because he was hidden, initially in a monastery attic, by the Ukrainian archbishop of the Uniate Catholic Church. He was an imposing figure in full uniform and had made an impassioned speech at the funeral of the Kielce victims.

A familiar figure at the displaced persons' camp in Bad Ischl, he helped to fund Drucker's project through American benefactors. He was a close enough friend to attend Chaim Spielman's wedding before he left for Israel in 1949, becoming Chief Rabbi of the air force. He later fulfilled a similar role in Argentina.

I continued to travel extensively, but as things evolved, we began to concentrate our efforts in the Galicia region, which spanned south-eastern Poland and what is now western Ukraine. I was not involved in the more formal processes of documentation, but within a year we had in the region of 600 children in our care.

The Mizrachi believe Jewish nationalism has a religious dimension, and I had become increasingly interested in the role that Palestine could play in offering a future for the orphans. With the British regime in the Holy Land resistant to large-scale Jewish immigration, this meant investigating the possibilities of working with Bricha, an underground movement whose word means 'flight', or 'escape'.

They were involved in a clandestine, illegal form of immigration to Israel, known as Aliyah Bet. In more modern terms, it is referred to by the Hebrew term *Ha'apala*, or Ascension. It featured other Zionist organizations, such as the paramilitary Haganah, which was eventually absorbed into the Israeli Defence Force when statehood was achieved in 1948, but I wanted to make our initiative as non-political and neutral as possible.

That was difficult since the issue was so highly charged. I secretly made contact through more orthodox channels with the Jewish Agency, where Yitzhak Rafael, who later became Israel's Religions Minister and Deputy Health Minister, and Eliezer Unger, a leader of the *HaShomer HaDati* movement, worked on a plan to get our children to Palestine.

These were men who helped shape modern Israel, both practically and philosophically. Rafael defied critics to organize the officially sanctioned influx of 685,000 Jewish refugees from 1948 to 1951. His father, Yehuda Leib Maimon, helped draft the new state's declaration of independence and became the first Minister of War Victims. Unger is popularly regarded as the first man to calculate that six million Jews were lost during the Holocaust.

They facilitated an introduction to Rav Yitzhak Herzog, the Chief Rabbi of Palestine. A great man, whose son Chaim and grandson Isaac both became President of Israel, he had made it his post-war duty to help abandoned children in Europe. He pressed the Vatican for assistance, and though officially rebuffed, he received clandestine support from Poland's Karol Wojtyła, the future Pope John Paul II.

Communication was difficult, and usually conducted through telegram, but the Chief Rabbi understood our intentions, and our need for financial and organizational help. He more than fulfilled his promise to find money, people and practical resources. Our plan took shape, even though we had to give the impression of it being business as usual.

It was a bittersweet time. I had developed an enormous amount of affection for the children in our care, and naturally worried about their welfare, but, logically, I knew we had done as much for them as we could. I had to entrust them to others, who had greater experience of covert operations. They knew which border officials to bribe, and what routes to take.

My involvement in the flight of our children ended when they were loaded into lorries, forty at a time, and taken through Czechoslovakia and Austria to Italy. It broke my heart to see them leave, and I followed their progress to the port city of Trieste as best as I could. From there I was told they were put on a boat, which docked in Haifa, where it appears they were intercepted by the British authorities and sent to a detention camp in Cyprus.

Most of these boats, which had inspirational names like *Lo Tafchidunu* ('You Can't Frighten Us'), were escorted by the Palyam, the maritime arm of the Palmach, an elite fighting force within Haganah. Voyages began from places as far afield as France, Algeria, Romania and Sweden. Over half were intercepted by the British Navy, which had eight ships on armed patrol.

I learned that our group travelled to Israel, soon after independence, in May 1948, but there the trail goes cold. Due to the secrecy involved, I suppose it is unsurprising that I have been unable to find records identifying them, and any progress made in their new lives. The closest I came was by accident when I met two ladies on a visit to Auschwitz-Birkenau. They told me they had stayed in Rabka-Zdrój as children. I was so taken aback I forgot to ask for their names and contact details.

My children, and grandchildren, have often suggested I should take out newspaper advertisements in Israel, seeking information about the orphans' fate. If any are alive, God willing, they will, like me, be of an advanced age. They would not recognize me, and I would not recognize them. Perhaps some will recognize themselves by reading this book, but my real reward is the memory of a great mission. My involvement remains one of my greatest privileges.

Back then, in the danger zone of post-war Poland, I had to move on very quickly. It wasn't safe for me to visit the market or walk the streets. I received regular death threats and came under fire several times. The UB men threw me to the ground to protect me, whenever they heard shots. On one occasion, travelling in a jeep, I had an axe thrown at me from a balcony. Luckily, it only grazed my foot, after brushing against my trousers.

I handed over responsibility for what remained of the project to Moniek Sarna, my second-in-command. To put pursuers off the scent, I then sent a false telegram to myself, stating that my father was seriously ill in Vienna, and requesting my presence as a matter of urgency. In reality, I travelled to Bad Ischl, where Chaim Spielman happily employed me, on behalf of UNRRA, as his deputy.

I oversaw security at the displaced persons' camp, a hotel which is now an apartment block, and worked from a small office at its entrance, recording who came in and who went out. Tensions were high, with local residents resentful at what they saw as preferential treatment for Jews. Our milk rations, I remember, caused great offence, and led to skirmishes, which I had to report to the local police commander.

This small town, in which the Habsburg Emperor Franz Joseph I spent his summers, was, like the rest of Europe, in a state of flux. Old myths were colliding with new realities.

219

Our people, around 300 survivors of Mauthausen and its sub-camps, were stateless, and living five to a room. There was no privacy. They had no families. They worried they had no future.

It was there I made the decision that would shape the rest of my life.

15

New Horizons

I confess that, immediately after my liberation, I was so disgusted with the human race I wanted to run away and hide. I had witnessed the atrocities people were capable of committing and struggled to contain my fear of my fellow man. I wanted to settle on an isolated farm, and live simply, among chickens, cows, dogs and horses.

The animals could not hurt me. They would not persecute me for my faith and family background. I know that might sound silly, but they represented a wonderful, fleeting fantasy that I indulged before I realized I had a duty to make the most of my survival. Nazi mass murderers had to be brought to justice. The orphans they created had to be given a second chance at life.

When those missions had been achieved, the world began to come to me. A succession of immigration officers from various countries visited Bad Ischl, promising to give us a fresh start. I didn't want to go to Australia, the ends of the Earth. Ironically, since I later spent many years in Montreal, I initially turned down the chance to go to Canada, where I thought, in my ignorance, Eskimos lived in igloos.

America, a traditional land of opportunity, had its pull, but I was attracted philosophically to the notion of helping to build Israel as a new nation state. I had participated in demonstrations calling for a Jewish homeland, and carried the old flag, half blue, half white, without the Star of David, through the streets of Vienna and Munich.

I belonged to an independent club known as Chovevei Zion, or Lovers of Zion (a biblical name for Jerusalem). A global network of such clubs, first formed by persecuted Jews in Romania and Czarist Russia in the late nineteenth century, had developed national pride and were dedicated to the principle of a return to the ancient homeland of Eretz Yisrael, the Hebrew term for the land of Israel.

It was a cultural rather than political movement, its ideals expressed by a Yiddish nursery rhyme from my childhood. With apologies for the looseness of my translation, it goes something like this: 'The land of Israel is my dear land. It is known all over the world. Between rivers and lakes and valleys there is nothing like it. There are no comparisons to my dear country.'

I realize that many other nations have songs in a similar vein but, to me, the simplicity of that nursery rhyme cuts through the polemic. I can imagine it being sung hundreds of years ago, when the dream of returning to the land, given by God to Abraham, Isaac and Jacob, was as powerful as it is today, when some regard Zionism as a dirty word.

The political dimension was the focus of the Mizrachi, of which I have already mentioned I was a member. It formed the first official religious party, which strove to enforce *kashrut*, the set of dietary laws governing kosher food, and the observance of the Sabbath in the workplace. We considered the Torah central to Zionism.

Mizrachi also laid the grounds for statehood by establishing a system of religious schools that operates to this day, but activism is as much about people as ideas and beliefs. I had used networks of Mizrachi members in my post-war work. There was a sense of hope and happiness. Almost without daring to say so, my generation was preparing for power.

The Schreiber family, to whom I had been introduced by Lolo, the friendly Kapo, were at the centre of the social and political hub in Austria. They linked individuals and organizations, fostering an atmosphere in which natural leaders emerged. The optimism that this aroused did not go down well with the existing establishment.

On one evening, returning from a particularly successful gathering at the Schreiber apartment in Vienna, we found our suitcases and personal belongings stacked on the sidewalk outside our hotel. The management claimed we were disturbing other guests with our singing and cancelled our reservations. Moshe Shapira, one of our group, offered to settle our bill, but was simply told to go away.

Moshe had bigger battles to fight. Within a year or so, he was among those who signed Israel's declaration of independence. He was appointed Minister of Health and Minister of Immigration in David Ben-Gurion's provisional government. Pinhas Scheinman, another friend, became secretary general of Hapoel HaMizrachi, another settlement movement, and rose to become Deputy Speaker of the Knesset.

These were the best and brightest. Moshe Krohne became secretary of Torah V'avoda, a religious Zionist movement that preaches tolerance and equality, and continues to encourage debate on Jewish law. Chaim Chamiel went on to become a celebrated author. Zerach Warhaftig, a rabbi, lawyer and politician, who was active in the Jewish Agency, was another acquaintance who signed Israel's declaration of independence.

The Mizrachi leadership saw something in me and, since I had never had the chance to undergo a formal education, offered to organize and underwrite my studies at Oxford. Rabbi Shmuel Belkin, dean of Yeshiva University in New York, also sent several letters offering me a place. A distinguished Torah scholar, he was in the process of turning the university from a small college and rabbinical seminary into one of the most important educational institutions in North America.

In reflective moments, I still have pangs of regret that I passed over such opportunities. I was obviously earmarked for political office in the new state, which I identified with as a sacred cause. I remained active in Jewish life in exile, mainly through the fraternal lodges of B'nai Brith, and founded the Mizrachi movement in Colombia in 1956.

I related to how the best politicians balanced fierce ideals with a mixture of pragmatism, boldness, and occasional ruthlessness. I formed a close friendship with Menachem Begin, a future Israeli Prime Minister, after first meeting him as part of a delegation that greeted him at the airport, on a visit to Argentina in 1950. I used my security clearance to board his plane and handle immigration formalities on his behalf.

He would go on to achieve great things, sharing the Nobel Peace Prize with Anwar Sadat after signing a treaty with Egypt in 1979. But at that time, as leader of the relatively recently formed Herut (Freedom) Party, Begin retained the rougher edges of his character, emphasized by his command of the militant Irgun underground opposition to British rule in Palestine.

The British had placed a 'dead or alive' bounty of £10,000 on his head during the revolt, but as so often in history, one man's terrorist was another man's freedom fighter. I admired Begin greatly for his humility and passion. I was immediately struck by the plainness of his dress. His suit was old, and his shirt well worn. His shoes could have done with a polish. It was only later, in his public appearances, that he dressed according to his status, in a blue coat, with white scarf and hat.

Argentina had a large Jewish community, of around 500,000. His main goal was to persuade people to buy Israeli bonds, and to improve business links with the new nation. Begin was a great speaker and delivered an eloquent speech in front of 180,000 in Luna Park in Buenos Aires, but he was equally impressive in small groups, in local synagogues and halls.

I had the privilege of spending quite a bit of time in Begin's company. We spoke in Yiddish about our respective backgrounds. We both had a traditional *cheder* education and discussed how each of us had been shaped, in our own way, by wartime experiences. He was hardened by his arrest and torture by the Soviets, who had sentenced him to eight years in a gulag.

He had no regrets about his role in the bombing of the British headquarters in the King David hotel, which killed ninety-one people and resulted in the splintering of Jewish armed resistance, arguing that it hastened the British withdrawal. His sorrow was reserved for Dov Gruner, a relatively inexperienced Irgun operative, executed by the British after being captured during an arms raid on a police station in Tel Aviv.

He was eager to hear of my experiences in the camps, and as so often happens, we were bonded by our private, personal tragedies. I tried to explain what it meant to be the only survivor from such a large extended family; Begin spoke of his parents and his elder brother Herzl, who were also murdered in the Holocaust.

Those memories triggered our most striking exchange. The Germans were offering a lump sum of between $5,000 and $8,000, a huge amount at the time, as reparations to young Jews denied an education because of the war. When I confessed I was thinking of accepting, Begin stiffened. His eyes, behind those familiar horn-rimmed glasses, suddenly blazed.

'Jossele,' he said, jabbing a finger at me. 'Don't sell the blood of your father, the blood of your mother, the blood of your siblings, the blood of your whole family, for a few stinking dollars. Don't do it.' He paused for a few seconds, with a stony stare, before repeating, 'Don't do it.' Though I later regretted it, I promised I would not.

Looking back, that moment explained why I was in Argentina in the first place. I felt alone in the world when I was in Bad Ischl, despite the friendships I made and the dreams we shared. I yearned for the refuge of family which, until I read an announcement from the International Red Cross, I feared I would be denied.

The Red Cross mentioned that someone in Argentina had sent letters and was looking for members of my family. I could not have pointed out Argentina on the map, but it summoned childhood memories of colourful stamps, on envelopes that came to our home from a faraway place. I used to trade those stamps with my friends.

The person who sent those letters, my great-uncle Israel, was looking for any surviving relatives. I could not believe my good fortune. It is hard to understand how empty you feel when you have no family around you. You can speak honestly, fearlessly and emotionally to those who are your flesh and blood but cannot share your secrets with friends in the same way.

My mind was instantly made up. I resolved to travel to Argentina and build a new life in South America. My great-uncle was overjoyed to find me and crushed to discover the fate of so many people he held dear. He quickly followed up on his promise to send me a ticket for the *Formosa*, a ship once used to transport cattle that had been refurbished to hold around a thousand passengers.

My immediate problem was one of identification. I had only an ID card issued by the American authorities in Austria, which stated: 'This is a personal card of an ex-prisoner Haftling, Num 85314. Liberated from Concentration Camp Mauthausen-Ebensee. Staatenlos (Stateless).' It featured my birthplace and date of birth, but these were irrelevant because I had simply made them up.

I needed a passport and contacted a *sofer*, a Jewish scribe employed by the Schreiber family. He bought me a train ticket to France and advised me to tell his friend, the Polish consul in Toulouse, that he had sent me. He also gave me the address of a family who would put me up for the night.

My hosts could not have been more helpful. They arranged my passport photographs, and when the consul's office was closed on my first visit, allowed me to stay for as long as necessary. They took me to the consul's home, where I explained my experiences as he prepared the necessary documentation.

Some things were left unsaid. The consul was obviously of Jewish descent but could not admit it because of the government he worked for. He seemed unusually used to dealing with passport applicants who had no formal means of identification. Inevitably, most of these would, like me, have been Holocaust survivors.

The next step, on returning to Bad Ischl with a new Polish passport, was to secure a visa from the Argentine consulate in Vienna. I proved to the clerk that I had the necessary ticket, and duly filled in the form. When the consul appeared from a back office, he greeted me warmly, and said he would issue the visa on the spot, provided I described myself as Christian, rather than Jewish.

I exploded. How dare he challenge my birthright? What gave him the authority to instruct me to deny my faith? I had suffered grievously because I was a Jew and would not lie about it to fulfil the needs of a functionary. 'Well, my friend,' the consul replied calmly, 'in that case I can't help you.' The same thing happened a couple of days later, when I tried to get a visa from the Argentine consulate in Munich.

The *Formosa* was due to sail from Le Havre, so I tried again at the consulate in Paris, with the same outcome. I was close to despair. I had tried all my sources and failed. This, remember, was at a time when many Nazis, and their collaborators, were quietly being welcomed throughout South America. Natural justice seemed to have been abandoned.

I pride myself on never taking a backward step and was determined not to give up. As on many occasions, I relied on a combination of charm and cunning to get what I wanted. I realized that the *Formosa* was first due to dock in Rio de Janeiro, to load local coffee, and so visited the Brazilian consulate, where I fixed the clerk with my best smile. I told him I had heard so many wonderful things about his country that I wanted to explore it, before completing my journey.

The plan worked. I did not have to lie about my religion and was issued with a transit visa. I spent the next five weeks or so on the *Formosa*, where hundreds of men, women and children slept in makeshift beds on, and below, deck. It was a time to reflect; I devoted many hours to studying the Torah with a new friend, a young Hungarian refugee named Chanania Grunblatt.

I landed in Rio with only $7 in my pocket, and my worldly goods in a small suitcase, a problem which grew more acute when I was quickly refused a visa to enter Argentina at the local consulate because of my continued refusal to masquerade as a Christian. I didn't know the language, and it was very hot. I slept on a bench in a beautiful park for several days, eking out the last of the food I had taken from the ship's kitchen.

My faith might have been complicating my travel arrangements, but it offered salvation. I was welcomed into the local synagogue, where I was given a few cruzeiros to buy bread and milk and had offers of accommodation. It was a relief to be among my own, speaking Yiddish and praying to God. Everyone wanted to know who I was, why I was there, and where I had come from. They were only vaguely aware of what Polish Jewry had gone through in the Holocaust.

The community found me a job, labouring in a mattress factory. That enabled me to earn enough money to rent a room and allowed me to explore the city. Rio was a revelation, a place of light and colour with fruits and food I had never before experienced. I extended my transit visa, and

229

secured a job with higher pay, in a factory that knitted sweaters.

All the while I was practising my rudimentary Portuguese, in markets and on the streets. In what I didn't realize was a taste of what was to come, I became friendly with a group of diamond dealers who had fled from Belgium. I remained in contact with my great-uncle Israel in Buenos Aires, through letters and telegrams.

The breakthrough came when he suggested I visit a business contact in Paraguay, a Mr Schneiderman. He sent money for a plane ticket to Asunción, and the connection was enough for me to be offered a visa. Much to my surprise, when I arrived, a civil war, which had begun four months earlier, in March 1947, was in its decisive final stages.

This was the so-called Barefoot Revolution, whose name seemed appropriate since I was stopped by a soldier with no shoes and a torn shirt. I spoke little Spanish, but understood the message of his rifle, pointed at my chest. As carefully as I could, I offered him my Polish passport. The Paraguayan visa had been issued by the country's diplomatic mission in Rio, which the uneducated soldier took to mean that I was a diplomat.

His mood changed instantly. He smiled and escorted me from the airport to the address I had for the Schneiderman family. They vouched for me and filled me in on the details of the war, between the existing dictator Higinio Morínigo and rebels supported by the majority of the armed forces, bankers and businessmen.

My host was well connected and suspected, correctly, the rebellion would fail because Morínigo was being supported by Juan Perón, the Argentine dictator. Mr Schneiderman bribed the wife of the local police commander to get me false papers and an official identification card, which suggested I had been born in Colonia Nuevo Germania, in rainforest in a remote part of Paraguay.

I chose to ignore the stain of being linked to a settlement established by anti-Semitic German nationalists, who believed in Aryan supremacy, and concentrated on the benefits. Paraguay was dangerous and unstable. Nearly a third of the population had fled. My false papers looked authentic enough to fool the Argentine immigration officer who boarded the hydroplane that took me from Asunción to Buenos Aires.

My great-uncle Israel was waiting for me with his wife Malka and daughter, Esther. They took me to their home in Canning, south-west of the city centre, and set me up in a bedroom. Israel had heard of the passing of my great-grandfather but had many years of family news to catch up on. The loss of his four brothers hurt him deeply.

Israel was the spitting image of my grandfather, though he was not quite the free spirit he had once been. He gave me a job in his factory, making ornate bed headboards, picture frames and mirrors, which we sprayed with gold leaf. It was dirty, dusty work; despite wearing face masks, we had to ease our throats by constantly drinking milk.

Everything seemed set fair until one evening, when, sitting with my great-aunt on the porch, she raised what she obviously thought was an important subject. The local boys were no longer taking her daughter out because they assumed I had been brought in to marry her. The unintentional inference, that I was causing unnecessary problems, enraged me.

I regret my reaction to this day. I was hot-headed, proud, and walked out of their home without a backward glance. It was an incredibly stupid thing to do. I was only twenty-one, and had no one to guide me, to tell me how to behave. I ignored everything I thought I held dear. I had left irreplaceable things behind and had nowhere to go.

It would be five years before I returned. I did so when I heard my great-uncle was sick. Esther, his daughter, was indeed married, and had two children. My life had changed, yet again. I was by that time a relatively successful diamond dealer. The wandering Jew, living on his wits, learning so many languages in so many countries, had finally grown up.

But I am getting ahead of myself. My survival instincts had seen me through the self-inflicted crisis in my great-aunt's house. I slept on a pile of newspapers in an attic owned by a *yekke*, a German Jew, and bluffed my way into a knitting factory by telling the owners I knew how to work the machines when, previously, I had only swept the floors. They threw me out, physically, after a couple of days in which I broke many needles, which were like gold dust.

A pair of Polish brothers gave me a job in a similar factory on the other side of Canning. Determined not to make the same mistakes, I watched my new workmates and learned on the job without doing too much damage. The brothers liked my appetite for work; I lived for Friday, when my wages would come in an envelope.

I first bought a mattress for the attic, then a bed, and a small table. I gambled I could earn more in commission, working as a salesman for a hardware factory. That involved lugging a heavy suitcase, full of cabinet handles and hinges, and though I gained many orders, the move failed because the company was unable to buy raw materials.

Fortunately, I had already met one of the key figures in my

new life, Izzy Lerner. He arrived in Argentina six months before me, from Antwerp, where his family were diamond dealers and manufacturers. He was taking his first steps in the trade after settling in by buying and selling on the streets.

It would be a little while before our friendship became a partnership. Acting on his advice, I would take the subway to the *pletzl*, the equivalent of a town square. The Jewish community congregated around a restaurant named Bar León. Most dealers set up outside, trading from small tables. Izzy taught me the rudiments of their business, while I set about making a few pesos by using my negotiating skills to buy something like a watch and reselling it at a profit.

By doing this, I began to understand the value of gold, and whether it was 12, 14 or 24 carat. I traded coins, small rings and pieces of jewellery, learning about diamonds on the side. I quickly realized that it was a social business. Conversations had to be relaxed enough to be enjoyable, but precise enough to avoid misunderstandings. People had to trust you.

These lessons held me in good stead for the rest of my life. My livelihood depended on my reputation. From my earliest days, if I offered someone a price I would stick to it, even if it meant losing money. A man was only as important as his word. I knew I had to work hard to prove my honesty, but before long I had my own table in the square, and a long list of customers.

Some in the square resented me because I was the youngest dealer. Others thought they could pull a fast one, because I was inexperienced. They quickly realized I knew what type of diamonds to look for, and what to pay. If I bought from private individuals I would check the quality of the merchandise with the Gemological Institute of America. Gradually, I reduced the risks by only buying from manufacturers I had previously worked with.

I did well enough to acquire an official licence and opened my first bank account. I began to travel regularly to Rio to buy rough diamonds, but had to be careful on my return, because customs officers and policemen had a nasty habit of 'confiscating' supposed contraband.

Corruption was everywhere, and you had to be clever enough to use it to your advantage. It went against my principles, but I got out of mandatory national service by handing officers and army doctors well-padded envelopes, containing large amounts of money. They showed their gratitude by registering me as officially unfit for military duties. It was a win-win deal.

Others were more troublesome. Secret service agents were notorious for tracking down diamond dealers so they could steal from them. They murdered two in cold blood when they objected. My fears were justified one morning when two men who announced themselves as 'government officials' intercepted me in the lobby of the small apartment I rented.

They told me I was under arrest. I asked why, as politely as I could, and somehow got them to agree to accompany me to a local restaurant, since I had not had breakfast. While there, I received their permission to visit the bathroom. I was followed in by one of the secret agents, who resisted my attempt to discover how much they needed to walk away.

He insisted they were determined to take me to the commissariat, their government department. I played along with the ruse, asking with as much innocence as I could muster how that would benefit them. Sure enough, that opened negotiations on a deal. I had a fair amount of money on me, since

I had intended to visit the bank, so I handed that over, and promised to return the following day, with the balance of what we had agreed.

The bribes were a business expense, but I vowed never again to be so vulnerable. If it could be fatal to try and beat them, I needed to join them. I didn't ask how, but a wealthy friend, a well-connected figure in the ruling party named Kempler, arranged for me to become a member of the Consejo Superior Peronista, a body led by Admiral Alberto Teisaire, a future vice-president of the Republic. That gave me full security clearance, and the protection of the system.

As business improved, I agreed to become Izzy Lerner's partner. That confirmed my status within the community, where I led Bnei Akiva, a religious youth movement, and was involved with AMIA, Asociación Mutual Israelita Argentina. I was also a member of Daia Amia, an umbrella organization, and chairman of Culture, Arts and Religious Affairs for the Mizrachi.

I was invited to join a delegation from the Jewish community to see the president, Juan Perón, in Casa Rosada, the pink-tinged mansion at the eastern end of the Plaza de Mayo in Buenos Aires that served as his office. He received us cordially, offering espressos as we lobbied him to recognize the state of Israel.

As headstrong as ever, and oblivious to political protocols, I pointed out to the president that he had a Hebrew name. His upper body stiffened and, as my fellow delegates looked daggers at me, he looked at me, directly in the eye. 'How can this be?' he asked, as the room took an intake of breath. 'Your Excellency,' I replied. 'Pe Ron is Hebrew. *Pe* means a mouth and *Ron* comes from the word "Rina", or singing.'

'So, what does it mean?'

I answered in Spanish: 'Boca-cantante, a singing mouth.'

He roared with laughter and instructed me to write it in Hebrew, together with the Spanish translation, in pencil on the pad his staff had provided. I handed him the page, which he made great play of trying to study, holding it upside down as if attempting to decipher its meaning before folding it in half and putting it in his pocket.

'I like it,' he exclaimed, ordering a uniformed officer to serve another round of espressos. I am not saying this had anything to do with me, but our audience was not in vain: Argentina established diplomatic relations with Israel in May 1949. A second visit, asking the president to use his influence with the Soviets to counteract Stalin's murderous campaign against Jewish doctors, was less successful.

I travelled with increasing regularity to the biggest diamond markets, in Belgium, South Africa and the United States, where the largest bourse was on 47th Street in Manhattan. I was increasingly confident in my business acumen but, as I discovered when randomly approached one day, at my table outside Bar León, I was far from infallible.

Mario, a strikingly handsome man, bought a small batch of diamonds from me, and asked to take some more to a contact in Spain, on consignment. I took him on trust and was willing to risk a couple of thousand dollars on the venture. When he returned, he was buzzing with excitement about a highly profitable new market.

It turned out that his contact was a lady called Olga, the estranged wife of a painter. Mario showed me seven of his canvases, which the painter's wife was willing to sell for $2,000 each, to fund the proposed partnership between us.

All I saw was strange shapes and colourful splodges. I didn't know the top of the paintings from the bottom.

Mario protested they would be worth a lot of money, but I told him I thought his idea was stupid. He was not my type of guy. It was clear he had been with that lady, dancing, drinking and a lot more besides. How was I to know that her estranged husband was Pablo Picasso, and those seven paintings would fetch tens, if not hundreds of millions, on today's market?

I had more profound and immediate things to worry about, like the start of the Korean War in the summer of 1950. My diamonds were traditionally set in platinum, which suddenly became scarce because the American government exhausted global stocks in support of the war effort. My jewellers did not want to mount diamonds in gold, so I was faced with the prospect of going out of business.

The price of platinum rose almost overnight, from $350 a kilo to $7,000 a kilo. I searched for supplies in Africa and Asia without any luck but heard a rumour that some might be available in Colombia. There were no direct flights from Argentina, so I flew, with successive overnight stays, via Santiago, in Chile, Lima in Peru, and Guayaquil in Ecuador, reaching Bogotá on the fourth day.

It proved to be one of the most important journeys of my life.

16

Love Story

Holocaust survivors form a unique self-help group. We might have contrasting personalities, conflicting beliefs, and different lifestyles, but only we can fully understand the horrors we experienced. If any of us asks a favour, it is delivered. No one who falls on hard times is left alone to struggle. We may be growing old, but as long as we are able, we are there for each other.

Word tends to travel fast on our grapevine, so it was no surprise that I received several requests from survivors, asking me to contact relatives in Colombia on their behalf, when they heard I was travelling to Bogotá. I did do willingly, because I appreciated how important human contact could be for people whose families had been so badly fractured.

When I finally arrived, and was settling into my hotel, I decided to try to find the first man on my list, Naftali Lederman. There were around twenty people with that surname in the local telephone book; I had tried six, without success, when I made my breakthrough. A voice on the end of the phone said: 'That's my father.'

The questions came quickly: 'Who are you?' 'Why are you here?' 'What do you want?' 'Where are you staying?' When I explained that I had been asked to link his father to a friend

239

of mine in Buenos Aires who happened to be his niece, I was told Naftali was out, tending to his business. His son promised that he would get him to call me on his return.

Naftali was as good as his son's words. Though I had to retell my story, he seemed thrilled to learn of his niece's survival. We arranged that he and his son would visit me when their four haberdashery stores had closed for the day. I accepted their invitation to tea at their house after giving them more background to my story over a drink in the bar of my hotel.

I had become used to the curiosity of strangers but was taken aback by the number of people who were waiting to greet me. Naftali had invited the world. Several generations of his family and many of his friends were eager to hear a first-hand account of life and death in the camps. Just how big an impact I made became clear when I was approached by one of Naftali's guests, Avram Liff.

He explained that he and two sisters had been saved by being hidden in a monastery during the war and that he was preparing to settle in Israel. When he visited me many years later, he was a general in the Defence Force, and very close to Yitzhak Rabin, the Prime Minister who would be assassinated by an extremist in Tel Aviv in November 1995.

Avram Liff gave me a gift for my friend in Buenos Aires, as did Naftali, on behalf of the entire family, when he gave me a lift back to my lodgings in a beautiful car, a black Buick Roadmaster. He did not personally know anyone in the platinum trade, and was not particularly religious, but he put me in touch with someone in the synagogue who did. I was welcomed warmly and given contacts in three cities.

Those in Cali and Barranquilla were unable to help, but

240

area. He explained he was so well known in the docks that he was never asked to show his papers.

Naftali took a life-changing decision, throwing his coat into the sea after going below deck to retrieve his few belongings and shave off his beard. His friend, Dovit Maya Rubenstein, gave him a bed and helped set him up in a local market, where he carried a board containing small mirrors, combs, razor blades and shoelaces.

Both men flourished. Dovit, the labourer hauling sacks of coffee, bought a machine to make scarves, hats and sweaters. He purchased several more, and ultimately became a multi-millionaire textile manufacturer. Naftali's business also grew quickly, and he was among the earliest Jewish settlers in Bogotá. He bought his first shop, invested in manufacturing, and earned enough to bring a succession of relatives to South America from Poland, throughout the 1930s.

He became a community leader, and hired a scholar called Menashe to give local children instruction in Hebrew and prayer. When Menashe died, Naftali bought a piece of land that became the city's first Jewish cemetery, so that the scholar could have a fitting final resting place. Naftali's influence extended to the highest ranks of Colombian society.

He and Dovit knew Mariano Ospina Pérez through the coffee trade. They were members of the same Masonic lodge and strengthened their friendship when Pérez rose through the political ranks in the Colombian Conservative Party. When Pérez became president, during a turbulent period immediately after the war, he approached Naftali for a favour.

As a young man, the president had studied in Louisiana, London and Paris. He valued education highly and sent his daughter to the Sorbonne in Paris. His problem was that her fees had to be met in hard currency, and foreign exchange was prohibited. Naftali, who had accumulated a secret stash of Swiss francs and US dollars, agreed to organize the payment. In return, he received a handwritten IOU on presidential notepaper.

Naftali left me that IOU in his will, but it remained uncashed. I passed it on to my wife's nephew, David, who was seeking to establish a family archive. A graduate of Cornell University who settled in Boston, he founded Abiomed, developers of the first artificial heart, in 1981. Tragically, he died at an early age, leaving his wife and two young children. Unfortunately, but perhaps understandably, the IOU was lost without trace.

The Ledermans, then, were a large, popular, and quietly powerful family. When I returned for a third visit to Colombia, in 1953, they gave a dinner in my honour, at their home. I was chatting to Naftali over pre-dinner drinks when I noticed a beautiful girl in the corner of the room. Naturally enough, I asked him who she was. 'Ah,' he said. 'That is my baby girl.'

Gambling that I could get away with such cheek, I replied, 'Wow. Where have you been hiding her?' He explained she had been in the United States, studying bacteriology at the University of California in Berkeley. His only daughter, among three sons, she had been born in Ostrowiec, around 180 kilometres from Krakow.

Her name was Perla. I spoke to her in Spanish, her mother tongue, though she also knew English and Yiddish. She agreed to go out to a club with me on the Saturday night, just before I was due to return to Argentina. We danced, drank and talked. We clicked. She was smart, beautiful, intelligent.

I was smitten. I had discovered something more valuable than platinum.

She had tightly layered blonde hair and wore the pillbox hats that were fashionable at the time. The inner person shone through. She was full of life, knowledgeable and practical. I had been out with lots of girls previously, usually in groups with friends to clubs, restaurants and the cinema, but I had never felt this way about anyone. I was in love. I couldn't stop thinking about her.

She was a woman of great principle. Her original intention, when she travelled to North America, was to study at McGill University in Montreal, but she was outraged to discover it operated a mere 10 per cent quota on Jewish students. The consul supported her in making a public complaint, but she accepted the counsel of community leaders, who suggested it could make a bad situation worse.

You cannot imagine how impressive she was when she studied in California. She not only excelled academically, but also contacted major corporations, and negotiated exclusive deals for Colombia, on behalf of her family. She was a natural businesswoman, with a razor-sharp memory and an uncanny ability to do complex numerical calculations in her head.

She imported Ronson cigarette lighters, which were exported, in turn, to other South American countries. She was the exclusive supplier of Arrow shirts, which were well cut, fashionable and expensive. She oversaw the sale of Anson and Swank tie clips and cufflinks, which were made of gold and inset with rubies and blue moonstone. When we met, she was setting up a laboratory in Bogotá with a friend.

We stayed in touch through long, increasingly romantic

letters and telegrams. I sent flowers and presents. I returned as quickly as I could, with a ring I had made, featuring a special diamond I had kept for several years. I didn't know if the ring was the right size – we can always work around that in the jewellery trade – but when I proposed, she accepted, and it fitted like a glove.

I saw the tears in her eyes and very quickly we were both crying.

The family gave us a lavish engagement party, and our marriage plans accelerated. Perla and her father visited me in Argentina to check me out. I was pretty well known in the community and had to interrupt dinner one evening to do an interview for the *Yidishe Zeitung*, the first daily newspaper for the Jewish community in Buenos Aires. When the article was published it contained a photograph of me with my fiancée. That helped to convince Naftali that I would be a son-in-law of suitable stature.

We were married on 7 March 1954, after I agreed to liquidate my business in Argentina and move to Colombia, which seemed more stable, politically and economically. I rebuilt my reputation as a fair and honest diamond dealer, while Perla, who had passed on her share of the laboratory to her friend, made a great success of her store, which catered to the elite.

On 28 December 1954 she gave birth to our first child, Symcha Meir, who we named after my father. His name in Spanish, Segismundo, explains his nickname, Ziggy. Our daughter Sheila, named after my mother Sheindl, was born on 12 October 1957. Life was good; we employed a nanny for the children, and a housekeeper.

I had never been better placed materially but felt undernourished spiritually. My priority was to give my children the education I never had. Perla and I both wanted to give them a strong moral and religious grounding. Though we decided against moving to Israel, where the diamond business was in its infancy, we felt we had to do something to help the new nation.

We organized a dinner party at our home and invited Perla's prominent customers. The Ministers of Foreign Affairs, Finance, Justice and the Economy attended, together with the head of the Armed Forces. The food was plentiful, and the range of whiskeys met with their approval. When we retired for after-dinner drinks I seized my chance and asked why Colombia had no diplomatic relations with Israel.

Predictably, the politicians regarded Colombia as a Roman Catholic country, which took its lead from the Vatican. Relations with the Jewish state would be complicated. My counter-argument, that a mutually beneficial commercial opportunity was being missed, must have registered because I was asked a couple of days later if I would travel to Israel as a matter of urgency, as a government envoy.

I was given three large suitcases, with official diplomatic seals, to share with their Israeli counterparts. These contained examples of local produce, such as coffee, tobacco and textiles. I handed them to my old friend Moshe Shapira, who was then Minister of the Interior, on my arrival at Lod airport in Tel Aviv, where I made the symbolic gesture of kissing the ground.

Moshe took me to the office of the Prime Minister, Moshe Sharett, who also acted as Foreign Minister. I explained the background to my mission, and he passed on responsibility for its success to the Minister of Trade and Industry, Peretz Bernstein. He, in turn, placed it in the hands of his South American desk.

That's when the bureaucrats fought back. Leading officials sent me a stinging note, in Spanish, condemning the supposed impudence of undertaking such an initiative without official permission. They suspected I did so because I had ambitions to become the Israeli ambassador to Colombia, but they were eventually put in their place.

I asked for, and received, nothing for my efforts, and within a year or so the two countries had established diplomatic relations. By that time Perla and I had decided to uproot our young family. Ziggy was nearing school age, and I was examining our options with increasing urgency.

Our initial plan was promising. We were negotiating with the American owners of Arrow to build a shirt factory in Rio de Janeiro. The Brazilian government undertook to give us land, without cost, on which to build it. We were given tax exemption for ten years but could not make the numbers work. The business would not have been viable because local factories flooded the market with cheaper shirts, of lesser quality.

My problem was that I had been a little rash. In anticipation of us moving to Brazil, I had been to Panama's free port of Colón, through which I arranged to send all our household goods and personal belongings to Rio. These were placed in storage, free of charge since we were new immigrants, so I didn't make an immediate loss.

Since we had abandoned our plans to settle in Brazil, I faced a dilemma. There was no point transporting our things back to Colombia. I knew these goods would be valuable on the Brazilian market, and knew I needed to do a deal. I put feelers out through existing business contacts and got into discussions with Hanoch Chaderitzky, who owned a diamond mine.

He was interested in buying everything I had in storage. I, in turn, was interested in a batch of rough diamonds he was in the process of polishing. This collection of twenty-eight coloured diamonds ranged from 1.60 carats to 7.00 carats. They were beautiful objects, in red pigeon blood, blue, pink, green, cognac and transparent black. I felt sure they would sell well on the international market, so shook hands on a straight swap.

In my defence, I was probably ahead of my time. Dealers in Europe and North America knew little, or nothing, about coloured diamonds. I kept them in a safe for a couple of years, and sent them to my agent in New York, Moshe Elias. He, in turn, took several more years to find a potential purchaser in Paris. Eventually, after negotiating for another year or so, I sold the collection for what I felt was a fair price.

It quickly became apparent I had misread the market. Coloured diamonds, especially pink and yellow ones, were becoming fashionable and very valuable. To give a recent example, a pink diamond of less than one carat was sold for $1 million at Sotheby's Auction House in Geneva. I reckon that batch of twenty-eight stones would be worth around $50 million today.

Let's just say I got nowhere near that.

There is no point in dwelling on such missed opportunities. It was just not meant to be. God, in his wisdom, gave me what he decided I should have, and not a cent more. He can give and He can take away. I accept that, without hesitation. That attitude helped me come to terms with another questionable decision, made when Perla and I were considering relocating in New York.

I had around $300,000 to invest and contacted a broker

about potential opportunities. He took me around Manhattan, to a building on 66th street. It was available for around $1.2 million. Since mortgages were 1 per cent, or a couple of points more, I could probably have afforded to buy it, but would have had most of my income swallowed up by repayments.

When I explained that I wasn't interested, because I needed to fund the family move and sustain our standard of living, the broker replied: 'You're not thinking right. This is not for today. It is for the future.' Oh, boy, was he right. But, in my own way, so was I. We couldn't eat future earnings. We needed security and stability, rather than a speculative venture.

I have passed that building many times over the years, when in Manhattan on diamond business. I always speak to it, under my breath. 'You could have been mine so easily,' I tell it. 'I lost you.' Obviously, I am no property expert, but those who are tell me that piece of real estate is now worth in the region of $100 million.

I tried something similar when we decided to move to Montreal, instead of New York. A friend in Argentina recommended a broker, and this time I took the plunge. Unfortunately, this building was not a great investment. It needed constant repair, the tenants rarely paid their rent on time, and, just as it was about to turn a profit, it burned down due to an electrical fault.

I just about broke even. Losing money, or even the promise of profit, loses its sting when you have lost so many lives. I have been blessed in countless other areas. I have been very, very lucky to have had my family.

Tuvia, our third child, was born in July 1961. We wanted

more children, but Perla, who had delivered all three by cae-
sarean section, was warned by doctors, mistakenly as it
turned out, that she would be in mortal danger if she became
pregnant again. My wife was a treasure. My children, grandchildren and great-grandchildren have been the source of so
much joy.

Friendships are also beyond price. I found a distant cousin,
Elaine, in Montreal. I was her only surviving relative from the
Holocaust, and knew her by her maiden name, Potok. Like
me, she had established a new family, having three children
and six grandchildren with her husband, Ralph Abramov-
itch, another Holocaust survivor. She passed away peacefully,
aged ninety-five, on 2 January 2021, a little more than seven
years after her husband.

We felt at home in Canada. There wasn't an igloo in sight.
We started by renting an apartment, and later built a house to
our own specifications. We lived on the ground floor, and
rented out the basement and two upstairs rooms. My diamond business evolved; average income was higher in
Montreal, so my clients demanded larger stones of better
quality.

I established the Blue and White Diamond Company,
secured an import licence, and looked farther afield, to the
Far East, Soviet Union and Africa. I even founded a diamond
factory in Fidel Castro's Cuba, because of low labour costs
and their need for foreign currency. This worked well, until
the regime changed focus and sacked the entire management,
in favour of hard-line communists without a shred of expertise.

I pulled out but was making a good living. We had settled
in a big house, on a large plot, in the exclusive neighbourhood

251

of Richmond on the island of Montreal. Around 75 per cent of the residents were Jewish, the highest percentage of any area in Canada, and the third-highest globally, outside Israel. We were so happy to lead active lives within a vibrant religious community.

Our children received a brilliant, balanced education. Our home hummed to the sounds of them playing with friends. When they graduated from high school, they went on to study in Israel and the United States. Perla volunteered to work with a Sephardi girls' school for Hispanic Jews. She also acted as treasurer for Emunah, an organization that helped vulnerable children.

I was heavily involved in the community, as a founding member of B'nai B'rith in Montreal, and as the vice-president and treasurer of Mizrachi in Canada. We built a special *shtiebel* to sustain the traditional form of Jewish prayer, and hosted Reb Shlomo Halberstam, who had re-established the Hasidic dynasty in the United States.

As a result of the success of his visit, which raised a lot of money for his *yeshiva*, a school focusing on the study of Rabbinic literature, a group of rabbis from Europe and North America asked us to organize a reception for Chiune Sugihara, the only Japanese citizen honoured as one of the Righteous Among the Nations for his heroic efforts in the war.

He defied his government while vice-consul in Lithuania, saving more than 5,500 lives by issuing Jews with transit visas so they could flee through Japanese territory. This risked not only his job, but the lives of his family. As he explained to me, he had no real choice. Far better to disobey the orders of his political superiors than to disobey the law of God and humanity.

He issued the last of those visas from the platform of Grodno station, just across the border in Belarus, minutes before the train taking him to a new post in Berlin departed. I was hugely impressed by his serenity and quiet strength. His example is inspiring since it teaches us that what we do today influences tomorrow.

Many of those he helped save became community leaders; it is said that there are 100,000 descendants of Sugihara's Survivors. None would have existed without him. I truly believe in God's plan. Some people are put on this Earth to perform a single act that defines them.

Life, of course, is unpredictable. Perla's mother Esther passed away in 1961, and Naftali, her father, came to live with us in Canada. His businesses had gone into a steep decline; he passed on what little was left to his sons in Bogotá. He seemed a lost soul, and married twice more in quick succession before he, too, passed away. It hurt me to see my wife grieve.

I suppose it is natural, as we grow older, to look back to formative experiences. Perla was two years younger than me and had viewed the Holocaust from afar. She had been spared the most disturbing detail, and wanted to know more, perhaps to understand me better, so we visited Poland twice, in 1990 and 1993.

Though she had no real memories of her birthplace, Ostrowiec, it was poignant to return just as the house in which her parents lived was being demolished. My childhood stories of oppression and murder became somehow more real when I took her to Krakow and Dzialoszyce. We visited the graves of *tsaddikim*, spiritual leaders, and other sites of Jewish cultural interest, but the camps called out to her.

Everywhere we went, it felt as if we were walking on graves. Like many first-time visitors, Perla was haunted by the discarded shoes, spectacles and suitcases of victims at Auschwitz. Plaszow lacked that immediate emotional shock, since so little of the camp remained, but the mounds that signalled mass graves did terrible things to her imagination.

I relived the worst of times and dealt with dormant demons. That was, to an extent, to be expected, but I was particularly distressed when I saw and heard history being subtly rewritten. I felt I had to make my point to the supervisor in Auschwitz's administration office when I noticed a sign on the wall of a room showing vivid film from the camp. It read: '1.5 million Polish people lost their lives here.'

I explained my background to the supervisor, who listened to my views politely. 'Please tell me,' I began, 'were there no Jews exterminated in Auschwitz?'

'Sure, there were,' he replied.

'So why do you say only Polish people on your sign?'

'They were all Polish citizens. We don't make discriminations of the religious beliefs of our people. All Polish citizens have the same rights.'

It was a politically correct answer that disguised the truth, or at least blurred the boundaries.

Though some Polish Christians protected their Jewish neighbours at great risk to themselves, many more collaborated against them. I still sense deeply rooted anti-Semitism in the country and seek justification in the facts: three million Polish Jews, 90 per cent of the pre-war population, were murdered by the Germans and their collaborators of various nationalities.

The survivors were forced to choose between their faith

and their country by the post-war communists. Those who stayed in Poland had to hide their identity and deny their heritage. A renewed purge in 1968 led to the departure of half the existing Jewish population. Historians insist only about 1 per cent of the pre-war Jewish population remained.

I felt compelled to do what I could to protect my traditions. On my second visit to Poland, I secretly bought a *Sefer Torah*, a scroll containing the Torah, from a non-Jew, who had hidden it with the intention of cutting it into framed sections, sold as Jewish antiquities. It had been stored in damp surroundings and was in poor condition.

I donated it to Jagiellonian University in Krakow, since I was unable to take it out of the country, and later arranged for it to be sent, as part of a cultural exchange, to the University of Havana. I travelled to Cuba, essentially bought it again, and, through contacts of the late David Feuerwerker, who created the university's department of Jewish studies, sent it to the University of Montreal for safekeeping.

People ask me about a survivor's mentality, but it cannot be summed up simply, or neatly. Only those of us who went through the camps, and were spared to once again breathe the clean, fresh air of freedom, can truly understand the experience. Many books have been written, but it is so hard to explain.

I attempted to protect my children from the horrors, but as they raised their own families, they urged me to write down my experiences. I heeded the word of Joel 1:3: 'You shall tell your children, and they will tell their children, and their children's children.' I tried to leave the past behind, but the past did not want to leave me.

Looking back, I was in shock for a couple of years after

liberation. But I vividly recall General Dwight Eisenhower, the commander of the Allied forces, calling on US Congressmen, journalists and photographers to visit the camps so they could share with the world the 'overpowering evidence of bestiality and cruelty'.

He knew a terrible truth; he had seen piles of dead bodies, strewn across the Ohrdruf concentration camp in Germany, and foresaw a day when the horrors of the Holocaust might be denied. In addition to inviting politicians and the media, he ordered local residents and off-duty American soldiers to witness for themselves the evidence of the atrocities for themselves.

Denying the Holocaust is a crime against humanity, because it is so well documented. I have not met anyone who does so, but if I did I would ask an excruciating question: 'Where, then, is my family? Where are my parents, my brothers, my relatives?' It is in that spirit that I decided to write this book. I hope this does not sound too presumptuous, but I do so for future generations. We have to confront and fix in the collective memory the terrible crimes that took place.

Education is very, very important, because evil is on the rise.

I look around and it appears to me that we are returning to the 1930s. I see anti-Semitism around the world, swastikas being daubed on memorials. People being persecuted, threatened, spat at. When Polish nationalists shouted 'Death to Jews' as they burned a book representing a historic pact protecting the rights of the country's Jewish community, my blood ran cold.

A friend in New York recently sent me a video, shot from

the balcony of an apartment building. A Jewish-looking guy with a beard, a delivery driver, was taking some goods from his van. The two back doors were open; a passer-by slammed them shut. The driver silently opened them again, in order to continue his work, and was suddenly attacked.

The passer-by kicked and punched him before throwing him from the sidewalk, into the oncoming traffic. I was sure he would be killed, but a car stopped and his assailant ran off. I'm sure many will identify with the delivery man, who slowly got up, straightened himself, and got on with his job. What did we, the Jewish people, do that the world still hates us?

I had thought that we were healing, but now I am not so sure.

Nelson Mandela was a great man. They said he led his people, his nation, and this world, from behind. By that they meant he set an example, and allowed others to follow it, on their own merits and in their own way. In my own small way, I can tell people what there once was, and what there could be again. Mine is a cause of common humanity. We must not section people by race or religion, creed or colour.

I have witnessed with my own eyes the work of truly terrible people, but I still believe in human beings. I have trusted many people in my life. I still do. When they talk to me, I listen. When they tell me something, I believe. I have been disappointed many times, though, because I cannot look into their hearts and know whether they are telling the truth.

If someone knocks on the door of my third-floor flat in Jerusalem and asks for charity, I do not really know if they need it, but I still give them money, from a stack of coins I keep on a nearby shelf. It is in my nature. I thank God that I am able to help. You have to give in order to receive or take.

Charity is society's medicine. I was brought up to believe that if you save one person, you save the world.

We are living in a time of epidemics. There is war in Europe. There are so many destructive forces at large in the world. Like many others, I question what is going on. Is it just circumstance? God created a beautiful world, and we human beings are ruining it. To my way of thinking He is sending us signals. We have to break the code, solve the riddle. What does He want?

I think we are not good enough. He is not happy with us. He wants us to be better. How do we get to be better? A Hebrew phrase, '*Tikkun olam*', refers to fixing the world, through a search for social justice. What can we do? Every individual, each one of us, should look into our hearts. Where are my shortcomings? Where do I fail? Where am I not doing what I should?

If we were committed to fixing ourselves we would have a better world, but I am a realist. We have a problem. We are never satisfied. We tell ourselves we never have enough. Help can only come from within. We are spoiling the world, and have to repair the damage. There are limits to what an individual can do, but we need to talk honestly, with an open heart and an open mind.

17

Choose Life

I continued working throughout my seventies but one awful morning in March 2006 changed my life irrevocably. I was sitting with Perla, chatting over a cup of coffee, when she suddenly blurted out: 'Oh, my head! Oh, terrible, terrible! Call 911!' They were the last words she ever spoke.

I made the call, and, hoping it was something like a fainting spell, tried to gently massage her neck. Her head moved to the side, and she turned an unusual shade of white. I was terrified. This was a woman who had never had a day's sickness. The paramedics came quickly, but I knew it was the end of her.

She spent the next three years in a coma, first in a hospital and then in a third-floor room in section C at the Jewish Eldercare Centre in the Côte-des-Neiges area of Montreal. I spent every day sitting beside her bed, praying with and for her. Our children and friends were a constant presence, but I felt empty. How I wished we could have said goodbye.

She didn't open her eyes, or raise as much as a finger, before she passed away on Tuesday, 24 March 2009, nine days after her eightieth birthday. She left a hole in my heart that has yet to heal.

Death is the final release, for those accepted into the afterlife by the Almighty, but what of those who are left to mourn? In my faith there are six phases of the bereavement cycle, established centuries ago by the rabbis who created the Talmud. The rituals are comforting, and memories are sacred, but we all react differently to grief.

I felt empty for five years after Perla's passing. My family stayed close; I spent each Sabbath and every Jewish holiday with my eldest son Ziggy and his wife Rivi. My other son, Tuvia, and my daughter Sheila called every day. My friends were kind and attentive. I was treated with tenderness and respect, but waves of sadness washed over me.

My wedding day had been the happiest day of my life. My wife was such a treasure. Hair of gold, heart of gold. She brought our children up beautifully. She was the perfect *bubbi*, the traditional Jewish grandmother. She made my survival worthwhile. Then, in a single second, she was gone, consumed by a brain aneurysm. We enlisted experts from Israel and Canada, but nothing could be done.

There are still times I glance around, half hoping she will be there. Her *neshama*, her soul or spirit, is strong.

I once tried to explain what that means to an American friend of my grandson, who was clearly struggling with mixed emotions while on a study visit to Poland. He approached me, and immediately stressed he did not believe in God, as young men have the right, and the tendency, to do. He said he saw me as a God-fearing man and wondered why I believed. 'Could you try to convince me there is a God?' he said.

'This beautiful world,' I asked him in return, 'do you think it is man's creation?' Predictably enough, he did. 'It's nature,' he answered. 'OK,' I said. 'You hear me, and I hear you. You see me, I see you. That's God's work.' He was still unconvinced and began telling me about his expensive watch and fancy car. How could he be expected to believe they were gifts from an invisible deity?

I observed that such belongings didn't seem to make him happy and proceeded to shock him further by asking: 'Have you ever seen a relative who has passed away?' He looked at me strangely, and said, 'Sure, my great-grandmother, when I was a little boy.' I asked him what he remembered: 'Did she have her distinguishing features? Her nose? Ears, hands? Was she dressed beautifully? Did she look pretty?'

He spread his arms wide, as if to say, 'What sort of question is that?' but admitted she almost looked more beautiful, more peaceful, in death, than in life. 'Tell me, then, did you talk to her?' That look again. 'No. She was dead. Why would I do that?' He missed the point of the question, so I placed it into perspective: 'You've told me she looked beautiful. Outwardly, she had the same features. So, what was missing?'

Again, he looked puzzled. 'I'll tell you what she didn't have. Something called *neshama*, the spirit. That spark of godliness in us is life itself. It is given to us, borrowed as collateral, from God. We have to thank Him for leaving it with us. It is His. He gave it to us, and can take it away whenever he wants, so we pray that He should leave it with us for as long as possible, into old age. Once it is taken away, we are nothing, a piece of material.'

I'm not sure I won him around, but I clearly made him think. He sought out my grandson on the plane home and poured out his family problems. His mother had run off with another woman and his father, who was more than sixty years old, was living with his twenty-six-year-old secretary. There was no anchor point in his life.

Understandably, he came across as being very confused. Perhaps that is as much my fault as his. It is especially difficult to come to terms with fundamental matters of faith as a young man, when your view of the world is not yet fully formed, and the example set by those closest to you is so lacking in wisdom and certainty.

I did not know him that well but took the liberty of sending him a message. He needed to get out of the family home and embrace the Jewish community. It was okay to strive for the nicer things in life, but it was time for him to become a real person. The ethics, morals and behaviours ingrained by the disciplines of religious belief would offer him comfort and security. I truly believe we have a free will, to shape our lives as we see fit. We are commanded to do good, but it is in our hands to obey, or disobey. Some people are blind. Others have a clearer vision. I don't think I am a wise man, but I believe in goodness. I trust people are well intentioned until I am disappointed. We are blessed with the power to choose.

Choose life. Choose goodness. That's what I tell anyone who asks.

I've already said, in this book, that any time the Almighty calls, I am ready. What will I say to Him when that time comes? I will apologize for not doing more good works than I did. I tried to be a better person, once I understood the personal faults I was trying to correct, but probably did a lot of bad things.

I confess to saying unkind words to people who were already unhappy, making things worse for them. I unnecessarily added to their bitterness and lack of self-esteem. That happened to me, in return: occasionally I would go to someone for advice and be treated harshly. That made me aggravated. It hurt so much more because I felt as if I had been dismissed as unworthy of attention.

The only consolation is that even the most righteous among us is not good, all the time. We all have human faults and failings, but we have the opportunity to help others. I firmly believe we take the good deeds we did in this world on to the next. If you have a positive spirit and a charitable nature you have a better account in the world to come.

There's a folk tale about a successful businessman, who gathered his children around him when he realized he was dying. He left them his factories, his houses and other buildings, but didn't give them his gold coin collection, worth millions, because he wanted to take it into the afterlife.

He goes to Hell and is burning, suffering and sweating. Suddenly he sees a kiosk where someone is selling soda water. He rushes towards it, carrying his precious collection. 'Give me water,' he pants, taking out a gold coin as payment.

'What is that?' says the Angel, through the serving hatch.

'You don't know?' the man exclaims. 'That coin is worth a million dollars.' The Angel tells him, 'That currency doesn't work here.' The man is scared. 'Well, what does work?' he asks. 'The dimes and quarters you gave to the poor people,' the Angel replies. 'That is the money you can spend here. You did not give in the other world, so you cannot receive here.'

My advice? Be as friendly as possible to as many people as possible. When you sense someone with a broken heart, try to approach him, or her. Try to talk to them, get close to them. You never know what they may be feeling, how they may be suffering. You can be the balm on wounds you cannot see.

When I see people doing bad things, I am not angry at them. I pity them. I pray they should have a better understanding of their actions. They need to be spiritually healed. My principles are pretty straightforward: Build families. Learn from good and bad examples. Trust in something bigger than yourself.

There are times when, to put it mildly, I don't feel great. I am usually remembering my losses in the Holocaust. I think about my mother and brothers a lot. I imagine how they were brought into the gas chambers, how they choked. They were children, little boys. They probably grabbed my mother for comfort. I wonder what she felt throughout it all, what she told them in those final moments.

Once, after a restless night dwelling on these unsettling, unanswerable questions, I went to a shop, intending to buy something. The server was rude and unfriendly, so I walked out in disgust. I felt worse than I had done when I left home, because the man's unhappiness affected me. I learned an important lesson: think of the other person when you see someone in a sad mood. Look beyond the obvious.

Each of us has our own troubles. Maybe business was not going well for that shopkeeper. Maybe he had lost money. Maybe there was trouble at home. Who knows? Maybe his children were ill. I should have sensed his despondency, invited him to sit and have a cup of coffee once his work was done, to talk of this and that. I could have picked up his mood and raised his morale.

I am proud that my attempts to pass on these lessons to my children seem to have been successful. To give an example, as an internationally renowned economic strategist on Wall Street, my youngest son Tuvia became accustomed to dealing with presidents, prominent politicians and influential corporate leaders.

His day was measured in minutes, because so many people

sought his advice. Yet he treated whoever approached him with courtesy and respect. It didn't matter if it was a great man, or someone of lesser stature. No matter how busy he was, he never cut them short. He did them the honour of listening to their stories, irrespective of whether he would benefit from his consideration.

He gave of himself and used his wealth and influence wisely. He funded a state-of-the-art CAT scan for Tel Aviv's biggest hospital as a gesture of gratitude for their assistance in his mother's care. When New York's Yeshiva University needed a keynote speaker for its annual Hannukah Convocation, former US president George W. Bush happily accepted Tuvia's invitation, as a personal friend, to speak to an assembly of nearly a thousand Jewish students and philanthropists.

Human beings are complicated creatures. I am no different. The course of my life was dictated by my craving for a family, which took me to Argentina. I have been blessed with three children, nine grandchildren, and thirteen great-grandchildren. So why, at the age of eighty-eight, did I choose to isolate myself from them, physically if not spiritually, by making what we call *Aliyah*, moving to Israel?

I mulled it over for several years and changed my mind several times. I was emotionally bereft, following the loss of my wife, of blessed memory, but had many friends. I proudly took Canadian citizenship in 1969. Montreal was a comforting, familiar place. I liked its mood and wanted for nothing. My children pleaded with me not to leave. Yet the pull of my Jewish homeland proved irresistible.

I was helped immensely in planning my emigration to Israel by Nefesh B'Nefesh, a non-profit organization also known as Jewish Souls United, that has aided more than 60,000 *olim*, the collective term for those making *Aliyah*, since 2002. They worked with the Jewish Agency to guide me through the logistics of the process, and the inevitable period of transition.

I sold my home in Canada and most of my possessions, sending those I most treasured ahead of me, before, on 21 July 2014, boarding an El Al flight from JFK Airport in New York to Tel Aviv's Ben Gurion Airport. A pre-flight party was thrown in our honour and, since it was my eighty-eighth birthday, I was upgraded to first class. I was the oldest *oleh*; the youngest was a babe of barely three months.

There was a lot of media interest. I'd had a four-man Israeli TV crew following me around for a week. Their producer convinced me to share my story because she thought it reflected well on the nation, and when the time came, they used their influence to persuade the Israeli Defence Force to give my grandson Noam temporary leave to greet me.

It is difficult to put into words the feelings that hit me when we embraced. Joy was mixed with pride and something intangible. Perhaps it was the sense of a circle being completed. A lot of my grandchildren have studied in Israel, but Noam, Ziggy's son, who eventually worked his way up to the rank of IDF commander before earning a degree in business administration, was the first of the new generation to make *Aliyah*.

I was luckier than most since I already had my apartment, in a housing development in which I had been involved, as an investor in a North American company that operated building projects across Israel until it collapsed in the wake of the devaluation of the shekel. The apartment had been empty for some time, so I took the opportunity to renovate it before I moved in.

I felt at home immediately, in a closely knit, largely Orthodox neighbourhood. I enjoyed the simplicity of life. I visited the synagogue in my building each morning and immersed myself in Torah and Talmud study sessions. I was astonished by how many people recognized me, when I took to walking every day in a nearby park; they could not have been kinder.

I'm told the social status of survivors improved immensely after the trial and execution of Adolf Eichmann, who was famously caught in a suburb of Buenos Aires on the evening of 11 May 1960, and secretly flown to Israel nine days later. I still find it astonishing that Eichmann used to take tea with another Nazi monster, Josef Mengele, in an adjoining neighbourhood to mine in the Argentine capital.

So near and yet so far . . .

When I look back, maybe I was wrong to want to run away from my past. It took time for me to appreciate the value of my history. I had a grand plan when I got married. I worked hard, with the intention of giving my children a tremendous Jewish education, but didn't want them to grow up with the complex that, to be Jewish, you have to suffer.

I used to sit with them and talk about anything other than the Holocaust. I enjoyed them, treated them as my friends. I am proud of their values, and the way they chose to live their lives. They have passed those values on to their children. They call each day and ensure that, although I am on my own in Jerusalem, I never feel lonely.

Ziggy, my oldest son, became a rabbi and is a qualified doctor. He takes a scholarly approach to the scriptures and is often consulted on their meaning. He specialized in child psychology, working in a hospital and in private practice before suddenly quitting the medical profession. His answer, when I asked him why, was revealing: 'I can no longer bear the suffering of my patients. I cannot live with their agonies. I simply can't do it anymore.'

He has not had my luck in business, but he is a great speaker and a genius with his hands. He can fix anything from a car to a computer. He is happy, a wonderful father and grandfather. His wife Rivi has a master's degree in literature and prepares test papers for universities. She taught online courses in English to Chinese students until their education system caught up with the rest of the world.

My daughter Sheila is a treasure, like her mother. She has taught for thirty years in a large school in Cedarwood, New York. The aim of HALB, Hebrew Academy of Long Beach, is to 'develop compassionate and proud Jews who answer the call of moral, civic and communal responsibility'. Lately, she has been talking of retiring, but why stop doing something you so obviously enjoy?

You have to keep your brain active. I effectively retired in 2007, though I occasionally did a little something on the side if asked. Money didn't matter that much, because my children made a living and I had enough to hand out monthly gifts, but it's hard to switch off completely. I still have a couple of small interests in New York. They send me a few dollars every now and again to top up my war reparations pension, which gives me the princely sum of 23 Euros a month!

At the risk of repeating myself, families are priceless. They have a richness and depth which can bring great joy, and great sorrow. Daniel Pearl, the great-grandson of my wife's uncle, Chaim, was the Wall Street journalist kidnapped and decapitated by terrorists in Pakistan in 2002, largely because he was Jewish. I remember him as a lively little boy; his name and principles live on in a charitable foundation run by his parents, Judea and Ruth.

Four generations of my family gathered to celebrate my ninetieth birthday in Israel in 2016. I cherish the photograph of us all together that day, and still love spoiling the little ones with ice cream, which drives their parents crazy. One of my grandsons summed it up really well: 'Saba,' he said, using the Jewish word for Grandpa, 'if you hadn't made it, none of us would be here.'

I also ache when I return to that photograph. There, directly behind me and with his arm on the shoulder of his brother, is Tuvia. He has a lovely soft smile. I still cannot quite believe he passed away on 1 October 2021, a month after being struck by a car, crossing a street in his home town of Hewlett on Long Island, New York, as he walked to his synagogue at 6 a.m.

Police reported he was initially in a stable condition in hospital, but the force of the accident was such that the silver five-zloty piece that hung around his neck, the one reworked by a Chinese prisoner in Melk as a gesture of gratitude for the piece of bread I scavenged for him from Julius Ludolf's villa, was found in someone's front yard.

Tuvia was sixty and had been Citigroup Inc.'s chief American equity strategist for thirty-three years. He was hailed as a Wall Street icon and as an *Ish Anak* (a Massive Man). When he was laid to rest his son Arel remarked that his father exemplified one of the parables in the Talmud: *'Eizehu Chacham? Ha'Ro'eh Et HaNolad.'* Loosely translated that means, 'Who is a wise man? The person with the ability to see the outcome of any effort.'

Such a son. World famous. A diamond to his father every

day. A busy man: 'Daddy, I'm running. I have two minutes between meetings. I want to say hello, how are you doing?' Had a lot of responsibility. Very educated, very giving. Suddenly, after losing a child, the world is built differently. Children should bury their parents.

I sat *shiva*, mourning for a week, not washing, or shaving, as tradition demands. People came in their hundreds to visit. Sages, prominent rabbis, even the Mayor of Jerusalem, who knew of Tuvia and explained that he wanted to pay his respects to me, as a Holocaust survivor. They brought so much food the kitchen was full; we ensured it was distributed in the neighbourhood.

My daughter Sheila wanted me to sit with the family in New York, but when I preferred to remain in Israel, she flew in to be with me. She was accompanied by a group of her friends, incredible ladies who cooked and cleaned while she comforted me. Our rituals dated back to biblical times. We discussed our loss, honoured the memory of our loved one, and confronted our grief.

It was not until much later that I realized the impact my son had on those he came across. People praised his spirit, compassion and humanity. He was described as 'a modest man with great international prestige and accolades'. I was particularly touched by the reflections of one of his close friends, Doug Kass.

'Tuvia was a special man,' he wrote. 'Kind, humble and even-tempered. He had a sense of justice. He sought out the good in people – and people like me sought out his advice. He was fiercely committed, and he developed a personal connection with his friends, his fellow workers at Citigroup, his clients, and many outside of the investment world.

'He loved his family and community. He was righteous, charitable, and deeply religious. He befriended everyone, the successful and the unsuccessful – it didn't matter – and developed thousands of sincere personal connections within and outside of the investment community. He realized we live in this world not for ourselves, but for others. To be with Tuvia was a delight.'

He had sponsored a special volume of the scriptures just before he passed away. His dedication read: 'In loving of memory of our parents, grandparents and great-grandparents who imbued us with Torah values.' That's our role, isn't it? We keep the flame burning.

Wall Street knew him as Tobias. To his family, friends and the Jewish community he was Tuvia. In Hebrew, the name means 'God is Good.' Sometimes that is hard to reconcile, but I have to believe it is true. What is a man without faith?

18

Survivor

My great-grandfather once spoke of a man called Shimon Yaroslavova, who came from an ancient city just north of Moscow. He was a pious man, who had never been rewarded with a good day in his life. He was bedridden. He had seen his children pass away. He was without a penny to his name. Yet he was content and had reached a great age, 100.

One of the celebrated sages of his generation heard about Shimon and resolved to discover his secrets. He knew he had to act as quickly as possible, since in those days men were considered old at fifty. He sent messages to Shimon, via his followers, but it took months for them to reach him. The rabbi used that time wisely, saving enough money to buy a balogola, a horse-drawn carriage.

The rabbi's journey was long and arduous, but rewarding. Shimon greeted him graciously, if a little cautiously. He thanked his visitor for his interest, and agreed to answer his questions, though he took a long time to answer the first one, about the reasons for his longevity. Eventually, he said: 'I have no questions.'

The rabbi was puzzled, and, after pausing to gather his thoughts, wondered how the old man had remained happy with his lot, despite his many setbacks and tragedies. Again,

Shimon took his time, and said: 'I have no questions.' This confused his famous visitor, who exclaimed: 'No questions? How can that be, after all that has happened to you?'

Shimon stirred a little in his bed and cleared his throat before addressing the rabbi directly. 'In this world, I have no questions,' he said, so slowly it was as if he was measuring every word. 'You want the answer? Come up, come up, to the other world, heaven. Up there, there are no questions, only answers, in illuminated letters.'

I have a number of questions. Why did God allow the Jewish race to suffer such a catastrophe? What was His purpose in allowing the innocents to be slaughtered? Could we have done more to defend ourselves? These are deeply personal, extremely troubling, but I understand the point Shimon was trying to make.

There is so much to talk about, but nothing to say. I will not dwell on the questions raised by what happened to me, because I know they will not be answered until I am in another place. God has granted me the serenity to accept that, and the strength to share my experiences. When people tell me that I am old, I reply that I am merely older than most. To accept being old is like giving up.

I believe we experience three different stages of life. The first is in our mother's womb, where the scriptures tell us we absorb the knowledge of the Torah. We live there, eat there. It is a residence. The second stage is that journey from birth, through childhood, adulthood, seniority and death. The third is spiritual, eternal.

In earthly terms, my generation is thinning. Holocaust survivors cannot avoid the limitations of our mortality. I read somewhere recently that only 300 or so of us, who endured the clearances and the concentration camps, remain in Israel. I personally know only one other Polish Jew with that background, a man a couple of years younger than me who lives in Tel Aviv, who is alive in our homeland.

When I meet fellow survivors, I try to talk to them about anything other than our shared experiences. We profoundly understand fear and barbarity, suffering and sacrifice, so there is little to be gained from brooding on memories of them. I prefer to ask my companions how many children they have, or whether they have been blessed with grandchildren.

I try to talk to them about their working lives after the war, the friendships they made and the places they saw. Inevitably, because of our age, we discuss our health. We all have our aches and pains. Many of us have lost our spouses. We reminisce about them, share the happiness we experienced with our soulmates. In that way we celebrate the tiny miracles of our lives. We have all beaten tremendous odds to be here.

I feel, in my own way, that I have taken revenge against the Nazis. Not in a malicious, vindictive way, but through a reassuringly human method. My revenge is the joy of a large family gathering, the renewal of a wedding ceremony, the laughter of my grandchildren. The Final Solution was designed to ensure that the Jewish family would be eradicated. The Nazis chose hate over love. Monsters like Amon Goeth shot young children in the head without a second's thought.

When I see people possessed by evil I wonder where it comes from. Is there a point where it is normalized? I can't conceive of an SS officer sitting down at the dinner table after spending his day killing Jews. When he tells his wife of his pride in his work, does she say, 'Great job, darling. Bravo'? I cannot hope to understand this, but I suppose she must have done.

There is so much that is unfathomable. How did Hitler, a nobody, manage to poison educated minds in one of the most cultured nations on Earth? He wasn't a parliamentarian, a senator or a governor. He hadn't even been a village mayor. Yet this lonely bachelor, a painter who was an anonymous lance corporal in the First World War, became an Angel of Death who destroyed European Jewry and started a conflict that claimed 55 million lives.

We are not the masters of life. Giving and taking life is in God's hands. He is responsible for creation.

I have a nephew who is a very famous doctor. He was not religious but one day he came to me, knowing the depth of my devotion, and said, 'Uncle Joe, I believe one hundred per cent there is a God.' I smiled quizzically and replied: 'Thank you very much. How come you have changed?' His answer intrigued me: 'I know the human body. It works so perfectly that it is beyond our comprehension. It couldn't be anyone creating such a thing but a God, so I am a believer.'

I am often asked why or how I survived, when millions succumbed. I have no real answer, though it involved a series of miracles. What I can say is that I was, and am, a man of faith. That meant that, in the worst of times, I had something to hold on to. If you have no belief system, what do you cling to? A lamp post? A new car? An expensive watch?

I believe everything happens because it is God's will. I believe in the separation between right and wrong. By doing the right thing I believe I am doing what God commands me to do. In my darkest moments I believed He was by my side.

276

We have a free will, and can choose the way we live our life. Some are blinded by modern attitudes devoid of any spiritual meaning.

I felt compelled to justify my survival by doing something to help others, like those orphaned children who had been left in stables, farm buildings, churches and monasteries by desperate parents who knew they would die during the liquidation of the ghettoes. People expect me to be angry at what was taken from us, and them, but anger is like a rocking chair. You keep moving, but it doesn't take you anywhere. Our job is not to exact revenge, but to repair our communities.

I am not a wise man, but I was recently visited by a general from the Israeli Defence Force, who was to give a keynote address to senior officers. We were about two hours into our conversation when I asked him to explain why he considered my testimony to be so important. 'We want to motivate them to be prepared for any event, anywhere in the world, that might endanger the lives of the Jewish people,' he said. 'We must use the past to learn how to react and behave in the future.'

I always tell people to choose life, choose goodness. Darkness may be descending, but the light of life will still shine through. While God gives me the fortitude, and the years, I will continue with my mission. My final job in life is to keep talking, telling, teaching. I ask you to remember, to share, to challenge anyone who doubts the reality of the clinically organized annihilation of my people.

I am passionate about educating the young. They give me energy with their ideals, and their zeal to forge a better life. Of course, there are times when I am dog-tired. If I am at home, I sit down on my sofa, and settle into a special cushion that supports my lower back. I take my shoes off, close my eyes for ten or fifteen minutes, and then I feel refreshed.

It is not so easy to rest when I am addressing students, but the rewards are immense. One group came up to me and asked whether I liked the song they were singing. Truth be told, I only half-listened, but I said, 'Sure, it was very nice.' They can't have been convinced because they then asked: 'Did you listen to the words?'

I had to admit I hadn't, fully at least. They laughed, and began singing again, clapping and swaying in unison. It was only then I realized they were singing about me: 'Rab Josef, you really changed my life, you *mamish* ['surely' or 'certainly' in Hebrew] changed my life.' I didn't deserve such an honour; all I had done was remind them of their heritage.

Am Yisrael Chai. The people of Israel live.

My memories remain painful, but in the last ten years or so, as the voices of my generation begin to fade, attitudes to survivors have changed. If we speak about the sanctity of life, of spiritual nourishment and identity, more people are now willing to listen. I have taken to heart the wisdom of Rabbi Israel ben Eliezer, the eighteenth-century founder of Hasidic Judaism: 'In forgetfulness are the roots of exile and in remembrance are the seeds of redemption.'

That's a beautiful concept, and it explains why I was not truly alone when returning to Belzec, where I retreated into myself. I was accompanied by a group of Jewish students. I watched them closely as I spoke of my feelings and experiences. Some self-consciously wiped away silent tears. I was particularly struck by one boy, who sat staring into space, lost in thought and kneading his forehead with his knuckles.

The youth will, I hope, carry the torch. Despite the complications of the pandemic, I have made a dozen or so educational visits to the camps, through charitable organizations like JRoots, whose founder Rabbi Naftali Schiff is a source of such support and spiritual comfort. In Israel, I speak at schools and universities, to companies and community groups. I ask for nothing but the chance to be heard.

I spoke recently to another group of about one hundred students, who had been to Poland and had followed the course of my life, through a series of associated visits. They visited my childhood haunts in Krakow and paid their respects in the camps. They, like me, found Belzec a ghostly place. They told me they had held a commemoration service for my family while they were there.

As masses of them crowded around me after I had answered as many questions as I could, asking for a blessing or a photograph, I noticed they were all wearing different-coloured wristbands. Each bore the name of my mother, or one of my brothers, as a tribute. It was such a uniquely emotional moment. It moved me to tears.

I see so many young people who appear to be lost. They know nothing about our history. They are spoiled by a world of wealth and waste. They do not go to bed hungry. It is too easy to concentrate on what you have, without appreciating what you have lost.

Yet all is not lost. There is reason for hope. At that moment with the students crowding around me, I felt a surge of contentment, and renewed commitment. How can I not continue to spread the word, when those who will shape the future take the time to appreciate the life and times of people like me? I must do so because it is so important.

This story is much bigger than me, though commemorative books, containing messages from students I have met, are flattering. The feedback has a theme: 'Your strength is a light for our people . . . thank you for showing me a flame can still be illuminated in the darkest of times . . . your light shone through all the darkness and destruction and inspired an infinite amount of Jewish pride . . . you are filled with such light and positivity . . .'

The light of life. It is an image I return to regularly.

In the modern world, it can be snuffed out too easily, and for no real reason. I despair when I read of soaring suicide rates in the young. Each death is a terrible tragedy, an incomprehensible loss. It seems that some youths are simply bored with life. There is an emptiness to their existence. It is fashionable to believe in no one and nothing. The inner being is thereby never nourished.

What would I, as a ninety-six-year-old man, say to a sixteen-year-old youth, with his future stretching before him?

At that age I was in the camps, and in real trouble. I would tell him what I told myself at the time. Be strong. Don't give up. Embrace life. The will of life is so important. If you give up, then you are lost. Hold onto life. Have faith. Don't collapse, don't fall. Do everything, flatter, cajole and even deceive, to get an extra piece of bread.

Fight for everything. If you go into business, try almost anything in order to be competitive. If you are lucky enough to find the right companion, and have a family, you will have to leave it from time to time. I used to travel, to find the source of the goods I wanted to sell. I hated being away from my loved ones, but in that way I eliminated the middleman.

Remember, if you are an inch ahead of your rival, you are already successful.

Fight with all your might, but also do good whenever you can. That will pay off. Charity is a medicine. Kindness heals. When your enemy is hungry, give him a piece of bread. When he's thirsty, give him a drink of water. If you help your enemy, he will become your friend. We cannot live alone. We have to understand others and be sensitive to their needs and motivations. Above all, to lapse into Hebrew for a moment, I would say *Chazak v'ematz*: Be strong and courageous.

Talk is cheap, unless, of course, you are speaking to or through a lawyer, but a lot depends on your audience. To mark Holocaust Martyrs' and Heroes' Remembrance Day in late April 2022, I was invited to address more than a hundred dignitaries, including thirty-five ambassadors. It was a fitting opportunity to speak truth to power, on a sombre, symbolic day.

Sirens blared across Israel, and the nation came to a standstill in honour of the six million Jews murdered during the Holocaust. Pedestrians were rooted to the spot. Drivers stopped their cars, got out of their vehicles, and joined the crowds bowing their heads in silent prayer. Ceremonies were staged at Yad Vashem, our national Holocaust memorial, and in parliament.

I meant no disrespect, but I did not have a prepared speech. I spoke not from a script, but from the heart. I began by telling the VIPs of my original hope, that the world had learned a terrible lesson. I stressed the obvious, that the Holocaust could not be allowed to happen again. But then I looked back through my lifetime, and emphasized my greatest disappointment, that my original optimism could not be justified.

We were, once again, in a time of war, in the Ukraine, so close to where I grew up. The Russians were killing for no other reason than national aggrandizement, and the wicked political ambitions of a despot. Closer to home, children from Iran to Palestine were being taught that Jews should be wiped off the face of the Earth. Truly, Hitler would have approved.

We had all seen the murderous consequences of ethnic cleansing, in places like Rwanda, Biafra, and across the former Yugoslavia. A generation had been slaughtered in Cambodia, to serve an insane political philosophy. Afghanistan's agony continued. God had created a beautiful world that was imperilled by human weakness.

Anti-Semitism was a growing threat. A subtle form of Holocaust denial was taking root at the highest levels of certain governments. Neo-Nazi organizations were becoming bolder. I challenged my audience directly. It was their responsibility to use their influence wisely. They had a duty, to never forgive or forget.

I overran my allotted time by about twenty minutes and wondered how people would react. The moment I stopped, waves of applause broke over me. The standing ovation continued when I moved to the side of the stage to drink a glass of water. It lasted for fully five minutes, before the audience came forward, and over to me.

The French ambassador was the first to reach me. He praised the honesty of my speech, and I in turn congratulated him, since his boss, President Emmanuel Macron, had just beaten off the challenge of his far-right opponent, Marine Le Pen. The Spanish ambassador proudly told me of his country's policy, of offering citizenship to Jews of Spanish descent.

I appreciated the earnestness of the German ambassador, who hugged me and said: 'I felt I must come. I have to apologize that my ancestors caused you personally so much suffering.' He was a good man in what must have been a difficult situation. I would have liked to have spoken to the Polish ambassador, but he did not approach me.

In general, though, the rest of the evening passed in a blur of embraces, kisses, good wishes and best intentions. Maybe they were obeying diplomatic protocols, but I felt honoured that my message had been taken on board by such important people. I hoped that I represented all Holocaust survivors with dignity, and a little defiance.

As so often in such situations, I was too busy talking to eat what was on offer. A lovely lady recognized my difficulties and whispered that she would make up a plate for me. I took home a lovely mixture of canapes, small sandwiches, cookies and cake. It was one of those small gestures of human kindness that gives me faith that all is not lost.

I hope to be around for many more years to come, but if I am deemed worthy of remembrance, when my time comes I would wish to be thought of as being humble, down to earth, nothing special. I am no hero, as I said right at the start of this book. I am an ordinary man, who survived through a series of miracles.

I tried to care for others. If I had a piece of bread that was not big enough for two, I would still share it. My fear is that, in saying things like that, I am drawing attention to myself. But I am not an egotist. I try to avoid boasting, and the sin of pride. I take heed of the saying in the Torah, that God takes the haughty and brings them down. I simply did what I had to do.

Life is precious, a privilege. The act of remembrance should not prevent us savouring the small pleasures of each day. One of those pleasures, for me at least, is a nip of Scotch whisky. I thank you for your interest in my story, and wish nothing but the best for you, and future generations. I would be honoured if you would join me in a toast.

L'Chaim. To life.

Acknowledgements

'Maybe their tomorrows will be enriched by my yesterdays.'

Josef was speaking specifically of his grandchildren, great-grandchildren and future generations of the family whose existence defies and repudiates the enduring evil of Nazism, but the universality of his message hopefully resonates with you, after reading this book.

Working with him has been one of the most enriching experiences of my life, personally and professionally. He is a man of natural warmth, great faith and serious intent, which is often offset by an infectious, impish laugh. I thank him for the privilege of touching history, through his humanity and humility.

There are days when the pain of injuries, sustained in slavery, is difficult to bear, but he is in remarkable physical condition for a man of his age. He is extremely sharp mentally; online reminiscences of fellow survivors, from his home village of Dzialoszyce, have occasionally confirmed or clarified his memories.

One of the beauties of being a co-writer is the intimacy of the process. I vividly recollect him listening to his deposition against Amon Goeth for the first time in nearly eighty years. As I read it to him, from my laptop screen, he shifted forward imperceptibly on his chair at the head of the table, as if the words, and the images they summoned, had a magnetic quality.

That archive document was one of thousands revealed, studied and contextualized by Jonathan Kalmus, a remarkable journalistic feat that deserves the highest praise and the widest respect. We thank him for his diligence; he was of particular help to me, a non-Jew, in understanding the Jewish culture and experience.

My research was extensive, but meagre by comparison. I was acutely aware of the responsibility on me to provide an authentic record of a remarkable life and must thank the staff at Yad Vashem in Jerusalem, particularly Lara Kwalbrun, for their time and insight in putting Josef's experiences into the broadest perspective.

I am in the greatest debt to Rabbi Naftali Schiff, without whom this book would not have been written. He is a global expert on the Holocaust experience, a blur of inexhaustible energy, instinctive kindness and indomitable spirit. His staff, in the JRoots charity, radiate his drive and idealism. They are a collective force for good.

Naftali was the first to recognize the power and potential of Josef's story. His foresight was acknowledged, appreciated and acted upon by Rory Scarfe, my literary agent at The Blair Partnership, which also represents Josef. We are additionally grateful to Neil Blair and Jordan Lees for their encouragement and wisdom.

Henry Vines, our publisher, shares our vision for this book. He has been a source of constant support, for which we thank him profusely. His team at Transworld, particularly Richard Mason, Viv Thompson and Richard Shailer, have done a wonderful job on our behalf.

As always, I am indebted to Christine Preston, who transcribed countless hours of interviews. She, too, was uniquely touched by the experience.

It has been an immersive process, so I must thank my wife Lynn, for her patience, in putting up with my pre-dawn writing sessions and seemingly perpetual distraction. I was moved by Josef's persistence in comparing notes on our respective families; he asked continually about my children, Nicholas, Aaron, William and Lydia, and my grandchildren, Marielli, Michael, Jess and India.

Faith, and family, are the twin pillars of Josef's life. I was deeply affected by the tenderness of his recollection of his wife Perla. The strength of his children, Tuvia, Sheila and Ziggy, whose long-held belief, encouragement and support for their father to share his story has been critical, reflects his character. The lessons he passed on to them are timeless.

The loss of Tuvia, to whom this book is dedicated, was grievous. He embodied the best traits of his father, and answered the call of *Chazak V'amatz*, to be strong and courageous. To borrow another Hebrew phrase, *ha`mishpakha hi akhat mi`yetsirot ha`mofet shel ha`teva*, the family is one of nature's masterpieces.

Michael Calvin
November 2022

About the Authors

Before the invasion of his hometown, **Josef Lewkowicz** lived with his family in Dzialoszyce, near Krakow in Poland. After the invasion, he spent three years in six different concentration camps before travelling around Austria and Germany as an intelligence officer searching for Nazis in hiding. Josef is now ninety-six and living in Jerusalem, after working as a diamond dealer in South America.

Michael Calvin is an award-winning writer and *Sunday Times* bestselling author, whose books have been hailed for their insight and influence.